PERSPECTIVES IN VERNACULAR ARCHITECTURE, II

EDITED BY CAMILLE WELLS

PERSPECTIVES IN VERNACULAR ARCHITECTURE, II

UNIVERSITY OF MISSOURI PRESS COLUMBIA

Contents

V. Buildings in Their Social Contexts

Acknowledgments

The editor is pleased to have received counsel and assistance from many colleagues and friends, including Catherine Bishir, Richard Candee, Barbara Carson, Cary Carson, Tom Carter, Edward Chappell, Betsy Cromley, Claire Dempsey, Mark Edwards, Bernie Herman, Gil Kelly, Carl Lounsbury, Turk McCleskey, Ozzie Overby, Adolph Placzek, Orlando Ridout V, Pam Simpson, Bob St. George, and Dell Upton. Early assistance with sorting and editing the manuscripts was provided by Carol Stiles and Lisa Mullins. Susan Berg and Mary Keeling, librarians at Colonial Williamsburg Foundation, kindly tracked down a number of references and bibliographical details. Stella Neiman applied her excellent skills to the making of the index.

Several institutions have made significant contributions as well. Members of the staff of the University of Missouri Press endured the assembly and production of this volume with remarkable patience and good humor. The appearance of the book is a direct result of their energy and talent. For support during the final stages of the project, the editor is grateful to the American Association of University Women for a Grace Ellis Ford Educational Foundation grant. Finally, the editor is indebted to the Department of History at the College of William and Mary—and especially to Graduate Director Jim Whittenburg—for sheltering the production of this volume.

C.W.
Williamsburg, Virginia   15 April 1986

1

CAMILLE WELLS

Old Claims and New Demands:
Vernacular Architecture Studies Today

What is vernacular architecture? Although it is entirely appropriate that definitions vary, a clarification of the issues is in order. Some scholars remain loyal to the conventional view that vernacular buildings must be old, rural, handmade structures built in traditional forms and materials for domestic or agricultural use.[1] Embedded in—or sometimes explicit to—this stance is the notion that vernacular buildings are the fragile remnants of a preindustrial, agrarian time when life was more cooperative, more humane, and, through manual labor, somehow more noble than the alternatives.[2] Although it enjoys some of the respectability of longevity, this view is becoming increasingly difficult to defend against charges of romanticism, nostalgia, and even ethnocentricity.

The study of vernacular architecture nevertheless owes its origins and many of its most important contributions to practitioners who maintain this perspective, and the restrictions on subject matter have not dictated similarly conservative limits on analysis. Approached as artifacts, the concrete results of architectural decisions made by common people in the course of ordinary lives, vernacular buildings have yielded new and sometimes startling insights into the cultures they represent. As a result, some scholars have been moved to proclaim that humble, unpretentious buildings represent the key to many fundamental questions. Historians might find among buildings information about the lives of documentarily mute people. For anthropologists, the complexity of architecture might yield evidence of ways of life or habits of mind that smaller artifacts conceal. These propositions have attracted the attention and, increasingly, the contributions of scholars from many varied disciplines that are often linked only by an interest in human behavior.[3]

Some history is useful here.[4] However it is defined, the study of vernacular architecture is part of a larger academic concern for what can be learned from all sorts of things that people make and use—from material culture. As it is now framed and practiced in North America, the field of vernacular architecture descends fairly directly from the work of cultural geographer Fred Kniffen. It was Kniffen's idea that folk housing forms might be used to track the

1. See Warren E. Roberts's untitled essay on material culture studies in *Material Culture* 17 (1985):89–93.

2. In a recent restatement of some of his classic positions, Henry Glassie distinguishes between vernacular and other forms of technology and asserts that the former has ennobling qualities. See his "Vernacular Architecture and Society," *Material Culture* 16 (1984):5–24.

3. See Dell Upton's claims for the potential of vernacular architecture studies in "Ordinary Buildings: A Bibliographical Essay on American Vernacular Architecture," *American Studies International* 19 (Winter 1981):57–75, esp. 57–58.

4. This essay outlines the descent of vernacular architecture studies that most readily comes to the mind of most scholars. For more complete discussions of the origins and developments of the field, consult Dell Upton's "Ordinary Buildings" and his "The Power of Things: Recent Studies in American Vernacular Architecture," *American Quarterly* 35 (1983):262–79. The latter essay has been republished in *Material Culture: A Research Guide*, ed. Thomas J. Schlereth (Lawrence: University Press of Kansas, 1985), pp. 57–78.

5. Fred B. Kniffen, "Louisiana House Types," *Annals of the Association of American Geographers* 26 (1936):179–93, reprinted in *Readings in Cultural Geography*, ed. Philip L. Wagner and Marvin W. Mikesell (Chicago: University of Chicago Press, 1962) pp. 157–69; Kniffen, "Folk Housing: Key to Diffusion," *Annals of the Association of American Geographers* 55 (1965):549–77, republished in *Common Places: Readings in American Vernacular Architecture*, ed. Dell Upton and John Michael Vlach (Athens: University of Georgia Press, 1986), pp. 3–26.

6. Henry Glassie, *Pattern in the Material Folk Culture of the Eastern United States* (Philadelphia: University of Pennsylvania Press, 1968).

7. James Deetz, *Invitation to Archaeology* (Garden City, N.Y.: Natural History Press, 1967); *In Small Things Forgotten: The Archaeology of Early American Life* (Garden City, N.Y.: Anchor Books, 1977).

8. Henry Glassie, "Eighteenth-Century Cultural Process in Delaware Valley Folk Building," *Winterthur Portfolio* 7 (1972):29–57, republished in *Common Places*, ed. Upton and Vlach, pp. 394–425.

9. Henry Glassie, *Folk Housing in Middle Virginia: A Structural Analysis of Historic Artifacts* (Knoxville: University of Tennessee Press, 1975).

10. John Michael Vlach, "The Shotgun House: An African Architectural Legacy," *Pioneer America* 8 (1976):47–70, reprinted in *Common Places*, ed. Upton and Vlach, pp. 58–78.

11. Edward A. Chappell, "Acculturation in the Shenandoah Valley: Rhenish Houses of the Massanutten Settlement," *Proceedings of the American Philosophical Society* 124 (1980):55–89, republished in *Common Places*, ed. Upton and Vlach, pp. 27–57.

12. See especially Dell Upton, "Vernacular Domestic Architecture in Eighteenth-Century Virginia," *Winterthur Portfolio* 17 (1982):95–119, reprinted in *Common Places*, ed. Upton and Vlach, pp. 315–35. Also consult Dell Upton, "Early Vernacular Architecture in Southeastern Virginia" (Ph.D. diss., Brown University, 1980).

course of a migrating culture.[5] His best perception—that buildings embody evidence of cultural patterns—was given fuller and more profound treatment by his student, Henry Glassie, whose doctoral dissertation in folklore was published under the title *Pattern in the Material Folk Culture of the Eastern United States.*[6]

The next most pressing series of questions concerned precisely how buildings represented their culture and what they have to say that is of significance. In *Invitation to Archaeology* and *In Small Things Forgotten*, anthropologist James Deetz proposed and explained the usefulness of the notion of "mental templates," or ideal prototypes that have currency within a culture. These are applied—more or less whole—to specific construction projects.[7] Glassie developed a similar idea in his discussion of the coming of the "Georgian mindset" to the architecture of the Delaware Valley.[8] In a subsequent path-breaking study, *Folk Housing in Middle Virginia*, Glassie solved the problems presented by individual deviation from these ideal templates by applying the principles of structural linguistics to an assemblage of houses in rural Virginia.[9] In effect, Glassie argued, every house is composed of distinct geometric components that are linked and integrated according to generally accepted rules of architectural "grammar." In this way, it is possible to explain the variety as well as the similarity that exists among the houses of a particular time and place.

In many respects, the study of vernacular architecture continues to function in the shadow of Glassie's work. The most influential of his ideas are those having to do with the importance of architectural form and type; attempts to follow his example appear in almost every study of ordinary buildings that has been produced since the late 1970s. His most inspiring contributions, however, have to do with the way in which artifacts relate to the more abstract aspects of culture and how changes in objects are sensitive indicators of changes in patterns of thought.

A number of scholars of vernacular architecture have worked with Glassie's ideas in particularly skillful ways. In his argument that the American shotgun house originates from African traditions, folklorist John Vlach applied what he learned from Glassie to questions of ethnicity.[10] Edward Chappell performed a similar operation on the issue of acculturation in his study of German immigrant houses in the Shenandoah Valley.[11] Dell Upton, who is trained in architectural history as well as in American studies, has not only worked in the anthropological directions that Glassie indicated but has also laid out new and promising avenues of inquiry by incorporating into his studies the methods of social history. Upton has offered the most useful criticism of Glassie's approach by asserting the importance of a specific historical context in the generation of building form.[12]

In thus reorienting vernacular architecture studies, Upton has been influenced by Abbott Lowell Cummings, a scholar of early

New England material culture. His work, exemplified by *The Framed Houses of Massachusetts Bay, 1625–1725*, is distinguished by intensive examination of standing buildings combined with extensive attention to related documentary sources.[13] Like Glassie, Cummings makes significant points about the necessity for rigorous architectural fieldwork, but his analysis of corroborating written material constitutes a sustained and subtle counterpoint to Glassie's anthropological approach. By example, Cummings has guided Upton and others toward a recognition that the persistence or alteration of artifactual characteristics must always be understood with reference to the particular historical environment.

Cary Carson, a social historian, has probably taken this perspective to its limit. He asserts that buildings can only prove their worth as source material when they embody the best, surest means by which historical questions can be answered.[14] This emphasis on the interpretation of architectural information in light of historical trends and hypotheses has been challenged by Fraser Neiman, an anthropologist who proposes that scholars of vernacular architecture, as well as other branches of material culture, must apply to their evidence rigorous scientific thinking—specifically, the model offered by evolutionary biology—if they are to avoid fallacious and soft-headed conclusions about complicated subjects.[15] Almost every study of vernacular buildings to date has been accomplished in the light of one or more of these influential works.

This linking of vernacular architecture as subject with the systematic thought of a constellation of disciplines has had the effect of releasing the term from any particular set of architectural characteristics. It has become defensible to assert that all ordinary buildings are the results of complex mental processes that have been shaped by learned—cultural—priorities and are therefore worthy of study. By now, it is generally acceptable to define vernacular architecture as common building of any sort. This means, for example, that nineteenth-century row houses and railroad stations and twentieth-century garages and diners are all potentially enlightening subjects of investigation.[16] The difference between a profound and a trite study is not the subject matter but the degree of skill with which it is examined. Buildings are supremely complex artifacts. Almost any aspect of them, given the right kind of inquiry, can be enlightening.

The next obvious step in this line of thought has not been so widely accepted. If what makes ordinary buildings interesting is that they are complex artifacts embodying important information about the people who built them, then pretentious buildings—monuments, palaces, cathedrals, the showcase projects of architects—are also worthy of attention. Although structures of this sort have long been coddled and scrutinized by traditional architectural historians, thoughtful attention has always focused on issues of style, on aesthetics, and on the contributions made by individual

13. Abbott Lowell Cummings, *The Framed Houses of Massachusetts Bay, 1625–1725* (Cambridge: Harvard University Press, 1979).

14. Cary Carson, "Doing History with Material Culture," in *Material Culture and the Study of American Life*, ed. Ian M. G. Quimby (New York: W. W. Norton and Company, 1978), pp. 41–64.

15. Neiman's work is not well known because it is still mostly unpublished. Fraser D. Neiman, "An Evolutionary Approach to House Plans and the Organization of Production on the Chesapeake Frontier," a paper presented at the annual conference of the Society of Historical Archaeology, Williamsburg, 1984.

16. For a recent and accessible statement on the inclusiveness of the term *vernacular architecture*, see Upton's contribution to *Built in the U.S.A.: American Buildings from Airports to Zoos*, ed. Diane Maddex (Washington, D.C.: Preservation Press, 1985), pp. 167–71.

designers.[17] Only rarely are these "great works" subjected to the questions that have come to characterize the best studies of vernacular architecture.

At this point in the argument, it is clear that vernacular architecture has become, for many scholars, less a *kind* of building than an *approach* to looking at buildings.[18] In a literal sense, then, the term is outmoded or inadequate. Nevertheless, it continues as a convenient denomination for a specific, if difficult-to-define, field of study. "Vernacular architecture" has been stretched—but not strained—to include the recording and analysis of structures of every age, form, and function. It can include consideration of architectural spaces as small as closets and as large as cityscapes. Accompanying this catholicity in subject matter is a similar range of issues that buildings are expected to inform. Furthermore, these formidable tasks may be accomplished by an increasing variety and combination of methods and theories proposed by scholars with an expanding diversity of specialties. Thus, though the term denotes nothing more than a kind of subject matter, it connotes much more. "Vernacular architecture" today is a mildly unstable and semantically indefensible mixture of evidence, method, and theory. It occupies a poorly worked-out frontier where new and significant things are likely to occur.

This book, the second in a projected series, is the product of an organization that was formed in response to the complex and stimulating qualities of the subject.[19] The Vernacular Architecture Forum is a North American organization established in 1980 to promote the study of vernacular buildings through various and multiple approaches. Because of the Forum's origins, most of its members resist the placing of limits on acceptable topics or ways of working. The result is a pervading sense that every established scholarly convention needs careful reevaluation and that every new perspective needs a fair chance. These characteristics gain energy and persistence from the quarterly *Vernacular Architecture Newsletter* and particularly from the Forum's annual conferences. At these meetings, tours of regional architecture impose limits on the hours devoted to paper sessions, completed projects share presentation time with works in progress, and informal exchanges bracket and flow from formal deliveries.[20] In all this, there is discernible a restless and uneasy attempt to consider or rethink every process by which the field of vernacular architecture defines, performs, and communicates its work.

The recent institution at Forum meetings of paper sessions devoted exclusively to methodology suggests correctly that this inclusive spirit is balanced by a pervasive commitment to scrupulous care in dealing with vernacular buildings. Most Forum members share a conviction that original fieldwork among standing structures is of primary importance. They acknowledge that even sturdy new buildings are actually fragile, unprotected source material requiring

17. For discussions of aspects of this issue, see Richard Longstreth, "The Problem with 'Style,'" in *The Forum: Bulletin of the Committee on Preservation, Society of Architectural Historians* 6 (December 1984):1–4; Elizabeth Cromley, "Six Mental Models of What Historians Do," a paper presented at the annual conference of the Society of Architectural Historians, Pittsburgh, 1985; and Jules David Prown's untitled discussion of material culture studies in *Material Culture* 17 (1985):77–79.

18. Upton, "The Power of Things," pp. 263–64.

19. Papers from the Forum's first two annual conferences, held in Washington, D.C., in 1980 and Massachusetts in 1981, are collected in *Perspectives in Vernacular Architecture*, ed. Camille Wells (Annapolis: Vernacular Architecture Forum, 1982).

20. The emphasis on architectural tours during the annual conferences was patterned after the example of the Vernacular Architecture Group, the Forum's thirty-year-old counterpart in the United Kingdom. See Cary Carson, "Whither VAG?" *Vernacular Architecture* 15 (1984):3–5.

thorough and exact attention. A part of this process involves the tools of graphic representation—including photography, mapping, and drafting—and methods of description and interpretation that do not obscure or misrepresent the complexity of the actual structure. In these ways, the eager attention to new approaches is always tempered by an awareness that many facile and sloppy ways of dealing with architecture need to be avoided. This creates a tension or urgency that may be the best environment in which to generate new techniques and ideas of lasting value.

If this book is successful, it will have preserved some of the permissive/demanding spirit fostered by the Vernacular Architecture Forum. Each essay in this volume is a refereed selection from among the papers presented at the Forum's conferences in North Carolina in 1982, Wisconsin in 1983, and Delaware in 1984. The twenty papers were selected because of the quality of their contributions to the study of vernacular architecture. While all of them are substantially the works that were originally presented, a number of the articles have been altered or slightly expanded by the authors during preparation for publication. The thirty other essays presented at the three meetings—many of which have been published or are in press elsewhere—are represented by abstracts at the end of the volume. In relevant cases, information is provided concerning where the full text of the paper may be found. Inclusion of abstracts as well as complete essays serves several purposes. First, it insures against loss the contributions of those authors whose work is incomplete or underway. It also allows the collection to function more fully as a record of the kind of work that is going on in the field of vernacular architecture. Finally, it permits a more complete representation of the texture of the annual Forum conferences, events that are fundamental to the continued vitality of the organization and the work to which it gives voice.

Where does this book fit into the developing body of studies on the subject of vernacular architecture? At the most basic level, it is the only serial publication in North America to be devoted entirely to the results of research and analysis of vernacular architecture. The diversity of topics and approaches in this collection of essays is also representative of the current trend toward consideration of all aspects of buildings. While most of the papers consider structures that may be readily classified as ordinary or unpretentious, a number of the authors have crossed the latest set of familiar boundaries: there is nothing ordinary about Wisconsin housebarns, nothing unpretentious about the Anglican churches of colonial Virginia. Moreover, the authors themselves reflect the diversity of disciplines that now consider buildings to be worthy primary source material. Counting only the most advanced degree in each case, the fifty contributors represent thirteen distinct fields of study.

The works in this volume also represent all types of contributions to the field of vernacular architecture studies.[21] A number of

21. Because of the interdisciplinary nature of many of these essays, they may be grouped and compared in a number of ways. The connections that are emphasized here do not always correspond with the similarities by which the papers are grouped in the body of the book. This need for multiple and overlapping categories is one of the factors that has frustrated those who are used to more crisply defined boundaries. This apparent disorder is necessary and even desirable, for scholars of vernacular architecture are in the process of working out ways of dealing with a varied and complex subject.

the articles are conceived as descriptions and comparisons. They remind other practitioners that, as long as many aspects of the complicated source material remain overlooked, there is an important place for plain, straightforward presentations. Recognizing this, Ken Breisch and David Moore deal with the stone houses of Norwegian immigrants to Texas and examine their relationships to Old World architectural precedents. With similar thoroughness, Bill Tishler and Chris Witmer present the surviving evidence for a tradition of housebarn construction in Wisconsin. As part of his continuing study of Paradise Valley, Nevada, Rusty Marshall describes the historical influences that have transformed the appearance of the community's orthogonal town plan.

The process of recording buildings—the "spade work" of vernacular architecture studies—is the subject of Edward Chappell's essay. He points out that even the most rigorous and seemingly objective recording efforts involve interpretations and priorities. Chappell devotes considerable attention to graphic systems of representing the complex information that fieldworkers invariably turn up. This issue of using drawings creatively to sort through and think about architectural information is also the subject of Frances Downing and Tom Hubka's paper. They demonstrate how architectural diagramming can be used to isolate or distill the significant components of a structure or site.

Among other possible uses, Downing and Hubka show that types of buildings can be graphically displayed. The matter of *how* buildings should be sorted among appropriate types—and the inability of conventional typologies to deal successfully with diverse building forms—is the principal concern of Richard Longstreth's article. In his analysis of American commercial buildings, Longstreth has found accepted criteria for constructing typologies to be inadequate. Paul Groth has arrived at a similar conclusion in his discussion of urban rooming houses. Both essays press at the limits common to anthropological systems for sorting artifacts in meaningful ways.

Classification and its potential for managing the recent explosion of information about vernacular architecture are the concerns of Barbara Wyatt's essay. She points out that, however inadequate it may be to sort buildings by style in the conventional art-historical manner, scholars of vernacular architecture have yet to develop categories and taxonomies that can serve in broad contexts to emphasize more important characteristics of buildings. Although a standardized continent-wide building typology may not be possible or even desirable, Wyatt is correct to emphasize that records about vernacular buildings are part of the public domain in a double sense: not only is most vernacular architectural fieldwork funded by public agencies, but the perceptions that may be gained by examining ordinary buildings are, like the structures themselves, part of a widespread heritage. Scholars have a responsibility to make their insights accessible—to teach what they learn.

In keeping with the interdisciplinary character of most vernacular architecture studies, many of the works in this volume experiment with tools and approaches that are more commonly applied to other subjects. Although vernacular architecture scholars tend to dismiss style and aesthetics as the concern of designers and art historians, Robert Alexander uses such matters to discern social and economic conflicts between different groups in turn-of-the-century Iowa City. Janet Hutchison's work, like that of most historians, draws upon documentary materials, but she critically examines the literature of the early twentieth-century Better Homes Movement to discern how house plans and embellishments were invoked to popularize a specifically Anglo-American, middle-class, paternalistic vision of homemaking and child care.

Some of the essays in this book employ a variety of careful recording techniques to refute established and often superficial notions about buildings and landscapes. In his study of New England villages, Joe Wood demonstrates that the stereotypical image of the colonial New England community is actually based on settlement patterns that did not evolve until the early nineteenth century. Paul Touart uses the evidence of surviving German buildings in Davidson County, North Carolina, to point out that acculturation can occur at different rates for ethnic building forms and construction techniques. Using both field and documentary material, Chris Martin refutes the popular belief that the nineteenth-century urban flounder house was conceived as an incomplete or auxiliary building form. Tom Hubka describes how the traditional and picturesque service ell of a New England connected farm was actually the result of an attempt on the part of nineteenth-century farmers to modernize their agricultural operations.

Other articles challenge the assumptions common to many recent vernacular architecture studies. In his examination of imagery associated with Quaker meetinghouses, Bill Moore shows that buildings are not the guileless embodiments of cultural values they are sometimes thought to be. Like documents, they can be biased, misleading, or ambiguous. Arlene Horvath questions the generally assumed relationship between the beliefs and the buildings of a specific culture. In her case study of a prominent Quaker's house in Chester County, Pennsylvania, she looks for concrete connections between culture as thought and culture as built.

In taking on the architectural relics of the colonial Virginia planter society, Mark Wenger and Dell Upton address subject material that might be considered more appropriate for conventional architectural historians. But in the questions they pose and answer, both authors demonstrate how the issues that concern scholars of vernacular architecture may be addressed effectively through any sort of structure. Wenger's principal concern is how one domestic architectural space was used and changed with time, while Upton considers how the symbolic content of Anglican churches—ostensibly public buildings—proposed and reinforced the social dominance of colonial Virginia's elites.

Wenger and Upton deal with the architecture of socially and economically advantaged people in order to explain something about the colonial world in which they prevailed. Other authors in this collection have framed topics around more recent subjects, permitting the study of less advantaged sectors of a population. Paul Groth suggests that vernacular architecture scholars must look among unlikely interstitial spaces to find the living patterns and material influences of such "invisible" social groups as downtown rooming-house dwellers. Gray Read shows how black working-class inhabitants redesign their nineteenth-century Philadelphia row houses, creating distinctive cultural statements among structures they had no part in building. In her study of the architecture of western North Carolina, Michael Ann Williams demonstrates that the techniques of oral history can reveal complex ideas about an apparently simple house form.

The sure-handed quality of some of the essays in this volume contrasts sharply with the groping, reaching quality of others. Tones vary because some of the authors have employed familiar ways of working with vernacular buildings, while others have adopted new tactics or materials. Most of these papers are representative rather than groundbreaking, but, collectively, they make an important statement about the current nature of vernacular architecture studies.

It is reasonably clear that the time for audacious declarations is past.[22] This is one aspect of the recent and pleasant acceptance that vernacular architecture studies are finding among established disciplines. But tenured positions and book contracts must deceive no one. Vast amounts of rigorous work and tough thinking remain to be done, and these tasks may be all the more difficult to perform precisely because of the field's increasing respectability, which will introduce to vernacular architecture studies the dangers of complacency and homogeneity.

Bold manifestos are also inappropriate among vernacular architecture studies because there continues to exist a wide disparity between postulated theories and satisfactory proof.[23] This is partly because the character of vernacular architecture as historical evidence has been misunderstood. When scholars of the subject began to pay closer attention to specific historical contexts, they discovered with alarm that the material record of the past is, like the documentary record, drastically skewed in favor of the powerful and affluent. In many cases, surviving buildings offer little or no better picture of life among common folk than do written sources.[24]

The gap between claim and performance also persists because of inadequacies in the methods and theories that scholars of ver-

22. John Vlach also has recently remarked that the time for material culture scholars to make strident manifestos is past. See his untitled essay in *Material Culture* 17 (1985):81–84.

23. Jules Prown has made the same observation of material culture studies generally. See his remarks in *Material Culture* 17 (1985):77.

24. Orlando Ridout V, "Re-Editing the Past: A Comparison of Surviving Documentary and Physical Evidence," a paper presented at the annual conference of the Society of Architectural Historians, New Haven, 1982; Dell Upton, "The Origins of Chesapeake Architecture," in *Three Centuries of Maryland Architecture* (Annapolis: Maryland Historical Trust, 1982), pp. 44–57; Cary Carson et al., "Impermanent Architecture in the Southern American Colonies," *Winterthur Portfolio* 16 (1981):135–96.

nacular architecture have applied to the study of ordinary structures. While the multidisciplinary nature of the field cannot be overemphasized, these various means of explanation might be conveniently designated as either historical or anthropological. Approaches to the study of vernacular buildings may be historical in the sense either that they are also used to manage more traditional documentary evidence, or that they focus primarily on the historical environment of the structures in question. They tend to yield results that are heavily descriptive, sometimes antiquarian, and only occasionally applicable to other contexts. Too often, historical approaches tend to use the information buildings offer merely to illustrate perceived historical trends. At best, buildings are elevated to the status of primary evidence for standard issues of concern to historians.[25]

By contrast, anthropological approaches are usually more likely to acknowledge that buildings are complex artifacts that can do far more than inform established questions. They can actually *change* the questions scholars ask. Anthropological methods of understanding buildings usually involve the application or development of analytical models, but once building forms and functions are sorted and dissected, interpretations of the results tend to be no more inspiring than are those derived from historical treatments. They may rely on a hard, "scientific" line of reasoning that makes the manifestations of culture indistinguishable from biological processes.[26] In other cases, anthropological analyses seem too intuitive, too dependent on the mental structures of the author. Like literary criticism, they are dangerously susceptible to the trim analogy or the persuasive phrase.[27] Although the anthropological treatment of buildings is often very brave, most discussions are erroneously prone to suggest that their results are universally applicable.[28]

Complacency about unfulfilled propositions is not the only danger that respectability poses for scholars of vernacular architecture. In its maturity, this field of study must also resist homogeneity. Arguments concerning how vernacular buildings should be recorded, sorted, and analyzed cannot come to rest on the illusion that a single encompassing system of analysis will fulfill every need or purpose.[29] Scholars must maintain a central place for the basic questions that first defined the field of vernacular architecture studies, and they must learn to live with the uneasiness of the resulting reevaluation, criticism, and disagreement.

Homogeneity in vernacular architecture studies can also take the form of compromises made among research conclusions in the service of wider acceptability.[30] This is particularly likely, for looking at buildings analytically can be a radicalizing experience. Structures constructed by every sort of person and in every sort of environment and period are attempts to modify the material world, often in order to shape the actions of others. At some level, most buildings can be understood in terms of power or authority—as efforts to assume, extend, resist, or accommodate it. In other words, those

25. See Carson, "Doing History with Material Culture."
26. See Neiman, "An Evolutionary Approach."
27. Glassie's work, for all of its inherent significance, often relies on the appealing qualities of his poetic style of writing. See his "Vernacular Architecture and Society."
28. Vlach, for example, occasionally argues that there are common forms and principles to be discerned in the manifestations of all cultures. See his argument that the venerability of the shotgun house can be inferred from the proliferation of subtypes in "The Shotgun House," esp. pp. 49–51 in the *Pioneer America* version.
29. Tom Hubka is one scholar who argues for the development of "a unified, historically comprehensive view of the whole" field of vernacular architecture. See his "In the Vernacular: Classifying American Folk and Popular Architecture," *The Forum: Bulletin of the Committee on Preservation*, Society of Architectural Historians 7 (December 1985):1–2.
30. A warning example is the way in which American social history—often called "history from the bottom up"—has been domesticated into the study of whole societies and how they function. While this reframing of the subject may seem fairer and broader in scope, it actually disarms a significant radical challenge to mainstream American history. The goal has been to make the methods and rhetoric of social history acceptable to a wide range of public agencies and private institutions. See Michael Olmert, "The New, No-Frills Williamsburg," *Historic Preservation*, October 1985, pp. 26–33.

who study buildings usually have access to a fairly rough story of conflict and exploitation, and they have an obligation to describe what they see. There should be no modifications for the benefit of employers and audiences.

If these dangers can be avoided, then scholars of vernacular architecture will be free to embrace their new respectability among established disciplines without fear that the flexible boundaries of their field will harden or that the sharp edges of their questions will be blunted. Moreover, there will be good reasons to take the next steps forward with confidence. Those audacious claims about recovering lost histories and recasting cultural analysis may remain unfulfilled, but they also remain worthy and recognized challenges. Furthermore, as this collection of essays emphatically demonstrates, vernacular architecture continues to represent a distinctive and enticingly varied assemblage of subjects for study—and no limits to the possibilities are in sight.

I. Methods for Understanding Buildings

2

RICHARD LONGSTRETH

Compositional Types in American Commercial Architecture

American commercial architecture is just beginning to be understood. Since the 1930s numerous studies have examined the history of the tall office building, yet until recently these have tended to be episodic, focusing on the inceptive period of development in Chicago and, to a lesser extent, in New York. Technological advances and formal devices employed on the exterior have almost always been the subjects of primary concern.[1] The architectural histories that have been written about many cities include a greater variety of commercial work. These monographs may be helpful in identifying relationships between urban growth and building form, yet stylistic properties and influences remain dominant issues.[2]

Commercial architecture has rarely been considered in broader terms—as it relates to the values of a consumer society, to the objectives of a complex managerial infrastructure, and as an approach to building whereby the capacity to generate revenue is the paramount consideration. Studies of buildings according to their function provide an obvious opportunity for such research, but these are rare and do not always pay sufficient attention to programmatic issues.[3] Several essays concerning topics such as interior spatial organization, architecture as a propagator of corporate identity, the role of a client in creating form and image, and how a building type fosters certain urban living patterns offer welcome departures and underscore the richness of subject matter deserving further attention.[4] Even here, the emphasis has been on major works. A sizable

1. The extensive bibliography of Chicago skyscrapers and their architects is well known. Broader geographic and interpretative analyses began to appear some fifteen years ago. See Winston Weisman, "A New View of Skyscraper History," in *The Rise of American Architecture*, ed. Edgar Kaufmann (New York: Praeger Publishers, 1970), pp. 115–60; Cervin Robinson and Rosemarie Haag Bletter, *Skyscraper Style: Art Deco New York* (New York: Oxford University Press, 1975). The first attempt to provide a complete overview of skyscraper development did not appear until Paul Goldberger's *The Skyscraper* (New York: Alfred A. Knopf, 1981). *Chicago and New York: Architectural Interactions* (Chicago: Art Institute of Chicago, 1984) demonstrates that fresh perspectives on the subject are by no means exhausted.

2. Among the cities covered are Boston, Portland (Maine), Philadelphia, Cleveland, Detroit, Kansas City, Minneapolis, Denver, and Los Angeles. One of the most recent and finest studies of this genre is Robert Stern et al., *New York 1900: Metropolitan Architecture and Urbanism 1890–1915* (New York: Rizzoli International Publishing, 1983). The subject is discussed further in Richard Longstreth, "Architecture and the City," in *American Urbanism: A Historical Review*, ed. Howard Gillette, Jr. (Westport, Conn.: Greenwood Press, forthcoming).

3. See, for example, Nikolaus Pevsner, *A History of Building Types* (Princeton: Princeton University Press,

1976), and James O'Gorman's review of it in the *Journal of the Society of Architectural Historians* 36 (1977):199–200. Among the few attempts to provide a comprehensive examination of a commercial building type are Carroll Meeks, *The Railroad Station: An Architectural History* (New Haven: Yale University Press, 1956), and Johann Friedrich Geist, *Arcades: The History of a Building Type* (Cambridge: MIT Press, 1983).

4. See, for example, Harry Resseguie, "A. T. Stewart's Marble Palace— The Cradle of the Department Store," *New-York Historical Society Quarterly* 48 (1964):131–62; Francis Duffy, "Office buildings and organisational change," in *Buildings and Society: Essays on the Social Development of the Built Environment*, ed. Anthony D. King (London: Routledge and Kegan Paul, 1980), pp. 255–80; Deborah Andrews, "Bank Building in Nineteenth-Century Phila-

accumulation of recent books and articles on roadside architecture has concentrated on representational design, but counterparts in the urban commercial center are seldom the objects of scrutiny.[5]

A concrete impetus for further research comes from the rapidly increasing efforts to preserve commercial buildings of all types and in virtually every kind of urban precinct. The typology presented here is an outgrowth of these circumstances: it began as part of a comprehensive survey of downtown San Francisco and was further developed under the auspices of the National Trust's Main Street Program.[6] The buildings studied were constructed between about 1800 and 1950. They were designed as retail facilities, offices, hotels, banks, and theaters, collectively representing the primary components of commercial centers. The immediate objective was to provide a means of classification that would lend greater insight into this architecture's salient qualities than does the plethora of pseudo-stylistic terms that have gained currency during the past two decades.

Concepts of style were developed during the nineteenth century as a way of analyzing distinguishing characteristics in the work of individual artists, and to give identity and meaning to broad tendencies in art over sustained periods of time. In applying this methodology to the myriad particulars of expression found in both eclectic and modernist work for nearly two hundred years, much of its value has been lost.[7] Nowhere is the problem more apparent than with commercial buildings, which, aside from small shops and market halls, scarcely existed as distinct entities before 1800. Style remains a pertinent matter in addressing many architectural developments—including those in the commercial sphere—but its full value can only be realized within a more holistic frame of reference, one that considers the entire range of salient physical characteristics of a given era.

Fundamental requirements for developing the typology were that it be simple and that it be nationally applicable. An underlying objective was that this classification method also provide an instrument for further research, raising questions that could lead to a better understanding of commercial architecture. The typology based on form devised by Fred Kniffen and others to trace cultural patterns through eighteenth- and early nineteenth-century rural

delphia," in *The Divided Metropolis: Social and Spatial Dimensions of Philadelphia 1800–1975*, ed. William Cutler and Howard Gillette, Jr. (Westport, Conn.: Greenwood Press, 1980), pp. 57–83; Susan Porter Benson, "Palace of Consumption and Machine for Selling: The American Department Store, 1880–1940," *Radical History Review* 21 (1979):199–221; and Charles Bohi and W. Roger Grant, "The Country Railroad Station as Corporate Logo," *Pioneer America* 11 (1979):117–29.

5. Besides numerous articles on roadside architecture, several books have appeared, most notably Chester Liebs, *Main Street to Miracle Mile: American Roadside Architecture* (Boston: New York Graphic Society, 1985); Paul Hirshorn and Steven Izenour, *White Towers* (Cambridge: MIT Press, 1979); and Warren James Belasco, *Americans on the Road: From Autocamp to Motel, 1910–1945* (Cambridge: MIT Press, 1979). Idiomatic examples in commercial centers have received some attention in urban studies such as Carole Rifkind, *Main Street: The Face of Urban America* (New York: Harper and Row, 1977), and John Jackle, *The American Small Town: Twentieth-Century Place Images* (Hamden, Conn.: Archon Books, 1982). The most detailed study of such work is British but could well be applied to American communities: J. W. R. Whitehand, "Commercial townscapes in the making," *Journal of Historical Geography* 10 (1984):174–200. Exemplary published inventories focusing on commercial architecture include Charles Hall Page and Associates, *Splendid Survivors: San Francisco's Downtown Architectural Heritage* (San Francisco: California Living Books, 1979); and Marie Louise Christovitch et al., *New Orleans Architecture: The American Sector* (Gretna, La.: Pelican Publishing, 1972).

6. In its original form, this typology was included as an appendix in Page and Associates, *Splendid Survivors*. Subsequent funding from the National Trust facilitated the study of work in hundreds of communities with populations of approximately fifty thousand or less in Arizona, California, Colorado, Connecticut, Illinois, Indiana, Iowa, Kansas, Kentucky, Maryland, Massachusetts, Missouri, Nebraska, Nevada, New Jersey, New Mexico, New York, Ohio, Oklahoma, Pennsylvania, Rhode Island, Utah, Vermont, and West Virginia, during the summer of 1980. A circuitous cross-continental route was selected to cover a wide spectrum of settlement periods, urban forms, economic bases, and topographical areas. Since 1980, an examination of buildings in almost as many communities in the same and other parts of the country has yielded no evidence for altering the typology. Yet, as with any such construct, more field testing may lead to modifications.

7. Meyer Shapiro, "Style," in *Anthropology Today*, ed. A. L. Kroeber (Chicago: University of Chicago Press, 1953), pp. 287–312; Richard Longstreth, "The Problem with 'Style,'" *The Forum, Bulletin of the Committee on Preservation*, Society of Architectural Historians 6 (December 1984):1–4.

houses affords an obvious model. At the same time, inherent differences in the nature of commercial architecture necessitate modifications to both the system itself and the purposes for which it can be used.

A commercial building's three-dimensional form may or may not be a revealing characteristic.[8] In the great majority of cases, mass is a direct response to lot configuration and therefore is not dependable as a basis for type differentiation. The forms of larger, and especially taller, buildings may be determined by factors such as zoning and building codes, available construction techniques, and interior functions. Form can help elucidate matters such as the development of office building design between 1890 and 1920, or building practices that became commonplace in St. Louis, but not in Boston. However, the possible combination of variables is very great and so dependent on local conditions that they are of little aid in identifying broad patterns.

A second distinction of this typology is the irrelevance of floor plans, which are either too amorphous or too particularized for general classification purposes. The layout of hotels, for example, sustained numerous substantial changes during the past hundred and fifty years. Moreover, during any one period, the plan might vary according to the type of clientele for which it was designed, the size of the building, its urban context, and its site configuration. Another complicating factor is that many commercial buildings were planned to serve more than one function: shops and lodge hall, bank and offices, hotel and theater. None of these variations necessarily bears direct correspondence to exterior form. Finally, numerous commercial buildings, especially those planned for the retail and wholesale trades, were constructed with an open plan that could be fitted and changed according to the needs of a succession of occupants.

The planning of commercial buildings thus differs considerably from that of houses, which are composed as a collection of rooms, each with its own special uses and relationships to the others. Domestic room arrangements tend to remain consistent over extended periods of time. By contrast, commercial buildings can be seen as vessels, efficient containers of flexible space, their form determined by one set of demands and their internal organization dictated by others. The resulting spatial order can be quite loose or very particularized and, in either instance, often modified or soon outmoded.

A third important difference in this typology is the absence of pronounced regional distinctions. Whereas early house typologies were developed as a means of delineating cultural regions, there is no comparable basis for classification of commercial architecture. Locational variations certainly can be found in the use of materials, elements, and historical references. Some types may be more prevalent in certain parts of the country than in others. But when viewed from a national perspective, these aspects are minor compared to the basic similarities that exist. Itinerant builders and architects con-

8. A typology based on commercial building form has been offered by Steven Holl in "The Alphabetical City," *Pamphlet Architecture #5*, 1980.

tributed to this homogeneity before manufacturers' catalogs and trade and professional journals helped to codify it.

From a pragmatic viewpoint, an architectural solution that demonstrated its economic soundness and popular appeal was bound to be widely used. Innovation in commercial architecture has always been essential to maintain a competitive edge. However, once a successful new scheme was created, it enjoyed a large following. Individual identity was important, but seldom to the point of radical departure from the basics of a current convention. Hence, a relatively small number of buildings, such as the Tremont House built in Boston in 1828, or A. T. Stewart's 1845 department store in New York, to cite two early examples, exerted an enormous influence in their respective cities and elsewhere.

Competition among communities further stimulated the tendency to conform. Hundreds, if not thousands, of American settlements were founded in the nineteenth century with the hope that they eventually would become great centers of commerce. As a result, cities strove to upstage one another in a battle for economic hegemony.[9] Architecture offered a potent symbol in these contests. Through commercial buildings, towns sought to look like cities, small cities to look like larger cities. Examples in the major metropolises set the standard. Under the circumstances, the conspicuous presence of ethnic roots or regional peculiarities in a commercial district was the last attribute community boosters wanted.

Among the most distinguishing features of commercial architecture, and one that best lends itself to broad categorical divisions, is the street front or facade. From the early nineteenth through the mid-twentieth century, the large majority of commercial buildings were erected abutting one another on deep lots of roughly standard dimensions. When exposed by service walks or alleys, the rear and side elevations were almost always treated in a stark, utilitarian manner. These sides were never intended to be "seen." In contrast, the facade gives the building most of its identity.[10] The importance of this elevation as an emblem of material progress is well conveyed by its abundant pictorial representation in advertisements, directories, atlases, and on the borders of urban views.[11] The facade does not just contain essential elements, it is composed. It boasts of ornament, signs, and other distinctive features. It exhibits the best materials and workmanship. Such edifices are not so much three-dimensional objects as they are decorated wall planes facing the street (Fig. 1).[12] The primary exceptions are buildings situated on corner lots and those erected with the expectation that they would remain considerably taller than their neighbors. In such instances, the exposed sides tend to echo the principal elevation and often play a subordinate role in the overall design (Fig. 2).

Commercial building facades are infinitely varied in their use of materials, elements, and decorative motifs. Save for speculative commercial rows and a relatively small number of cast- and stamped-iron fronts, no two facades are identical. On the other

9. See, for instance, John Reps, *The Making of Urban America: A History of City Planning in the United States* (Princeton: Princeton University Press, 1965) and *Cities of the American West: A History of Frontier Urban Planning* (Princeton: Princeton University Press, 1979); Richard Wade, *The Urban Frontier* (Chicago: University of Chicago Press, 1959); and Mel Scott, *The San Francisco Bay Area: A Metropolis in Perspective* (Berkeley and Los Angeles: University of California Press, 1959).

10. Major interior spaces in buildings such as hotels, department stores, banks, and theaters can be at least equally important in this regard.

11. Commercial directories composed of illustrations of building facades were published in at least three cities: for New York, *Pictorial Directory of New York* (1848) and *Illustrated Pictorial Directory of Broadway* (1948); for Philadelphia, *Rae's Philadelphia Pictorial Directory and Panorama Advertiser* (1851) and *Panoramic Business Directory of Philadelphia* (1879–1880); and for San Francisco, *The Illustrated Directory* (1894–1895).

12. This emphasis is evident in early plan books such as Samuel Sloan's *City and Suburban Architecture* (1859) and several others prepared by A. J. Bicknell between 1872 and 1878. In these volumes, store facades and their details are featured, but with scarcely any corresponding plans. The interior organization of buildings with more complicated programs was, of course, a concern for architects. This subject received considerable attention in professional literature by the turn of the twentieth century.

Fig. 1. York Gas Company in York, Pennsylvania, built in the early twentieth century. (author)

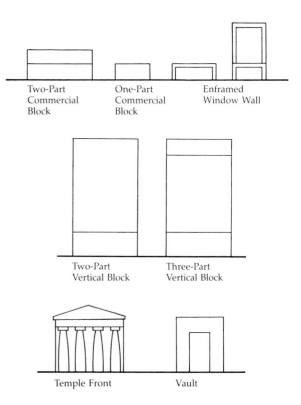

Fig. 3. Diagrammatic representation of commercial building compositional types. (Sherwin Greene)

Fig. 2. A mid-nineteenth-century commercial building in Covington, Indiana. (author)

hand, the great majority of examples constructed between about 1800 and 1950 do conform to a few compositional arrangements.[13] These basic facade patterns provide the primary characteristics for this typology (Fig. 3).[14]

The *two-part commercial block* is generally limited to buildings of two to four stories and is characterized by a horizontal division into two distinct zones. Each zone receives its own treatment, often with little direct relation to the other. The division reflects differences in use: the one-story lower zone tends to contain more public spaces, the upper zone more private ones. The type came into common usage during the first half of the nineteenth century and remained popular into the mid-twentieth century.

The *one-part commercial block* is used for one-story buildings and is characterized by a configuration akin to the lower zone of a two-part commercial block. The type appears to have emerged during the mid-nineteenth century as a means of imparting urban overtones to new communities and to rapidly developing service nodes in outlying areas of older settlements. It continued to be used into the mid-twentieth century in places where land values remained relatively low.

The *enframed window wall* is used for one-story and sometimes taller buildings. It is characterized by a large center section—often made of glass—that almost always suggests a thin membrane. This center is surrounded on three sides by a wide, more or less continuous border. The entire front is treated as a single compositional unit. The type began to be used around the turn of the twentieth century and maintained currency for about five decades.

The *two-part vertical block* is used for multistoried buildings and is characterized by two major zones, the lower one generally of two stories, serving as a visual base for the upper, multistoried shaft. The lower zone tends to be more embellished, but the upper zone is much larger and is the predominant part. As a result, the facade reads as a tall building with a unified ordering of elements, not just as layered stories piled atop the lower zone. Examples can be found on buildings of modest heights as early as the mid-nineteenth century, but the most prolific use was on considerably taller buildings constructed from the 1890s through the 1920s.

The *three-part vertical block* is used for multistoried buildings and is characterized by the same features as the two-part vertical block with the exception of a distinct third zone at the top that provides a visual cap to the composition. The periods of use are approximately the same as those for the two-part vertical block. In a number of examples erected during the 1920s, the upper zone is treated as one or more setbacks in the building mass.

The *temple front* is generally limited to buildings of one to three stories and is characterized by a composition derived from the fronts of temples of Greek and Roman antiquity. The facade may be either *prostyle* or *distyle in antis*, with freestanding or engaged col-

13. Because this typology is based on extant buildings and, with the exception of San Francisco, has not been derived from detailed examination of major cities, some gaps may exist, particularly for developments in metropolises such as Boston, New York, Philadelphia, and Chicago during the third quarter of the nineteenth century. Two essays by Winston Weisman provide a cornerstone for further inquiry: "Commercial Palaces of New York: 1845–1875," *Art Bulletin* 36 (1954):285–302; and "Philadelphia Functionalism and Sullivan," *Journal of the Society of Architectural Historians* 20 (1962):3–19.

14. Each type is discussed at length in Richard Longstreth, "A Topological Guide to Main Street Commercial Architecture," in the National Main Street Center's forthcoming book on commercial building design.

Fig 5. An early twentieth-century bank in Wells, Nevada. (author)

Fig. 4. York Trust Company in York, Pennsylvania, built in 1910. (author)

15. The author's research on other topics in California and in the central states has revealed that by the latter decades of the nineteenth century a number of carpenters and builders began to call themselves architects and that such men appear to have designed many commercial buildings, including rather simple ones in small towns. By the early twentieth century, the majority of commercial buildings were probably the work of individual architects, construction companies, or plan firms that employed trained designers. It can be argued that these idiomatic products remain quite different in some respects from those of the nation's leading architects, but exploring such distinctions is clearly the topic for another study.

umns, pilasters, or piers that allude to the column form. The type was popular for buildings of a number of functions during the first half of the nineteenth century. At the turn of the twentieth century it was revived and used in a more interpretative manner primarily for banks. Its common use continued into the 1920s.

The *vault* is generally limited to buildings of one to three stories and is characterized by a massive front penetrated by a single large opening in the center, sometimes with smaller openings on either side. The type was infrequently used during the nineteenth century. It became a popular composition for bank facades during the first three decades of the twentieth century.

The pervasiveness of such compositional types raises several issues concerning the nature of commercial building design. These types are standard for both high-style and vernacular examples; by themselves, they do not distinguish between the two realms. Thus, this method of classification emphasizes commonalities between the work of a nationally renowned architectural office, one with a localized practice in a small town, and a builder who may or may not have used detailed plans. Despite the many differences that can be attributed to such diverse authorships, the compositional language seldom varies to a substantial degree (Figs. 4 and 5).[15]

Fig. 6. Commercial buildings in Burlington, New Jersey, most built in the early nineteenth century. (author)

Origin is another matter. Some types, such as the temple front, were introduced through important buildings designed by leading architects of the day. From a few innovative and celebrated examples, this type became widely diffused by the middle of the nineteenth century. Its reemergence some fifty years later followed much the same course.[16] The development of the three-part vertical block is more complicated. The idea of a tripartite composition was employed over a period of several decades for narrow buildings of four to seven stories in probably no more than four major cities. Not until the 1890s did the type gain widespread use, and then it was for buildings that were considerably taller.[17]

The history of the two-part commercial block differs in a more fundamental way. The type has a centuries-old lineage among modest buildings that enclosed shops on the ground floor and living quarters above. This European vernacular tradition took hold in the American colonies, where it became a normative fixture in important trading centers. By the early decades of the nineteenth century, the shop/house pattern provided an important departure point for treatment of strictly commercial buildings (Fig. 6). Architects eventually adopted this compositional mode. By the 1840s, they were introducing new stylistic elements and materials to it. They never-

16. William Strickland's Second Bank of the United States in Philadelphia (1818–1824) is a seminal work for the first phase. McKim, Mead and White's Knickerbocker Trust Company building in New York (1901–1904) is similarly important for the second phase.

17. Sarah Bradford Landau, "The Tall Office Building Artistically Reconsidered: Arcaded Buildings of the New York School, c. 1870–1890," in *In Search of Modern Architecture: A Tribute to Henry-Russell Hitchcock*, ed. Helen Searing (New York and Cambridge: Architectural History Foundation/MIT Press, 1982), pp. 136–64.

Methods for Understanding Buildings / 19

theless continued to make use of the basic formula—as did their builder colleagues—for another hundred years (Fig. 7).

Likewise, the one-part commercial block seems to have had vernacular origins. It was accepted, somewhat later, by architects and persisted in both high-style and vernacular realms for a number of decades. This type, however, was probably developed in a short period as an expedient solution to strong pressures for commercial development in areas where available resources limited construction to what is, in essence, a fragment of the two-part type. Collectively, these backgrounds suggest that relationships between vernacular and high-style architecture can be intricate, with each sphere influencing the other in different ways.

Another subject that requires consideration is that of locational differences. Recognizing that these commercial types are not region specific can further the process of understanding the distinctions that do occur. A community in the Sierra foothills may appear quite unlike one in the high plains of Nebraska, the Virginia piedmont, or the upper Connecticut River Valley. Some of these differences are urbanistic, such as configuration and width of the streets, or density and extent of the district. Other distinctions are architectural. The time of settlement and periods of growth have a direct bearing on when and how expensively buildings were constructed. Related and equally consequential factors include the presence of skilled designers, builders, and artisans and the availability of local or imported materials. Climate may also influence the selection of elements. In regions where hot summers are the rule, wooden and metal canopies were generally used to shade the ground floor and adjacent sidewalk. However, all such differences are secondary and tertiary characteristics of commercial buildings. The primary characteristics derived from basic compositional arrangement remain constant.

The false-fronted emporium affords a classic illustration of how the matter of regional distinctiveness can become confusing. No

Fig. 7. Late nineteenth- and early twentieth-century commercial buildings in Florence, Kansas. (author)

Fig. 8. Turn-of-the-century false-front emporiums in Ramona, Kansas. (author)

Fig. 9. A false-fronted neighborhood store built in Middlebury, Vermont, in 1812 and remodeled around the turn of the century. (author)

image of a commercial building carries stronger perceptual ties to an area, in this case, the central and western states (Fig. 8). Yet, such buildings do not constitute a type. They are one-part or two-part commercial blocks, usually constructed of wood, and crowned by a planar vertical projection that makes a modest, normally gable-ended mass seem larger and more urban. Moreover, while examples are most commonly found in the western half of the United States, they are by no means exclusive to that area. Regional variations in this instance clearly result from the circumstances of development. In the West, where most towns were founded during the second half of the nineteenth century, false-fronted buildings dominated the linear commercial core, playing a decisive role in defining the character of each place throughout the first period of development. They remain a conspicuous presence in the numerous communities that have experienced little subsequent growth. By contrast, false-front emporiums in older well-established towns of the East tend to stand alone or in small clusters, serving the residential neighborhoods around them (Fig. 9).

Another potential source of confusion in identifying commercial types stems from the fact that local images were cultivated ac-

Fig. 10. Commercial buildings constructed in Santa Barbara, California, in the 1920s. (author)

tively during the early twentieth century, most often in fashionable suburbs, resort communities, and company towns. In the commercial centers of places such as Princeton, New Jersey, Santa Barbara, California, and Tyrone, New Mexico, design was consciously developed to be expressive of locale (Fig. 10). Yet the historical references employed are, as a rule, imported. They may nurture valued associations, but they seldom tap indigenous traditions. Work of this order also tends to represent singular initiatives more than regional practices. Furthermore, places in different regions and with dissimilar cultural heritages sometimes adopt the same imagery. J. C. Nichols's Country Club Plaza in Kansas City, Missouri, incorporates Spanish classical elements analogous to those concurrently used in Santa Barbara and Palm Beach (Fig. 11).[18] Finally, however distinctive such work may seem, its special character is usually derived from materials and surface motifs rather than from an unorthodox compositional arrangement.

Examining these types from a chronological perspective raises other issues. For most of the nineteenth century, the range of types was very limited. When the popularity of the temple front waned prior to the Civil War, the two-part commercial block enjoyed an almost universal presence. Alternatives were tested in the largest cities, while small towns and peripheral districts had numerous one-part commercial blocks, but it was not until the century's last decade that new types emerged as established patterns. Furthermore, it was not until the 1920s that the full compositional palate became integrated into the urban landscape across the country. Part of this change can be attributed to the rapidly growing number of formally trained architects. Of importance also was the ascendancy of French academic principles that emphasized composition as the essence of design. There may have been other factors at work as well, such as clients who invited greater variety, or a consumer public that welcomed this phenomenon.

18. Richard Longstreth, "J. C. Nichols, the Country Club Plaza and Notions of Modernity," *Harvard Architecture Review* 5, forthcoming; David Gebhard, *Santa Barbara—The Creation of a New Spain in America* (Santa Barbara: University of California Art Museum, 1982).

Fig. 11. Country Club Plaza in Kansas City, Missouri, begun in 1922. (author)

Much the same questions should be asked about the fundamental changes that occurred in commercial architecture after World War II, when many of these compositional types fell from favor or experienced substantial modification. The shift may be explained partly by the widespread acceptance among architects of a modernist approach to design that gives little credence to composition. Equally important was the new concentration of commercial development in suburban areas, where an abundance of available land and the need to accommodate large numbers of automobiles led to a prevalence of low, freestanding buildings and shopping complexes.

Addressing such changes is not an easy matter, in part because there is no evidence that builders, architects, their clients, or the public ever thought in terms of compositional types. Buildings were not so identified in writing, even, with very few exceptions, in professional literature.[19] At the Ecole des Beaux Arts and the American architecture schools under its influence, the compositional pattern or *parti*, as it is known among practitioners, was not conceived as a fixed thing, but rather as a fluid process whereby elements are combined in various ways according to the circumstances of a given project. The temple front, for instance, could also serve as the base for a three-part vertical block or as the centerpiece of a sequence of lateral masses appropriate to, say, a museum or university building.[20]

This typology, like many others, is an abstraction derived from physical evidence. As a concept, it is probably quite different from the conscious thoughts of the people who produced that evidence. Nevertheless, compositional types can render assistance, not only as a convenient form of nomenclature, but also as a vehicle for learning more about an architecture that so distinguishes the American landscape.

19. Louis Sullivan's "The Tall Office Building Artistically Considered," *Lippincott's Magazine* 57 (1896):403–9, is a rare exception.

20. Ironically, the Knickerbocker Trust, previously noted as a key design in repopularizing the temple front *parti*, was initially designed as the lower zone in a three-part composition. See Leland Roth, *McKim, Mead and White, Architects* (New York: Harper and Row, 1983), p. 301.

3

EDWARD A. CHAPPELL

Architectural Recording and the Open-Air Museum: A View from the Field

1. Personal interview, Philadelphia, 26 January 1983. For a brief portrait of early architects involved in the Williamsburg restoration, see Charles B. Hosmer, Jr., *Preservation Comes of Age: From Williamsburg to the National Trust, 1926–1949*, 2 vols. (Charlottesville: University Press of Virginia, 1981), 1:11–73.

2. See Sir Cyril Fox and Lord Raglan, *Monmouthshire Houses: A Study of Building Techniques and Small House-Plans in the Fifteenth to Seventeenth Centuries* (Cardiff: National Museum of Wales, 1951, 1953, and 1954); Adelhart Zippelius, *Das Bauernhaus am Unteren Deutschen Niederrhein* (Wuppertal: A. Martini und Grutteften, 1957); Henry Glassie, *Folk Housing in Middle Virginia: A Structural Analysis of Historic Artifacts* (Knoxville: University of Tennessee Press, 1975); Abbott Lowell Cummings, *The Framed Houses of Massachusetts Bay, 1625–1725* (Cambridge: Harvard University Press, 1979); Dell Upton, *Holy Things and Profane: Anglican Parish Churches in Colonial Virginia* (New York and Cambridge: Architectural History Foundation/MIT Press, 1986).

Charles Peterson once remarked that he conceived the idea of the Historic American Buildings Survey as a response to the practices of Colonial Williamsburg architects, whose weekend fieldwork, he unflatteringly suggested, was kept carefully locked away from the prying eyes of fellow draftsmen.[1] Typically, Peterson makes an interesting rhetorical point. Records and interpretations of our violable material culture are too valuable to be maintained like private stamp collections. The material is useful only if it is accessible and intelligible. In a half-century at Colonial Williamsburg, shifts in museum policy and personal initiative have resulted in a variety of approaches to architectural recording. This paper briefly discusses some of the current methods of fieldwork at that venerable institution, techniques that have been developed over the past five years. It is offered as a way of provoking others to consider the purposes and methods they apply to their own fieldwork.

Most of us have come to recognize that it is necessary to consider a broad range of buildings in order to begin understanding similarities, variations, and change. Yet it is also important to look carefully and intensively at individual structures, and to record precisely what is found. Sir Cyril Fox and Lord Raglan in Wales, Adelhart Zippelius in Germany, and several members of the Vernacular Architecture Forum have shown that a relatively limited number of buildings well recorded and analyzed can be more useful than volumes of photos and sketchy descriptions of hundreds of examples.[2] It is important, then, for each fieldworker to have a system, or group of systems, for understanding buildings. This does not mean that everyone's fieldwork should follow my own perhaps overwrought approach, but some sort of critical framework for study is always necessary.

In the present era of government and corporate aggression against cultural and environmental resources, museum workers have found themselves with a somewhat larger role to play in the task of artifact recording. Museum involvement in fieldwork has several purposes. In the case of open-air exhibits, one of these purposes is restoration and reconstruction. Bad reconstructions—and there are plenty of those—simply rob genuine buildings of random details in order to provide "period" design solutions when there is no direct evidence for what the reconstructed building originally looked like. Elaborate woodwork, rare fittings, and precious outbuildings are favored objects of such uncritical use (Fig. 1). This, therefore, is a caution that some serious pitfalls lie in the paths of fieldworkers employed by a museum. Architectural discoveries can find a place among an embarrassing array of three-dimensional might-have-beens that are viewed annually by thousands of tourists.

On the other hand, if a museum actively uses restorations as a means to teach about the variety of experience in the past, fieldwork can be an integral and intelligent part of a very beneficial process. Approached critically, fieldwork in vernacular architecture should knock sizable holes in traditional images of a happy, homogeneous, and genteel past. It can point toward more honest interpretations of, for example, industrial work spaces, ordinary dwellings, and places where social deviants were confined (Figs. 2 and 3). At Colonial Williamsburg, new fieldwork is intended to provide some plausible alternatives to a fairly entrenched Kate Greenaway image of the eighteenth century. A principal aim has been to examine variations in levels of buildings or, put another way, to study the architectural choices that were available to different types of people.

Relevant questions abound for the colonial Chesapeake region. What kind of house was a wealthy middle-class farmer likely to

Fig. 1. Gazebo at the Nelson-Galt house, Colonial Williamsburg. This building is an example of how "period" architectural details can be assembled to create fanciful buildings that probably never existed in the context where they are now found. Current plans call for removal of the building. (author; all illustrations for this essay appear courtesy of Colonial Williamsburg Foundation)

Fig. 2. The reconstruction of the James Anderson forges at Colonial Williamsburg is intended to illustrate both traditional labor-saving building techniques and an environment common to eighteenth-century American workers. (author)

Fig. 3. The Public Hospital at Colonial Williamsburg. Inside this 1984 reconstruction are exhibits that deal with changing perceptions of mental deviance and the institutional environments those perceptions created. (author)

3. For essays touching on some of these types of topics, see Edward Chappell, "Williamsburg Architecture as Social Space," *Fresh Advices: A Research Supplement to the Colonial Williamsburg Interpreter* 2, no. 6 (1981):i-iv; "Slave Housing," *Fresh Advices/Interpreter* 3, no. 6 (1982):i-ii, iv; "Beyond the Pale: Architectural Fieldwork for Colonial Williamsburg," *Fresh Advices/Interpreter* 4, no. 6 (1983):i-iv; "Looking at Buildings," *Fresh Advices/Interpreter* 5, no. 6 (1984):i-vi; "Deeper into Buildings," *Fresh Advices/Interpreter*, forthcoming.

build about 1750? How would it have differed from the house constructed by a person of similar means fifty years later? How would either dwelling compare in size and finish to homes of neighbors who had small landholdings? What levels of finish distinguished the farmer's house from his work buildings, and what sort of distinctions were there among the work buildings themselves? How did those service buildings function, physically and economically? What can be determined about the variety of living conditions experienced by slaves, and how did those conditions change through time? What techniques were used to segregate slaves' work space and domestic space? Similarly, how was the realm of storekeepers distinguished from the realm of their customers? What decorative systems reinforce social distinctions within houses, and what do they have to say about the changing functions of rooms?[3]

It is reasonably easy to frame questions like these, but answering them requires a systematic way of assessing buildings. Almost any useful approach to unstudied buildings should involve carefully measured plans and, if possible, sections, elevations, and details. Especially for unpretentious buildings—the ones most likely to suffer neglect from owners and other fieldworkers, drawings can provide a crucial permanent record. The preservation role of measured drawings has long been recognized, and it is one of the principal justifications for most recording efforts, including the resilient Historic American Buildings Survey. Equally important, though, is that measuring a building encourages the recorder to recognize relationships among different parts. Questions about room hierarchies and functions, circulation, and construction sequence follow naturally from the process of careful examining and recording. In short, doing measured drawings of a building is the best way to discover some of its consequential secrets.

This analytical quality should also make its way into the drawings. The principal fault with most HABS drawings is that they try to be objective records. Everything is recorded coolly and accurately, and no questions are asked of the material. There are defensible reasons for the unanalytical quality of HABS drawings largely having to do with the employment of student draftsmen who have backgrounds in architectural drawing rather than building analysis. Perhaps it is better for the national repository of historic building records to ignore periodicity than to run the risk of misinterpreting data. Yet the failure to distinguish between periods of construction tends to blend different building campaigns into a single product. There is no clarification of whose intentions resulted in what.[4]

To a large degree, the system of architectural recording currently in use at Colonial Williamsburg can be credited to or blamed on a group of volunteers that was formed in 1980 with the intention of recording threatened agricultural buildings in the Chesapeake region. The group refers to itself by a variety of names, the most publicly acceptable of which are the Chesapeake Farm Buildings Survey and the Friends of Friendless Farm Buildings.[5] The Friends' system—now that of Colonial Williamsburg—owes a considerable debt to archaeological methods of recording periods and details as well as materials and forms. On the other hand, Williamsburg's recording includes certain idiosyncratic approaches that might be frowned on by the Friends.

Essentially, we try to use drawings as a means of understanding things that might not be immediately obvious about a building. In order to accomplish this, the staff follows an anti-scrape policy, recording material from all periods. This approach sometimes verges on eccentricity, as when a twentieth-century cat-feeding platform is included on the plans, elevations, and sections of an early nineteenth-century post-set milkhouse. The intention, worthy or otherwise, is to show everything possible about how a building has been put together, used, and changed.

At first look, the John Hill house in Southampton County, Virginia, seemed to be a straightforward I house with an array of rear service-room accretions (Fig. 4). However, careful examination of physical evidence showed that the house had evolved in five major stages, with various lesser changes made at other times. It began in the late eighteenth century as a small house with a single room on each of two floors. Before 1830, the house was transformed into a better-detailed two-room-plan dwelling. Soon thereafter, another substantial construction project reduced the status of the original structure by the addition of a symmetrical two-story house with a different orientation, superior woodwork, and a larger principal

4. The HABS perspective is expressed in C. Ford Peatross, ed., *Historic America: Buildings, Structures, and Sites* (Washington, D.C.: Library of Congress, 1983), and Harley J. McKee, *Recording Historic Buildings* (Washington, D.C.: National Park Service, 1970). By contrast, recorders for the British Royal Commission on Historical Monuments do not hesitate selectively to interpret the buildings they draw. Two prominent examples are Peter Smith, *Houses of the Welsh Countryside: A Study in Historical Geography* (London: Her Majesty's Stationery Office, 1975), and Eric Mercer, *English Vernacular Houses: A Study of Traditional Farmhouses and Cottages* (London: Her Majesty's Stationery Office, 1975). On a slightly more modest private scale, there are Raymond B. Wood-Jones, *Traditional Domestic Architecture of the Banbury Region* (Manchester: University Press, 1963), and Barry Harrison and Barbara Hutton, *Vernacular Houses in North Yorkshire* (Edinburgh: John Donald Publishers, 1984).

5. See Orlando Ridout V, "The Chesapeake Farm Buildings Survey," in *Perspectives in Vernacular Architecture*, ed. Camille Wells (Annapolis: Vernacular Architecture Forum, 1982), pp. 137–49.

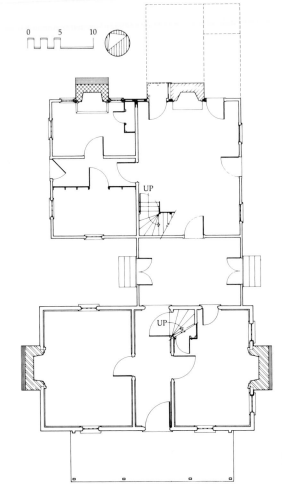

Fig. 4. Elevation and plan of the John Hill house in Southampton County, Virginia, showing the building's form in 1982. (Douglas Taylor and Willie Graham)

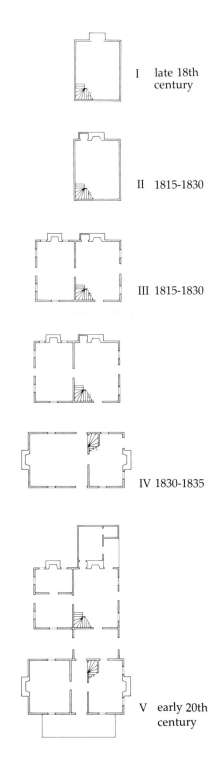

I   late 18th century

II   1815-1830

III 1815-1830

IV 1830-1835

V   early 20th century

Fig. 5. Simplified plans of the John Hill house, interpreting its evolution through two centuries of use and alteration. (Douglas Taylor and author)

room. It was not until the early twentieth century that a circulation passage was carved out of the big front room and the two buildings were connected by an enclosed hyphen (Fig. 5). Sadly, the house was cut into sections and moved to a new site soon after it was recorded in 1982.

A large-scale plan is used to record the building as it existed when measured, to note the presence of potentially informative details, and to indicate the period of all exposed masonry and wall framing. Since almost none of the wall framing was exposed at the Hill house and the sequence of change was complex, it was useful also to draw a group of small-scale plans that demonstrate our interpretation of how the house grew. In other words, the larger plan represents a relatively objective recording of conditions, though with emphasis on selected significant features. The schematic plans clarify deductions about evolution.

In most cases where framing is exposed, the succession of building campaigns is sufficiently perceptible that evolution can be indicated by a simple set of conventions on the principal plan. Additional interpretive plans are then unnecessary. On the William Beale farm in Southampton County, a fairly commonplace close-studded dirt-floored smokehouse was built during the second quarter of the nineteenth century (Fig. 6). It continues in use for its

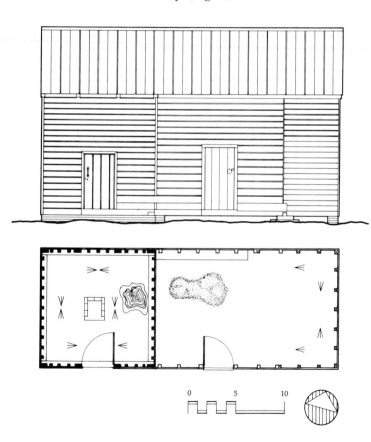

Fig. 6. Elevation and plan of the Beale smokehouse in Southampton County, Virginia. The simple series of changes is easily conveyed in these drawings. Arrow-like conventions indicate the location of wall braces. (Douglas Taylor and Harold J. Bradley)

original function, with hams and other pork parts dangling above a small smoky fire. During its first fifty years, however, two factors affected the form of the building: the scale of pork production grew, and two stages of the curing process were separated. To accommodate this change, a wood-floored preparation room was added and later expanded. The new sections were connected to the old smokehouse, but there was no internal circulation and the old building retained its original form. This simple history is easily captured by an elevation, a plan, and several sections.

Generally, our drawings do not show decay for picturesque effect. What is interesting is how buildings were made and altered, not how they fall apart. If parts of a roof have slipped from place but still survive, they are drawn in place. If, however, parts are missing—say, several rafters from the roof—they are shown as missing. On the other hand, decay is gladly shown if it helps explain the structure. Thus, we would not consider patching the crumbling infill of a rare surviving mud chimney when its deteriorated condition reveals the chimney framing. Obviously, these practices require thoughtful judgment. A good guiding rule is this: when in doubt, be honest. If something is missing, it should be drawn missing, along with any evidence for what was there. Otherwise, the drawings will reflect the preconceptions of the recorder and will omit useful but poorly understood information.

In fact, there is a benefit in recognizing that the physical history of most buildings is very messy. The original form of some buildings is almost unrecognizable, while others look deceptively intact. Something as plain and seemingly straightforward as the one-room eighteenth-century Rochester house in Westmoreland County, Virginia, has had three major renovations. The earliest of these improved the level of interior finish and the most recent involved removal of substantial nineteenth-century additions early in the present century (Fig. 7).

Alterations are more than obstructions to an understanding of original integrity, more than thoughtless accretions that must be stripped away in order to appreciate unblemished charm. With a few prominent exceptions, buildings do not survive because of fortuitous circumstances, but rather because they continue to fulfill needs. Sometimes these needs can be accommodated without alterations. Over the long run, though, most cannot. Every field-worker has stories about the villainous mistreatment of important architectural survivors, but there is nothing innately unfortunate about change. In fact, how and when buildings are altered represents important information about human activity and how it changed with time.

Slave houses provide an example. Although workers' housing in the South has consistently been poor, there has always been a range of quality within this subordinate system of design and construction, and the superior end of the scale has seen some improvement. The particularly mean level of most eighteenth-century Ches-

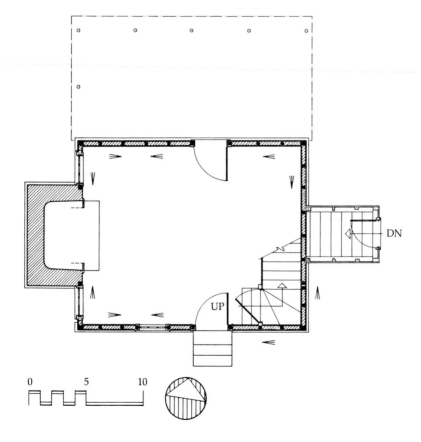

Fig. 7. Elevation and plan of the Rochester house in Westmoreland County, Virginia. This seemingly unchanged dwelling has actually sustained three major renovations. Part of the recent metal covering has been omitted in the drawing to show original weatherboard roof sheathing. (Willie Graham and author)

DN

UP

0   5   10

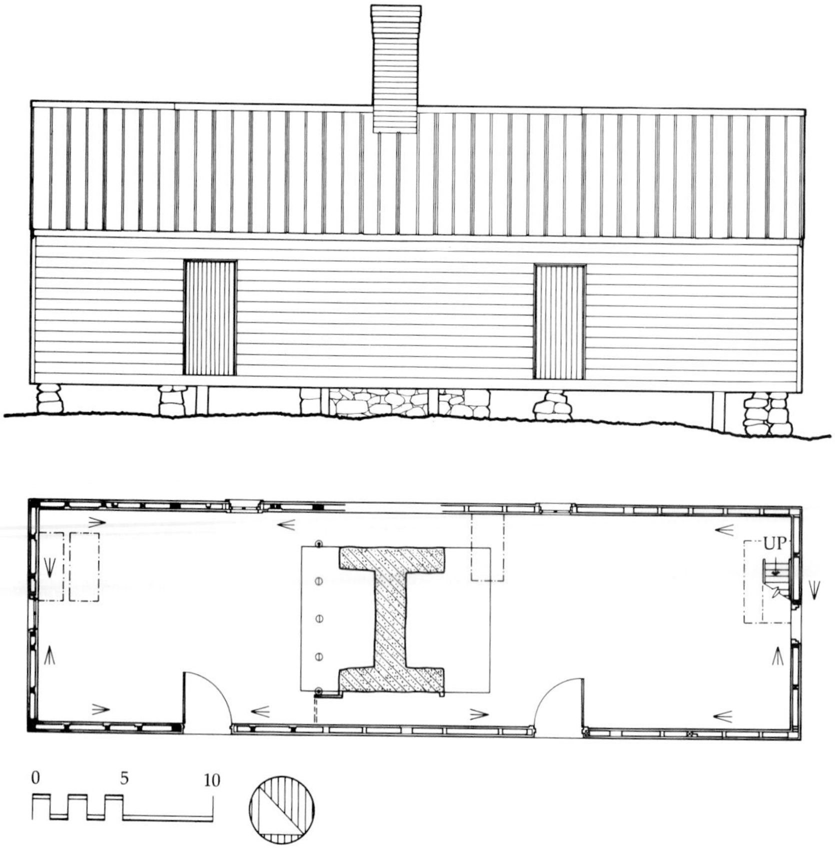

Fig. 8. Elevation and plan of a slave house at Prestwould in Mecklenburg County, Virginia. The house was later enlarged to provide somewhat better accommodations for two slave families. It was further rehabilitated about 1900. Circular conventions to the left of the chimney identify the position of framing joints in the original southwest wall. (Mark Schara and author)

6. Many slaves lived in secondary spaces of landowner's houses and out-buildings. Because of their more direct effect on the owner's comfort and status, these buildings were better built and hence more likely to survive than were those constructed specifically to house slaves.

7. Home quarters consisted of slave houses near the owner's principal dwelling and were intended to house people whose work was focused on the main complex or in the fields nearby. Like quarters at distant culti-vated fields, these houses could form their own group, removed from the work buildings clustered around the house.

apeake slave housing is implied by the almost total absence of surviving colonial examples.[6] A rare exception is a ruinous twelve-by-sixteen one-room building at the site of the late eighteenth-cen-tury home slave quarter of Prestwould, a large gentry plantation in Mecklenburg County, Virginia.[7] Constructed with skimpy framing, the building was originally sheathed with riven clapboards and had a minimum of window and door openings. It also had a wooden floor. In this feature, it is very likely to have been superior to most slave houses of any period.

During the first half of the nineteenth century, housing for some slaves—usually domestic servants and skilled craftsmen— was somewhat improved. In the Chesapeake, this improvement usually took the form of relatively well-built duplexes providing a single first-floor room and attic space for each of two families. Gen-erally, there was no interior communication between the two family units. At a fairly early date, the Prestwould slave house was trans-formed into such a central-chimney duplex (Fig. 8).

Virtually all surviving slave houses are standing because they continued to be used as housing for domestic and agricultural workers after the Civil War. In most cases, this function resulted in further alterations. At the Prestwould quarter, changes occurred slightly after 1900, when windows were upgraded, sheathing was added to the interior, and a rough ladder stair was introduced to provide stationary access to the attic. These changes are comparable to those made to most slave houses that were retained for laborers after 1865. In almost all cases, the two rooms have been joined by an interior door, and slight improvements such as mantels, cheap wall finish, and more windows have been introduced. The best re-modelings also include the addition of new rooms, generally either full second-story bedrooms or rear shed kitchens (Fig. 9). Offsetting any heady optimism about the truly superior living conditions that twentieth-century rural laborers enjoyed is a vast array of antique kitchens, smokehouses, and school buses that bear evidence of domestic occupation. A rather mild example is an Essex County dairy

Fig. 9. Transverse section of house A at the Howard's Neck slave quarter in Goochland County, Virginia. The second floor, porches, and almost all interior trim were added in the twentieth century. (John Bernard and Harold J. Bradley)

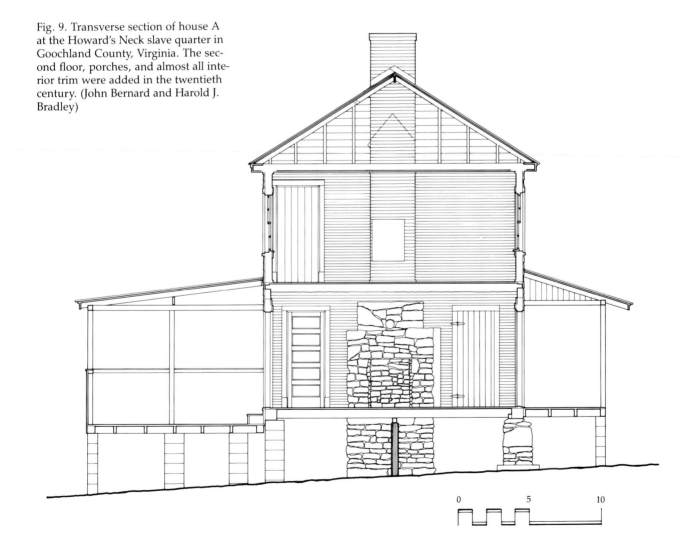

Fig. 10. Longitudinal section and plan of a dairy and smokehouse at Cherry Walk in Essex County, Virginia. The dairy has been converted to housing for a domestic servant. (Douglas Taylor, Mark Schara, and Harold J. Bradley)

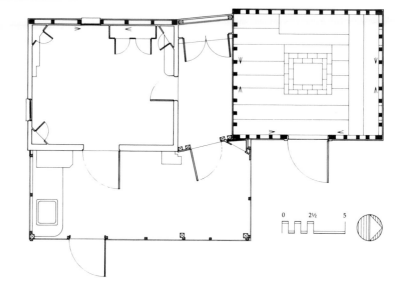

8. Living conditions of nineteenth-century workers have been a more popular subject for European museums, such as the Ironbridge complex in the English Midlands and the open-air museum in Arnhem. The latter institution is unusually forthright in its interpretation of day laborers' housing: "Compared with the hovels they usually lived in, the improvements here included walls of brick and wood instead of turves, and a floor of flagstones instead of mud. Refinements like these were gradually introduced towards the end of the nineteenth century and give a false impression of the standard of living of most casual labourers in the past, especially when carefully reconstructed, as in this case." *Guide, The Netherlands Open-Air Museum* (Arnhem: Association of Friends of the Netherlands Open-Air Museum, 1985), p. 47. At the Welsh Folk Museum, the subject has been more imaginatively addressed in print than in building exhibits. See J. B. Lowe, *Welsh Industrial Workers Housing 1775–1875* (Cardiff: Amgueddfa Genedlaethol Cymru, 1977) and *Welsh Country Workers Housing 1775–1875* (Cardiff: Amgueddfa Genedlaethol Cymru, 1985). For Ulster, see Alan Gailey, *Rural Houses in the North of Ireland* (Edinburgh: John Donald Publishers, 1984).

remodeled in this century as a dwelling for a family cook (Fig. 10). The cramped living space was not unusual.

The housing conditions of twentieth-century workers seem a regrettably distant topic for most American open-air museums, although some European counterparts have addressed the issue with powerful recent exhibits. A striking example is the Ulster Folk Museum, which avoids a single-minded bucolic scene by including modern urban housing not very different from that still occupied by many of its visitors.[8] Williamsburg remains largely an eighteenth-century museum, but it is hoped that current plans for the re-creation of a slave quarter at nearby Carter's Grove plantation will do much to alter visitors' perceptions of life and work in America's Golden Age.

To be of much worth, history museums must do more than illustrate the latest thinking about the use of flashy paint colors, parlor chairs, or rude building techniques. Such details are important, but only if they are employed to illuminate static or shifting social and economic relationships. The new Carter's Grove quarter should not simply adjust modern perceptions of eighteenth-century Chesapeake housing. It should also use the evidence of housing and furnishings to raise questions about the relationships among people involved. What economic decisions did owners make in housing their slaves? How significant was the issue of labor control? More importantly, what were the responses of the people who were forced to live most of their lives in these settings? To answer such questions, the fieldworker's observation of physical relationships is crucial.

Such observations may be about seemingly insignificant details, as well as about entire structures and their social and economic contexts. Several years ago, Colonial Williamsburg decided to open a new store that would sell reproductions of goods known to have been offered there in the third quarter of the eighteenth century. The building selected was Greenhow Store, a 1954 reconstruction of a store that was destroyed during the Civil War. The reconstruction had been based primarily on archaeological evidence that indicated several rather confusing stages of building. Since it had first been intended only as an exterior reconstruction, earlier architects had no reason to grapple with the design of the store's interior. When it was decided to reopen the Greenhow Store, architectural fieldworkers were asked to find ways to make the archaeological evidence intelligible.

Subsequent investigation of surviving eighteenth- and early nineteenth-century Virginia stores revealed several patterns. There was always a clear distinction between public and private zones within the store (Fig. 11). Sales rooms were usually subdivided by counters that acted as barriers to areas fitted with shelves for merchandise. In this way, quantities of goods could be displayed while access to them was controlled. Often, there was a heated office or "counting room" located in a position distant from the front door. In most cases, the office was finished in a manner superior to that of the sales room. For example, if the sales room had sheathed walls and exposed ceiling joists, the office might be plastered. Access to any finished second-story living space was through the office. Both the room treatment and the circulation pattern indicate that the occupant of these upper rooms held a relatively trusted position in the business. Most surviving stores were found to have been altered one or more times. Inevitably, the alterations represented encroachment of the sales area on the office. This was often achieved by combining the two rooms into one, extending the shelves and counters, and constructing a new office.

There continue to be mysteries about the precise form of Green-

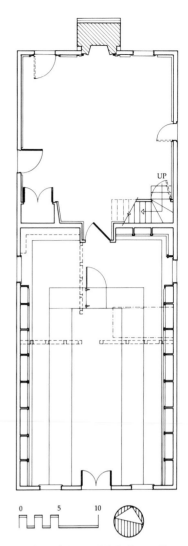

Fig. 11. Plan of Pitt and Sale Store, Essex County, Virginia. Partitions between the original sales room, office, and storeroom were removed to create a longer sales room, and a larger heated office was added at the rear. The fittings are contemporary with the remodeling. (Charles Bergengren and Harold J. Bradley)

how Store, but fieldwork offers a general sequence that agrees with the archaeological evidence. The newly created interior illustrates the functional zones found in other stores and presents some of the visual confusion that results from alteration (Fig. 12). The intention is that the new store have useful small lessons to teach, and that it be more realistic and intriguing than some of the stridently coherent restorations of the past.

Architectural fieldwork, in short, has considerable potential both for initiating complex questions and for resolving issues of importance to open-air museums. Whether dealing with the arcane details of eighteenth-century American store design or the larger issues concerning how oppressed people have been forced to live, it is a principal resource. Fieldwork is best if it is methodical and sensitive to complexity and messiness. Of course, pitfalls are numerous, and, especially for those working with museums, the mistakes in interpretation can be very public. But with perseverance and luck, new-found information will be used in a responsible and critical manner, encouraging fresh thought about old problems.

Fig. 12. The re-created interior of Greenhow Store at Colonial Williamsburg. The functional divisions of the store as well as its details are based on observations in early Virginia stores. A certain amount of visual confusion also reflects conditions found in surviving buildings. (author)

4

B A R B A R A   W Y A T T

The Challenge of Addressing Vernacular Architecture in a State Historic Preservation Survey Program

The National Historic Preservation Act of 1966 directed each State Historic Preservation Officer to "conduct a comprehensive statewide survey of historic properties and maintain inventories of such properties."[1] In the eighteen years since this federal-state partnership was established, SHPOs have surveyed and maintained inventories for millions of properties of historical, architectural, archaeological, engineering, and cultural interest. One of the key uses of inventory data is in evaluating eligibility for the National Register of Historic Places. In order for its significance to be assessed, a property can be compared with inventoried structures in the vicinity. Combined with other information, the inventory data can be a critical asset to a preservation office, particularly if the staff is aware of biases inherent in the inventory. Most SHPO staffs *are* aware of their inventory's limitations and attempt to compensate for them in making eligibility decisions. However, new generations of staffs, increasing complexity of the nomination process, growing interest in vernacular architecture, and burgeoning inventories are forcing SHPOs to consider resolving some problems that were all too easy to ignore during the early years of the historic buildings survey program.

Three issues seem to be of greatest concern to state historic preservation offices, and each one affects the study of vernacular architecture. First: because of evolving standards and poorly trained surveyors, surveys have been conducted unevenly. The sporadic occurrence of vernacular architecture in inventories is especially obvious. Second: in cases where vernacular architecture was surveyed, it was often inadequately described and only superficially evaluated. Furthermore, there was no standard system for identifying types of vernacular buildings. Third: inventory data is often inaccessible because of the sheer bulk of the material and the method by which it is organized. The inaccessibility makes studies of poorly understood building types even more difficult. As SHPOs begin to resolve these situations, their inventories will become more useful to the study of vernacular architecture.

The problem of uneven survey coverage is manifested in many

1. National Historic Preservation Act of 1966 (P.L. 89–665; 80 STAT. 915; 16 U.S.C. 470) Sec. 101 (7)(b)(3)(A).

states by an absence of vernacular architecture in early reconnaissance surveys. Later surveys tended to remedy the situation because of federal programmatic developments and an expanding consideration of the vernacular by preservationists in general. During the middle 1970s, the concept of the intensive survey was promoted by the National Park Service, and many SHPOs began undertaking such surveys. The theory was that a comprehensive, evaluated survey of a specific geographic area would expedite the review of federally funded projects by SHPOs and provide a basis for nominating large numbers of properties to the National Register in the "multiple resource" format. Many states began this more thorough accumulation of data both to thrust historic preservation further into the comprehensive planning arena and to promote historic preservation tenets among local governments. Intensive surveys provided many SHPOs with a basis of research that had been lacking in previous efforts. Survey data became more than a tool for locating properties; it became useful for broader evaluation and programmatic applications.

Fundamental to the intensive survey is an equal emphasis on historical research and architectural interpretation. In addition to encouraging an evaluation of properties and districts from an architectural and historical perspective, the intensive survey requires an examination of a wider spectrum of resources (Fig. 1). The increased popularity of the intensive survey coincided with a generally growing appreciation of vernacular architecture in its urban and rural manifestations. Results of an intensive survey of Eau Claire, Wisconsin, demonstrate the strides that have been made in one state's historic preservation program. In 1982, a district of early twentieth-century bungalows in Eau Claire was nominated to the National Register (Fig. 2).

The National Park Service provided another incentive for conducting more comprehensive surveys with the introduction of the Resource Protection Planning Process, dubbed RP3. One of the most comprehensible and laudable aspects of this cultural resource management planning process is its insistence on the interpretation of buildings in a historical context. Ideally, this means that even the simplest or most mundane of buildings is subject to careful consideration. While this expansion of the evaluation process is resulting in the recognition of more kinds of significance, it is also alerting SHPOs to gaps in their inventories.

A 1983 compliance case illustrates the value of approaching the evaluation of a property in the context of a comprehensive planning strategy. The case involved a rather ordinary agricultural building in Oconto County, Wisconsin. Although the 1975 survey of Oconto County and nearby counties had not recorded this or comparable outbuildings, information contained in the cultural resource management plan enabled its identification as a potato warehouse. The agency involved in the compliance case was required to provide the SHPO with additional information, and, ultimately, the building

Fig. 1. This house was overlooked in an early survey of Lake Geneva, a historic Wisconsin resort. In the 1985 intensive survey, this and many other modest buildings in the community were documented. (courtesy of Wisconsin State Historical Society)

Fig. 2. The "Emery Street Bungalow District" in Eau Claire, Wisconsin, was listed on the National Register in 1983. It contains this representative early twentieth-century dwelling. (courtesy of Wisconsin State Historical Society)

Methods for Understanding Buildings / 39

was determined "not eligible" for the National Register even though it reflected a historically significant agricultural pursuit in several counties. However, the SHPO was alerted to a significant type of vernacular building and to the fact that the building type had been routinely omitted in early survey efforts.

Most survey programs are improving in two other key areas: the standardization of survey methods and the training of surveyors. These factors are resulting in more uniform and comprehensive survey coverage. Even so, many areas recorded early in the program simply will have to be resurveyed as SHPOs are able to justify the effort both fiscally and programmatically. Until that happens, SHPOs would be wise to document and publicize known gaps and biases in their inventories so that users are aware of their strengths and limitations. In addition, SHPOs should insist on thorough historical and cultural information when little-known building types are evaluated for National Register eligibility.

The second major problem is lack of a uniform method for describing or typing vernacular architecture. An unfortunate aspect of today's broader survey coverage is that many SHPO staffs and surveyors are still unable to identify some of the building types they are recording. In many states, the inventory is overloaded with properties labeled simply *vernacular*. Applied to mundane buildings of all periods and descriptions, the use of this term will continue until more specific descriptors are adopted.

Although typologies for vernacular buildings have been suggested by various cultural geographers, folklorists, and architectural historians, none seems to fulfill the needs of a great number of SHPOs. On the other hand, many SHPOs are just beginning to examine this body of work, realizing the need to better identify the vernacular. It is interesting to speculate why the SHPOs have only recently turned their attention to the various ways of identifying vernacular architecture. Most SHPOs have evaluated buildings in the manner of traditional architectural historians, using exterior details and overall massing, and their knowledge of national stylistic movements. A key reason for this classification approach is that the National Historic Preservation Act required an SHPO to include an architectural historian as a member of the core staff. In the middle 1960s and early 1970s, when survey programs were being established, architectural historians were not as interested in or as informed about vernacular architecture as they are today. Thus, many survey programs were established by professionals unaccustomed to any nomenclature for vernacular architecture, and with no trained appreciation of it.

With the introduction of large numbers of unadorned buildings to the inventory, the traditional classification system fell short and the ubiquitous "vernacular" building was added to a list of architectural styles, as if "vernacular" itself was a style. The inadequacy was perceived, but some of the terms accepted by cultural geographers and folklorists were not readily interpreted and adopted in many SHPO programs. Many SHPOs were also reluctant to adopt the terms for primarily twentieth-century vernacular houses suggested by the *Old House Journal*.[2] Forced to action, some SHPOs began to develop typologies based simply on form, height, roof, and orientation of the major facade. The Colorado Historical Society published *A Guide to Colorado Architecture* in 1983, which suggests such a typology, recommending the use of basic descriptors to group similar vernacular buildings.[3] Although such typologies are helpful to individual survey programs, many SHPOs would prefer to adopt a terminology that has become generally accepted by both historic preservation and scholarly communities.

Because historic preservation combines elements of architectural history, history, and cultural geography, it may be left to SHPOs to develop a vocabulary for vernacular architecture that is appropriate to their own needs. It is imperative that a standardized vocabulary with universal application be established and implemented before fifty different systems are developed. Several SHPOs have endorsed the concept of a basic national vocabulary and descriptive method—with allowances for regional variation—to facilitate and standardize the study of vernacular buildings. These same preservationists have advocated that development of such a vocabulary and method be undertaken by SHPOs in consultation with scholars from related disciplines who recognize the special needs of the SHPO survey programs. Some SHPOs have initiated regional efforts to develop a standard nomenclature or survey approach for vernacular architecture. All SHPOs could benefit if these efforts are carried to completion, implemented, and published for wider application.

The third problem apparent in many SHPO inventories, one that directly affects the study of vernacular architecture, is the inability to retrieve information about surveyed properties. Only when computers became a generally accepted tool for the storage and retrieval of information did SHPOs fully realize their inventories' latent potential for research. Prior to that realization, manual searches of the inventory were the common manner of obtaining information. Thus, the inventory was accepted as a photographic collection, useful for retrieving information of limited scope and complexity. For that purpose, the inventory with a clear organization by geographical, alphabetical, or numerical factors was considered adequate. Searching the Wisconsin inventory for buildings of a particular style, form, or use would now require manually sifting through thousands of cards or forms. Because no public agency staff member has the time or patience for this, the identification of patterns and trends in the state cannot be fully accomplished.

It is becoming clear that the accessibility of information in the inventory is enhanced with automation. The SHPO is enabled to pursue questions of National Register eligibility more quickly and accurately when an automated inventory is available. Furthermore, with the ability that computers have to tabulate and search for data,

2. Sarah J. Pearce, *A Guide to Colorado Architecture* (Denver: Colorado Historical Society, 1983).

3. "The Comfortable House," *The Old House Journal* 10, no. 1 (1982):1–8.

Fig. 3. This building in Neenah, Wisconsin, was identified as a "vernacular" building in the 1981 intensive survey. Today, Wisconsin surveyors would identify it as a "one story cube." (courtesy of Wisconsin State Historical Society)

the inventory can become useful to a broader range of scholarly issues, and studies can more easily include material from more than one state. Although it is too soon to assess the full impact of computers on the national historic preservation program, it is clear that with automation the usefulness of the inventory can improve.

The relationship between automation and inventoried vernacular buildings poses a problem to many states. If all of the thousands of buildings identified in the manual inventory as "vernacular" are likewise entered in the computer, the essence of automation either as an index to the photo file or as a more sophisticated research tool is lost. Automation intensifies the need to develop a typology for vernacular architecture or a standard means for describing examples (Figs. 3 and 4).

The opportunity to improve an inventory through automation is obvious. As a state encodes or enters data, descriptions are often redefined or reevaluated, usually by a professional at least as qualified as the original surveyor. Thus, all sorts of information in the inventory, including type, style, form, or fabric, can be standardized. If the descriptors are not standard throughout the inventory, a search has to include several items that may have been applied to a given feature, and the retrieval may turn up buildings of no interest to the user. Thus, the search is both time-consuming and costly, and the result is cumbersome and, possibly, inaccurate. Most SHPOs are developing "code tables" for entering key information to avoid this problem.

Automation is revolutionizing more than the retrieval of infor-

Fig. 4. Wisconsin surveyors now provide full descriptions of buildings like this one that are not easily categorized by style. (courtesy of Wisconsin State Historical Society)

mation from the inventory. Perceiving problems with the encoding of early survey data, SHPOs are developing and refining survey techniques to facilitate the input of new information. More thorough and uniform surveys by SHPOs are resulting in many states. Although the complete integration of computers with the survey program will take several years, those states that have initiated automation are convinced that it is improving their inventories and are dedicated to completing the process.

This paper has attempted to delineate the three most pervasive problems affecting the integration of vernacular architecture into SHPO survey programs. However, the message is not intended to be thoroughly discouraging. Funding issues aside, the state survey program has never had a more positive outlook. The issues discussed indicate the level of maturity the program has achieved; they are not symptoms of a poorly conceived or executed program. With hindsight, it is clear that work on the resolution of some of the issues should have begun years ago. Good access to inventory data, however, was not possible until computers became a standard tool for storing and retrieving information. The problems apparent in SHPO survey programs directly concern vernacular architecture, a newcomer to many programs. The challenge is to continue to survey, interpret, define, and nominate to the National Register of Historic Places this important and less understood aspect of the built heritage.

5

FRANCES DOWNING AND
THOMAS C. HUBKA

Diagramming: A Visual Language

A picture, photograph, or any depiction of the world is often said to be worth a thousand words. Pictures, however, may also be worth too many words, barraging the viewer with too many ideas. In fact, most visual documentation is subject to multiple interpretations depending on the point of view, mood, or cultural perspective of the viewer. The diagrammatic process is particularly useful for architects and architectural historians who must analyze the visual world. Diagramming facilitates the extraction of discrete information or issues from a complex, multifaceted environment. For example, a diagram of All Saints Margaret Street Church can isolate the structural bay system from an exceedingly complicated interior space (Fig. 1). Diagramming allows the environmental researcher to identify and visually explain specific characteristics of an artifact,

Fig. 1. Axonometric diagram of the structural bay system in All Saints Margaret Street Church, London. (Hubka)

building, or experience while retaining an overview of the whole. Reference to both part and whole within the same drawing is one of the qualities that makes diagramming such a valuable method for analyzing the physical environment.

Diagramming can work two ways: as a graphic design, and as a method of thinking. Graphically, a diagram is less a mode of direct representation than it is an analytical visualization. Unlike verbal analysis, however, a diagram retains visual characteristics of the object or situation under investigation. As a method of thinking, diagramming provides a way of visualizing ideas and giving form to thought. Through a process of extraction and separation of attributes, diagrams make it easier for the environmental researcher to grasp ideas and arrange them in a visual field. As both a medium and a method, diagramming might be characterized as a strategy toward visualization that enjoys a distinct advantage over verbal analytical methods. The process of diagramming allows the researcher a flexibility to perform a delicate balancing act between understanding the world experientially and understanding the world intellectually.

Architects employ diagramming skills constantly (Fig. 2). Basic to the architectural design process is a need to visualize initial ideas, recall historical examples, synthesize complex systems into manageable wholes, test and compare multiple solutions. All of these processes require diagrams. In fact, diagramming is part of the highly developed visual language that architects use in design development. The same process can also enhance the study of material culture.

Diagrams can be categorized by their process or operational characteristics, and by their content. Certain basic processes are common to all diagrams: abstraction, visualization, and intensification. Abstraction and visualization are the parallel processes by which ideas are distilled and given spatial form. Intensification is the process by which diagrams isolate and focus on a particular characteristic or set of characteristics. Together, these processes re-

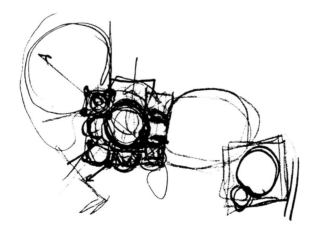

Fig. 2. A typical architectural design diagram analyzing inside and outside spaces. (Hubka)

duce information to a manageable form, but, unlike drawings or photographs, diagrams serve to magnify and emphasize information during the reductive process. The diagrammatic method of abstraction, visualization, and intensification can take several forms.

Isolation is the process of abstraction by which the diagram is used to focus attention on one of many phenomena (Fig. 3).

Emphasis is the process by which diagrams can be made to accentuate a particular attribute or idea. This usually involves the exaggeration or magnification of information (Fig. 4).

Juxtaposition is the process by which multiple or diverse phenomena are expressed in one diagram, usually allowing a comparative interpretation (Fig. 5).

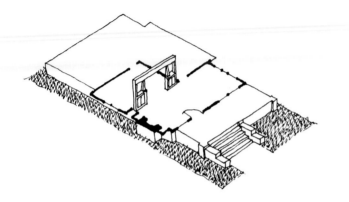

Fig. 3. A diagram isolating the screen wall in a bungalow plan. (Downing)

Fig. 4. A "fish-eye" perspective diagram emphasizing the invitational quality of a bungalow porch. (Downing)

Fig. 5. A diagram that compares the vibrant interior of a Polish synagogue with its stark vernacular setting. (Hubka)

Systemization is the process by which diagrams structure and compare relationships, as in hierarchies, typologies, categories, and taxonomies (Fig. 6).

Spatialization is the process by which diagrams give visual and three-dimensional relationships to ideas (Fig. 7).

Abstract visualization is the process by which diagrams depict nonvisual phenomena like sequence in time, spatial usage, quality of light, or even theories and ideas. This method also permits the expression of imaginary or magical interpretations (Fig. 8).

Five categories in which architects have traditionally employed diagrams also provide a starting point for investigators of the historic environment.

Fig. 6. A typological diagram of roof and porch organization of bungalows. (Downing)

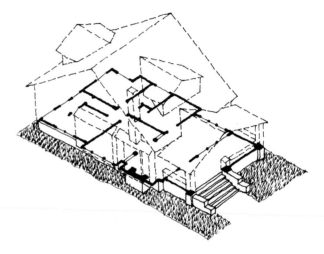

Fig. 7. An axonometric diagram that clarifies the form and plan of a bungalow. (Downing)

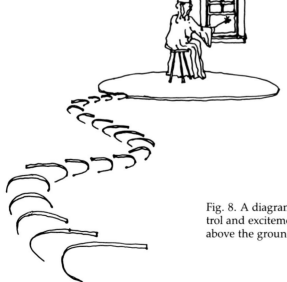

Fig. 8. A diagram expressing the control and excitement gained by rising above the ground plane. (Downing)

Methods for Understanding Buildings / 47

Space and form: Diagrams may be used to record and analyze the physical content of architecture including the traditional categories of volume, structure, materials, architectural style, and building systems (Fig. 9).

Context: Diagrams may be used to record and analyze the physical and cultural setting of buildings by including topography, climate, vegetation, and surrounding architecture, as well as the ideas, beliefs, and attitudes with which people respond to their environment (Fig. 10).

Usage: Diagrams may be used to record and analyze the spatial settings for human activities. They may depict specific users, different functions, and social organization (Fig. 11).

Time: Diagrams may be used to record and analyze different stages of development, including the relationship between permanence and change (Fig. 12).

Fig. 9. An axonometric diagram analyzing the entrance courtyard of All Saints Margaret Street Church. (Hubka)

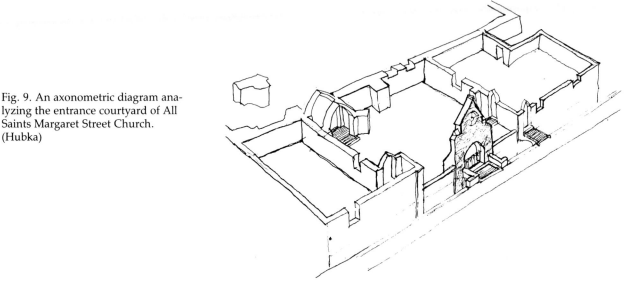

Fig. 10. A diagram showing typical building and yard usage for nineteenth-century New England connected farm buildings. From *Big House, Little House, Back House, Barn: The Connected Farm Buildings of New England*. (Hubka, courtesy of University Press of New England)

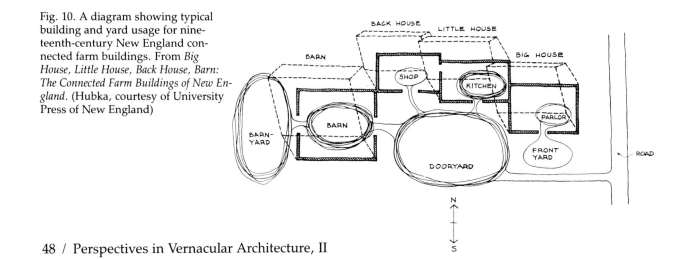

Design: Diagrams may be used to record and analyze the development of spatial ideas by builders, owners, and architects. Similarly, an environmental researcher may use diagrams to explore and formulate hypotheses about a building or environment of the past (Fig. 10).

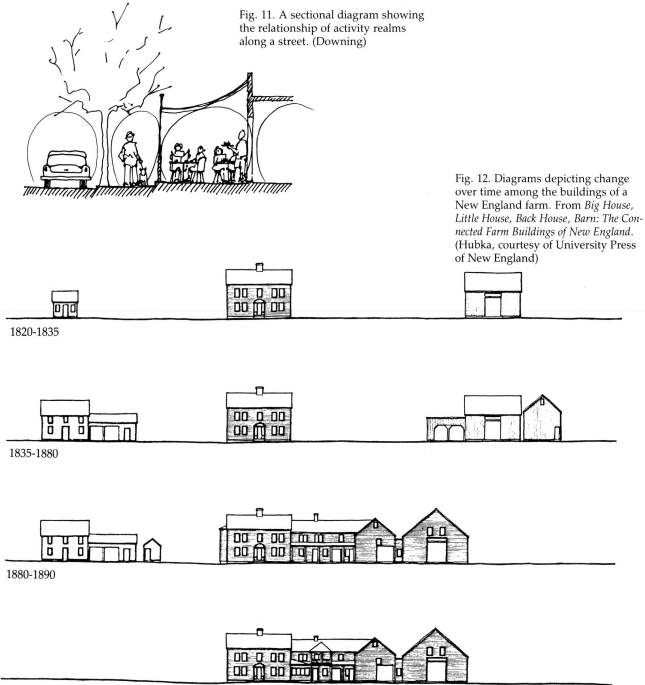

Fig. 11. A sectional diagram showing the relationship of activity realms along a street. (Downing)

Fig. 12. Diagrams depicting change over time among the buildings of a New England farm. From *Big House, Little House, Back House, Barn: The Connected Farm Buildings of New England*. (Hubka, courtesy of University Press of New England)

1820-1835

1835-1880

1880-1890

1890-1980

In order for scholars to apply diagrammatic techniques to the analysis of the architectural environment skillfully, it is useful to understand the philosophical and methodological assumptions behind the act of diagramming. There are at least three models of knowledge under which diagramming can function as a technique. Each contains different assumptions about how the world should be understood.

Rationalism is a model of knowledge in which an investigator of the environment might use diagramming. Rationalists tend to believe that knowledge is logical and embodied in precedents. A rationalist's scientific procedure involves the justification of plausible arguments through appeals to logical precedents. Truth is derived from deductive inferences that follow an acceptable premise and survive all reasonable challenges.

Another model in which diagramming has relevance is *structuralism*. A structuralist believes that knowledge is generic and embodied in taxonomies. Structuralist procedure involves the successive approximation of categories that interact to exhaust the naturally occurring events or characteristics of a given subject. Order is inherent when objects or ideas are sorted into related groups.

Finally, a model on which the American scientific community bases most of its exploration is *empiricism*. To empiricists, knowledge is provable and embodied in theories. The scientific procedure relies on unbiased observations to confirm hypothetically predicted events that are isolated through experimental or statistical controls.

In any one of these systems, diagrams are potent tools. Rationalists, including many architectural historians, utilize diagrams to explore a selective range of architectural examples that demonstrate preexisting laws or patterns. A rationalist employs diagrams to

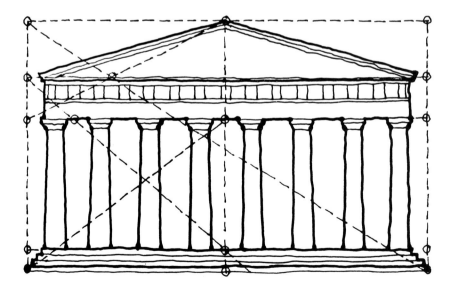

Fig. 13. A rationalist diagram using the "golden section" to explore the meaning and physical proportions of classical architecture. (Downing)

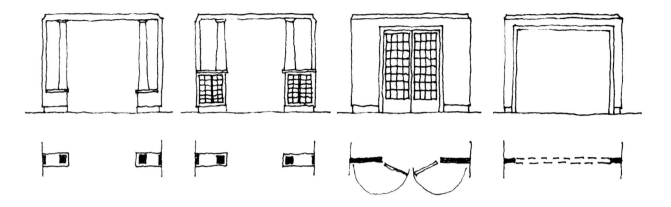

Fig. 14. A structuralist diagram exploring a typology of screens found in bungalows. (Downing)

identify the abstract ideal. Frequently researchers using rational logic attempt to emphasize proportions, rhythms, symmetry, stylistic orders, and other regulating patterns (Fig. 13).

A structuralist utilizes diagrams to explore a universe of objects in order to find inherent and systematizing elements. Less concerned with the particularities of individual buildings than with the elements common to many similar buildings, a structuralist produces diagrams to emphasize taxonomies, categories, and hierarchies (Fig. 14).

An empiricist uses diagrams to explore concrete instances derived from sensate data. The empiricist selects information that is scientific rather than abstract. Diagrams generated under this model tend to be place-specific and are more sensuously and experientially based than are the diagrams generated by rationalist or structuralist methods (Fig. 15).

Outside the hard sciences, most researchers tend to mix and overlap models, methods, and techniques, depending on their particular area of interest. Most architects and architectural historians have been enculturated and educated within the American system and may need to admit to a fourth model—*pragmatism*. Pragmatists believe that knowledge is, above all, useful. Pragmatism suggests that the value of any concept is determined by the results. Thus, a fluid mixing of ideal models is not uncommon. Combining models is a problem, however, if the researcher is ignorant of the assumptions implicit in each model.

Clearly the diagrammatic process can be a valuable means for analyzing historical environments. Diagrammatic thinking and drawing invite a healthy disregard for the rigid boundaries between academic disciplines by pushing the normal intellectual process of concept formulation into a less familiar realm—the spatial mode. Whatever the precise determinants, diagrams thrive in the sort of robust juxtaposition of intellectual philosophies that characterizes much of the best recent scholarship.

Another distinct advantage of the diagrammatic mode of analysis is its potential to become an extension of the analyzing mind—a tool for thinking and speculating about the environment. The diagram is also an egalitarian device. The ability to construct basic analytical diagrams does not require advanced or technical drawing skills. Of course diagramming is not easy, but the hard part is the thinking and analyzing—nothing new to those scholars of material culture who have been struggling toward an understanding of the built environment.

Fig. 15. An empiricist diagram interpreting the experimental qualities of the entrance sequence for All Saints Margaret Street Church. (Hubka)

II. Buildings in Their Geographic Contexts

6

JOSEPH S. WOOD

The New England Village as an American Vernacular Form

The common New England village is a vernacular form developed in nineteenth-century America. Despite conventional wisdom about a colonial landscape of nucleated villages, what seventeenth-century New Englanders called a "village" was an outlying community of farmers living on dispersed farmsteads.[1] From the beginning of settlement in the late 1620s, New Englanders avoided nucleation whenever they could. The settlement landscape inherited from the colonial period greatly affected the relative location and the morphology of the nineteenth-century village, but the form was distinct from seventeenth-century agricultural settlements in England and New England.[2] At most, the new village resembled the handful of inland commercial places established during the eighteenth century. Hence, villages, now as in the nineteenth century, are composed largely of commercial buildings and associated dwellings, not farmhouses.

Regardless of colonial New Englanders' penchant for dispersal, the fashion in which they organized the colonial settlement landscape is important for understanding how the contemporary village took shape. Notwithstanding religious motives for emigration, New England's colonists yearned to own land, and the control over its distribution was a crucial factor in directing the course of settlement. Expansion took place by replication of communities—by establishing new communities in a common mold—first around Indian old fields, salt marshes, and intervales, and very shortly thereafter on more marginal lands. The New England town system was designed to bring order to new communities as they established settlements (Fig. 1A). The town was an incorporation of settlers, an administrative unit to encourage orderly settlement within clearly defined geographical boundaries.

Because settlers came from different English backgrounds, no single model of how an agricultural community was to operate or how a settlement was to be formed prevailed.[3] Thus the early landscape was a patchwork of settlement forms, as settlers experimented with open-field agriculture—especially about fertile salt marshes and intervales—and with single-family enclosed farms. House lots in towns were commonly assigned but not as commonly

1. Joseph S. Wood, "Village and Community in Early Colonial New England," *Journal of Historical Geography* 8 (1982):333–46.

2. Joseph S. Wood, "Elaboration of a Settlement System: The New England Village in the Federal Period," *Journal of Historical Geography* 10 (1984):331–56.

3. Joan Thirsk, "The Farming Regions of England," in *The Agrarian History of England and Wales, 1500–1640,* ed. Joan Thirsk (Cambridge: Cambridge University Press, 1967), pp. 1–112; David Grayson Allen, *In English Ways: The Movement of Societies and the Transferral of English Local Custom to Massachusetts Bay in the Seventeenth Century* (Chapel Hill: University of North Carolina Press, 1981).

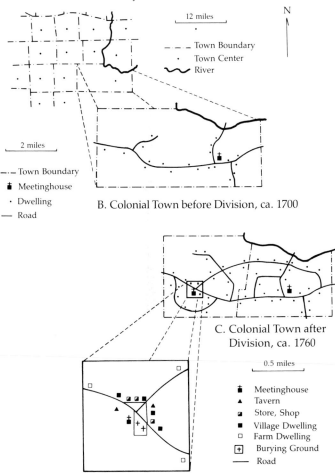

A. The Colonial Town System

B. Colonial Town before Division, ca. 1700

C. Colonial Town after
Division, ca. 1760

D. Commercial Village of the Federal Period, ca. 1810

Fig. 1. Morphogenesis of the New England village. During the colonial period, a mosaic of towns was formed across New England (A). If the location of a meetinghouse was too eccentric for a portion of the congregation (B), division of the town or parish took place (C). The commercial village of the Federal period developed about the town center (D). After *Journal of Historical Geography* 10 (1984):351. (Marvin Barton)

inhabited, for the abundance of land encouraged dispersal. Despite such apparently centripetal forces as community forebearance, Puritan tenets, and defensive precautions, towns were composed of dispersed farmsteads from the first (Fig. 1B).[4]

Preference for dispersed settlement does not deny that New Englanders shared a strong sense of community, nor does it imply remoteness or isolation. Regardless of settlement form, communities functioned quite well. Townsmen formed congregations, regulated land distribution, encouraged local enterprise, and coordinated communal activities. Ecclesiastical and political responsibilities were performed within an established social structure. Such community identity was important despite dispersed settlement.[5]

The colonial New England community's network of linkages

4. Wood, "Village and Community."
5. Ibid., p. 341.

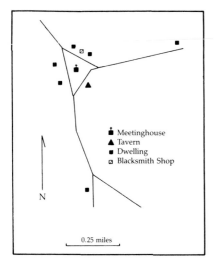

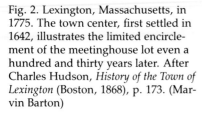

Fig. 2. Lexington, Massachusetts, in 1775. The town center, first settled in 1642, illustrates the limited encirclement of the meetinghouse lot even a hundred and thirty years later. After Charles Hudson, *History of the Town of Lexington* (Boston, 1868), p. 173. (Marvin Barton)

and interaction had a physical manifestation. The meetinghouse was the dominant feature of the settlement landscape, the focus of community activity. The lot on which the meetinghouse and parsonage were sited might in time be encircled by a tavern, a blacksmith, and a farmhouse or two, all forming a town center (Fig. 2). The town road network interconnected dispersed farmsteads with the meetinghouse, thereby enhancing its situation. As long as the town was not too large in area, the physical circumscription of town boundaries added to the sense of community.

Equitable organization of space within a reasonable distance for dispersed settlement was the overriding consideration in the formation of new communities. As seventeenth-century settlement reached farther from the established town center and more settlers were required to travel a considerable distance to meeting, colonial assemblies granted petitions for establishment of separate villages with their own meetinghouses (Fig. 1C). *Village* in this sense meant a secondary settlement within the bounds or under the auspices of a parent town and with its own ecclesiastical society, or parish. *Village* meant—as *town* always has in the New England sense—a corporate community, not a compact settlement (Fig. 3).[6] Division of dispersed communities into new villages and towns was important business in colonial New England, and it was an important part of the evolution of the New England settlement landscape.

A few nucleated agricultural villages, relics of feudal England, did develop in some New England towns. Such villages took a variety of forms, producing a distinctive regional pattern.[7] Hampton, New Hampshire, had a very compact agricultural village, while in Newtown, Connecticut, the village was linear.[8] Connecticut River towns like Wethersfield and Northfield, settled almost seventy-five years apart, developed highway villages stretching for miles along the river terrace.[9] On Long Island Sound, numerous compact places like Milford and Stratford combined open-field farming on salt marsh with sufficient commercial activity to distinguish these communities as much for trade as for agriculture.[10] In the first few inland towns about Massachusetts Bay—Dedham, Sudbury, Concord, Andover, and Haverhill—compact settlement took place initially about intervale, but within a generation inhabitants had dispersed.[11] Only at Concord, which became a major inland trading place, was a vestige of the agricultural village retained.

6. Ibid., pp. 337–39.

7. Joseph S. Wood, "Agricultural Villages, circa 1780," in *This Remarkable Continent: An Atlas of United States and Canadian Society and Cultures,* ed. John F. Rooney, Jr., Wilbur Zelinsky, and Dean Louder (College Station: Texas A&M University Press, 1982), p. 40.

8. Joseph Dow, *History of the Town of Hampton, New Hampshire* (Salem, Mass., 1893); James E. Johnson, ed., *Newtown's History* (Newtown, Conn., 1917); John N. Boyle, *Newtown, 1708–1758: Historical Notes and Maps* (New-

town, Conn.: Bee Publishing, 1945).

9. Charles M. Andrews, *The River Towns of Connecticut: A Study of Wethersfield, Hartfield and Windsor* (Baltimore, 1889); Josiah H. Temple and George Sheldon, *A History of the Town of Northfield, Massachusetts* (Albany, N.Y., 1875).

10. Leonard W. Labaree, *Milford, Connecticut: The Early Development of a Town as Shown in Its Land Records,* Con-

necticut Tercentenary Commission Publication, no. 13 (New Haven: Yale University Press, 1933); William H. Wilcoxson, *History of Stratford, Connecticut, 1639–1939* (Stratford: Stratford Tercentenary Commission, 1939).

11. Erastus Worthington, *The History of Dedham* (Boston, 1827); Kenneth Lockridge, *A New England Town, the First Hundred Years: Dedham, Massachu-*

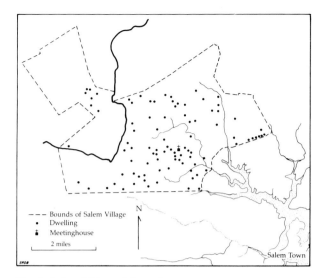

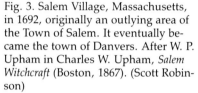

Fig. 3. Salem Village, Massachusetts, in 1692, originally an outlying area of the Town of Salem. It eventually became the town of Danvers. After W. P. Upham in Charles W. Upham, *Salem Witchcraft* (Boston, 1867). (Scott Robinson)

Fig. 4. Litchfield, Connecticut, in 1762. Settled in the 1720s and selected as a shiretown in 1751, Litchfield served as a market center for northwestern Connecticut. After a sketch by Ezra Stiles in *Extracts from the Itineraries and Other Miscellanies of Ezra Stiles, D.D., Ll.D., 1755–1794*, ed. Franklin B. Dexter (New Haven: Yale University Press, 1916), p. 185. (Gordon Riedesel)

Commercial places, ranging in size from small landings to cities like Boston, were in large measure concentrated along or within easy reach of tidewater.[12] Excepting Concord, which was established in the seventeenth century, inland commercial places of any stature—Worcester, Windham, and Litchfield—were settled in the eighteenth century. Each owes its commercial importance to its selection as a shiretown and market place for the surrounding region.[13]

These inland communities developed a unique form by the accretion of structures for administrative and commercial activities and by the construction of dwellings about the meetinghouse lot at the town center (Fig. 4). Because the settlement of each of these

setts, 1636–1736 (New York: W. W. Norton and Company, 1970); Alfred S. Hudson, *The History of Sudbury, Massachusetts, 1638–1889* (Sudbury, 1889); Sumner Chilton Powell, *Puritan Village: The Formation of a New England Town* (Middletown: Connecticut Wesleyan University Press, 1963); Ruth R. Wheeler, *Concord: Climate for Freedom* (Concord, Mass.: Concord Antiquarian Society, 1967); Abiel Abbot, *History of Andover from Its Settlement to 1829* (Andover, Mass., 1829); Philip J. Greven, *Four Generations: Population, Land, and Family Life in Colonial Andover, Massachusetts* (Ithaca: Cornell University Press, 1970); George W. Chase, *The History of Haverhill, Massachusetts, from Its First Settlement, in 1640, to 1860* (Haverhill, 1861).

12. Douglas R. McManis, *Colonial New England: A Historical Geography* (New York: Oxford University Press, 1975), pp. 72–85.

13. Wheeler, *Concord*; William Lincoln, *History of Worcester, Massachusetts* (Worcester, 1837); Ellen D. Larned, *History of Windham County, Connecticut*, 2 vols. (Thompson, Conn., 1880); Alain C. White, ed., *The History of the Town of Litchfield, Connecticut, 1720–1920* (Litchfield: Litchfield Historical Society, 1920).

14. Wood, "Village and Community," pp. 339–40; Abbott Lowell Cummings, in *The Framed Houses of Massachusetts Bay, 1625–1725* (Cambridge: Harvard University Press, 1979), argues for the simultaneous creolizing of architectural forms.

15. Wood, "Elaboration of a Settlement System."

16. Herbert Levine, "In Pursuit of the Nucleated Village" (typescript, Old Sturbridge Village, Sturbridge, Mass., 1971).

17. W. R. Cochran and George K. Wood, *History of Francestown, New Hampshire* (Nashua, N.H., 1895); Sumner G. Wood, *The Taverns and Turnpikes of Blandford, 1733–1833* (Blandford, Mass., 1908).

18. *Centennial Proceedings and Other Historical Facts and Incidents Relating to Newfane, The County Seat of Windham County, Vermont* (Brattleboro, Vt., 1877); Matt B. Jones, *History of the Town of Waitsfield, Vermont* (Boston, 1909); Helen N. Foster and William W. Streeter, *Only One Cummington* (Cummington, Mass.: Cummington Historical Society, 1974).

19. Edward A. Kendall, *Travels Through the Northern Parts of the United States in the Years 1807 and 1808*, 3 vols. (New York, 1809), 3:33–34, 216; Franklin McDuffee, *History of Rochester, New Hampshire from 1722–1890* (Manchester, N.H., 1892); George A. Wheeler and Henry W. Wheeler, *History of Brunswick, Topsham, and Harpwell, Maine* (Boston, 1878).

20. Martin Lovering, *History of the Town of Holland Massachusetts* (Rutland, Vt.: Tuttle Company, 1915); Ithamar B. Sawtelle, *History of the Town of Townshend, Massachusetts, 1676–1878* (Townshend, 1878); Edward L. Parker, *The History of Londonderry, New Hampshire* (Boston, 1857).

places was not tied to waterfront location, and because, except for Concord, they were developed long after much of New England was settled, they did not look like transplanted English market towns. By the eighteenth century, much early regional variation in settlement forms had disappeared and New Englanders shared a common and familiar landscape.[14]

The landscape in the nineteenth century was altered by the development, about town centers, of hundreds of commercial villages. Across New England after the Revolution, stores, shops, offices, and residences—material manifestations of a quickening of the rural economy—were gathered about meetinghouse lots (Fig. 1D).[15] Regardless of regional differences in how long a town had been settled or what form initial settlement had taken, full-time storekeepers, artisans, and professionals who located at town centers were creating villages that resembled Litchfield, Windham, Worcester, and Concord.

There was an opportunistic quality about these new villages. Few were planned, and speculation was rife as encirclement of meetinghouse lots took place. Village lots, like turnpike shares and mills of various sorts, proved to be sound investments. Lot subdivision and tenancy have been well documented for Sturbridge, Massachusetts (Fig. 5).[16] The land around the town center, initially a single lot, was partially subdivided by 1775. Development began in the 1790s, marked by considerable turnover of land, stores, and shops. Between 1795 and 1805, four new, substantial dwellings were built, doubling the number of residences at the town center and bringing some stability to the developing village. By 1815 the town center had become a considerable place, and by the end of the next decade the form of the village was set.

Not every town center was a commercial success. When the meetinghouse was poorly located with respect to activity in a town, the village might be situated near a mill or a landing. Competing villages might also emerge. Turnpike villages, often stretching out along one or more axes of movement, were especially likely to flourish.[17] By contrast, many hilltop centers did not develop and often failed, if access roads were too arduous.[18] Particularly in northern New England, where settlement was later than in the south, there was little vested interest in meetinghouse sites.[19] Nevertheless, the dispersed enterprises of the colonial period gave way to those that were purposefully relocated to the "right" central places in the early nineteenth-century Federal period. It was a cruel but efficient geography.[20]

The development of villages was concurrent with New England's cultural flowering, as reflected in architectural style. Villagers crowned their success—or at least their pretensions—with palatial town houses. The village of the Federal period was built to entice and impress, to enhance the prestige and influence of the villager, to show enterprise and good taste. As early as 1785, Sheffield, Massachusetts, was "a most beautiful village. There are sev-

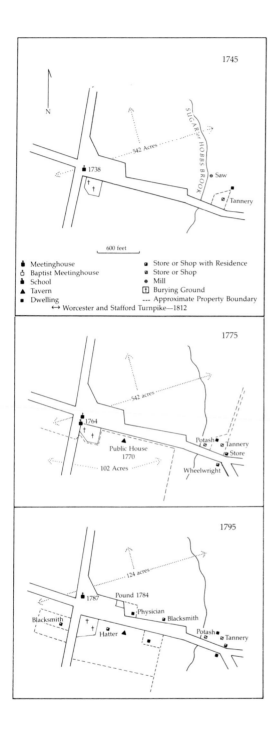

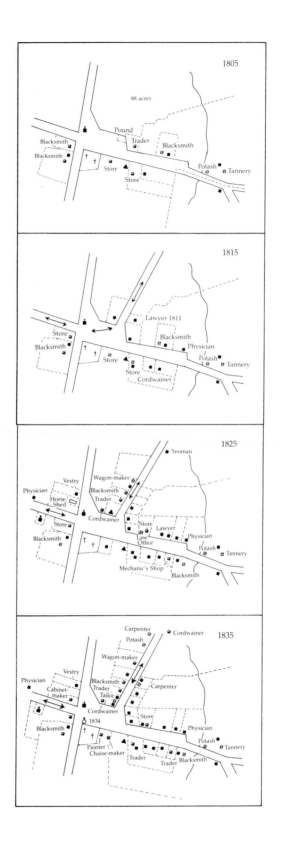

Fig. 5. Sturbridge, Massachusetts, between 1745 and 1835. After Herbert Levine, "In Pursuit of the Nucleated Village," typescript, Old Sturbridge Village, Sturbridge, Massachusetts, 1971. (Gordon Riedesel)

Fig. 6. Thompson, Connecticut, about 1835. The community had a three-story Federal house built in 1798 just to the east (right) of the new meeting-house. Woodcut from John Warner Barber, *Connecticut Historical Collections* (New Haven, 1838), p. 422.

21. Douglas S. Robertson, ed., *An Englishman in America, 1785, Being the Diary of Joseph Hadfield* (Toronto: Hunter-Ross, 1933), p. 173

22. Larned, *Windham County*, 2:270.

23. Milton H. Thomas, ed., *Elias Boudinot's Journey to Boston in 1809* (Princeton: Princeton University Press, 1955), p. 5. White became popular for exterior walls in the Federal phase of the classical revival. See Timothy Dwight, *Travels in New England and New York*, 4 vols. (New Haven, 1821–1822), 1:222; and Alan Gowans, *Images of American Living: Four Centuries of Architecture and Furniture as Cultural Expression* (Philadelphia: J. B. Lippincott, 1964), p. 168.

24. Larned, *Windham County*, 2:339, 359.

25. J. E. A. Smith, *The History of Pittsfield, Massachusetts, 1800–1876* (Springfield, Mass., 1876), p. 9.

26. Nathaniel Bouton, *The History of Concord, New Hampshire* (Concord, 1856), p. 515.

eral persons of easy circumstance and several buildings here."[21] In Connecticut by the early 1800s, "the south Killingly settlement though but a mere hamlet, three of four houses and a shop clustering around the meeting-house, had a very imposing aspect in the eyes of that generation, and by common consent was dignified as 'The City'—a name that clung to it for many years."[22]

Elias Boudinot, remarking on the changing countryside of southwestern Connecticut in 1809, found "the houses, along the road and in the Villages, are greatly increasing—well built—neatly painted (generally white) and beautifully situated."[23] Pomfret, Connecticut, had "fine houses" built on the street in the 1790s, and in Thompson, Connecticut, "many large and comodious houses were built along the line of the turnpike" (Fig. 6).[24] In Pittsfield, Massachusetts, at the turn of the century, "very shabby and uncomfortable abodes were, on the main streets, extremely rare."[25]

At the end of the eighteenth century, houses on the "Main Street" in Concord, New Hampshire "were built two stories, with what is called a hip-roof, with two front rooms, a door in the middle, and entry and hall running through, and an L, one story, on the back side, for a kitchen."[26] Houses of this Georgian style had been built in Boston for over a generation, but they were not common in rural New England. Because of this lag in the diffusion of architectural style, Georgian houses built about the town center in Royalston, Massachusetts, and Norwich, Vermont, were in the height of local fashion when Greek Revival was appearing in coastal cities. A Federal house of three stories with a symmetrical facade and a balustraded hipped roof was built in Thompson, Connecticut, in 1798, but few houses built in the new villages were as pretentious (Fig. 6). Most were plain two-story Georgian structures, perhaps

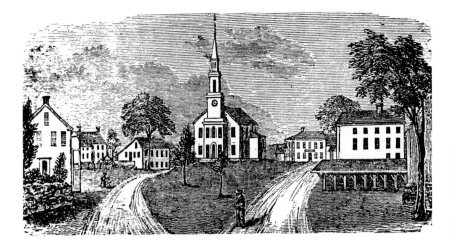

Fig. 7. Upton, Massachusetts, about 1835. "Grecian" became so pervasive in New England that one commentator called it the "New England style." Woodcut from John Warner Barber, *Massachusetts Historical Collections* (Worcester, 1839), p. 623.

with a flattish roof and a balustrade. The first such house in Royalston was built in 1806. Eight more similar houses were built before 1830, somewhat after the Federal style had declined in favor elsewhere.[27] By then, the Greek Revival was becoming common in the new villages, although few houses exhibited an exacting classicism (Fig. 7). Hence, the Reverend N. H. Chamberlain of Canton, Massachusetts, remarked, "Strictly speaking, the houses of our New-England villages have no style whatsoever; though, by numberless repetitions in building . . . most of our houses have to be considered as built in the New-England style."[28]

Rebuilding the meetinghouse was an important part of the development of villages. The 1780s and 1790s witnessed the culmination of the town division process, and by the 1800s many colonial meetinghouses were dilapidated and poorly situated. If a town center had not attracted or generated its share of commercial activities, it was necessary to resite the meetinghouse to accommodate the settled population of the mature town or parish. Hence, new churches were constructed near the places where townspeople shopped.

Style was used to distinguish the town-center meetinghouse from the new village church. Colonial meetinghouses had been barnlike structures with entrances on the long side, opposite the pulpit. Instead of a spire, there might be a bell tower at one end. For the new church, the entrance and pulpit were shifted to the gable ends. This design was also distinguished by a marked increase in ornamentation and the addition of a spire. An older meetinghouse might be renovated to conform to the gable-front style by turning the structure ninety degrees—or by moving the road to the new front—and by adding a pediment and a steeple.[29] Wealthy congregations could afford to hire a reputable architect, but most church designs, like those of houses, reflected a builder's transla-

27. Anderson, Notter Associates, "Royalston Common and a Plan for Preservation" (typescript, Offices of Notter, Finegold, and Alexander, Boston, Mass., 1974); Philip A. White and Dana D. Johnson, *Early Houses of Norwich, Vermont* (Norwich: Norwich Historical Society, 1973). See also Gowans, *Images of American Living.*

28. N. H. Chamberlain, *A Paper on New-England Architecture Read Before the New-England Historic Genealogical Society, September 4, 1858* (Boston, 1858), p. 11.

29. Marion C. Donnelly, *New England Meeting Houses of the Seventeenth Century* (Middletown, Conn.: Wesleyan University Press, 1968), pp. 79–80; Edward W. Sinnott, *Meetinghouse and Church in Early New England* (New York: McGraw-Hill, 1963), pp. 71–73; and Charles A. Place, "From Meetinghouse to Church in New England," *Old Time New England* 13 (1922–1923):69.

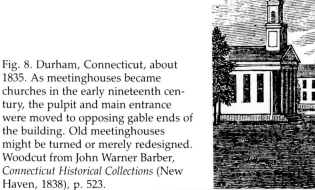

Fig. 8. Durham, Connecticut, about 1835. As meetinghouses became churches in the early nineteenth century, the pulpit and main entrance were moved to opposing gable ends of the building. Old meetinghouses might be turned or merely redesigned. Woodcut from John Warner Barber, *Connecticut Historical Collections* (New Haven, 1838), p. 523.

tion of Georgian, Federal, or Greek Revival notions into a vernacular that has remained popular in American church design to this day (Fig. 8).

The nineteenth-century village green or common was the colonial meetinghouse lot.[30] In the absence of a meetinghouse in later settled towns of northern New England, these essential features of the New England village were often added.[31] Thus, by emulation if not by initial design, town centers across New England came to look much the same. Clearing the lot allowed for militia drill. Fencing off the burying ground or a portion of the common allowed its occasional use for pasturage. Purposeful improvement and beautification were not common until later in the nineteenth century (Fig. 9).[32]

The social and economic revolution that gave rise to the New England village was short-lived. The village was not only the material manifestation of worldly enterprise, but its victim as well. By the second half of the nineteenth century, encirclement of the village green was complete, and the commercial and classical revivals had run their course. Little subsequent alteration of the villagescape took place. Scores of poorly situated trade centers declined in prosperity when economic conditions changed. Most villages survived, but few long remained the bustling places they were in the first several decades of the nineteenth century.

At that time, New England villages were still relatively new places, as an 1858 observer noted:

> The first marked trait in our houses in the rural district, and in large measure also in our cities, is a fragility,—a want of permanence exceedingly suggestive of the instability of our American life. A village, with its scattered white houses, often reminds one of an encampment, with its

30. The term *green* is used more in southeastern Massachusetts, Connecticut, and Rhode Island, while *common* is used more in the remainder of New England. Hans Kurath, ed., *Linguistic Atlas of New England* (Providence: Brown University Press, 1939), p. 13.

31. John B. Meyer, "The Village Green Ensemble in Northern Vermont" (M.A. thesis, University of Vermont, 1974).

32. John D. Cushing, "Town Commons of New England, 1640–1840," *Old Time New England* 51 (1961):86–94.

Fig. 9. New Canaan, Connecticut, about 1835. The meetinghouse lot became a green. The burying ground was enclosed by a stone wall (at left), and the remaining green was encircled by a road on which fronted various village activities. There was little purposeful improvement of greens themselves. Woodcut from John Warner Barber, *Connecticut Historical Collections* (New Haven, 1838), p. 386.

white tents, that to-morrow morning, at the sound of the bugle, will be struck, and disappear. . . . Most men, receiving no transmitted home of ancestry as their house of residence, build as though there was no posterity. Thus our village houses seem often to have had no past, and but slight promise of a future.[33]

Clarifying the origin of New England villages provides context for understanding this perspective. The New England village did not derive in any direct fashion from English antecedents. It was not a peasant agricultural village transplanted to colonial New England, nor was it modeled after the region's eighteenth-century water-side market towns. In form, the New England village of the nineteenth century most closely resembled the eighteenth-century inland shiretowns and marketplaces that resulted from a building up of commercial structures and associated dwellings about a meetinghouse lot. The rapid encircling of other meetinghouse lots in the nineteenth century, the consequence of serious speculation in real estate and investment in commercial enterprise, produced the early nineteenth-century New England village, a true vernacular town form.

It is unfortunate that the marketplace villages that proliferated in nineteenth-century New England have come to symbolize far more than just Yankee enterprise.[34] Concord's fame as a historical and literary site has, implicitly, at least, linked all New England villages with a stereotyped Puritan colonial past. These communities now carry this romantic burden that obscures the real origins of this significant element of the American vernacular landscape.

33. Chamberlain, *A Paper*, p. 12.
34. Donald W. Meinig, ed., *The Interpretation of Ordinary Landscapes: Geographical Essays* (New York: Oxford University Press, 1979), pp. 164–92.

7

KENNETH A. BREISCH
AND DAVID MOORE

The Norwegian Rock Houses of Bosque County, Texas: Some Observations on a Nineteenth-Century Vernacular Building Type

The area of Bosque County, Texas, originally settled by Norwegian immigrants, is an outstanding and intact example of a small, rural ethnic community that grew up on the American frontier in the latter half of the nineteenth century. Initiated in 1853, the community appears to represent the only substantial Norwegian settlement of this period in the entire southern half of the United States. Because of the self-sufficient nature of its social and economic structure, this settlement remained more or less isolated from the surrounding Anglo-American and German-American communities for more than five decades. It thus maintained, well into the twentieth century, much of its traditional Norwegian culture in terms of language, religion, agricultural practices, and architecture.[1]

A significant component of the Norwegian architectural heritage is a group of stone houses constructed between about 1855 and 1885. In form, plan, and siting, they differ markedly from the masonry homes erected by other contemporary Texas immigrant groups. These houses are referred to locally as "rock houses," and their presence clearly defines the limits of early Norwegian settlement in west-central Texas. The forms of these structures, as well as the overall arrangement of the surrounding farmsteads, have much to teach about the life-styles of these sturdy Texas pioneers.

Organized Norwegian immigration to the United States began when fifty-five settlers, led by Cleng Peerson, landed in New York in 1825. This small band eventually moved west, establishing themselves in 1834 in La Salle County, Illinois, where they founded the town of Norway. During the following years, Peerson continued to encourage immigration to America. By the time of his death in 1865, he had helped to start more than thirty Norwegian colonies in this country. The vast majority of immigrants who arrived during this period settled in the upper Midwest. A few, however, managed to find their way south into the newly created Republic of Texas. Peerson was eventually among them.

1. This study, which was undertaken in preparation for a National Register nomination written for the Texas Historical Commission in 1982, identified more than a hundred Norwegian-Texan homesteads. These were constructed in Bosque County between 1855 and 1919. Of these, there are approximately twenty individual stone houses that were built between 1855 and 1885.

64

Although Norwegian Johan Nordboe settled near the site of present-day Dallas as early as 1841, and the first permanent Norwegian community—Brownsboro—was founded only four years later, the total Norwegian population in Texas was never nearly as large as that of other immigrant groups, such as the Germans, Poles, and Czechs. By 1900, for instance, fewer than two thousand Norwegian immigrants had moved into the state, and only a handful more followed in this century. Nineteenth-century settlement was primarily confined to three communities. Two of these—Brownsboro and Four Mile Prairie—were established in the area east of Dallas. The third was founded in Bosque County, on land located some fifty miles west of Waco.[2] The majority of the Norwegian immigrants eventually settled in this last region.

By all accounts the first Norwegian to arrive in Bosque County was Ole Canuteson.[3] In 1850, he and his wife, Ellen, and their children, along with Cleng Peerson, had moved from La Salle County, Illinois. They initially located near the property of Johan Nordboe in Dallas County, but, by the early 1850s, Canuteson had begun to look for other land along the Bosque River to the west of Waco. In the summer of 1853, Ole and Ellen Canuteson claimed 320 acres of land that became Bosque County in the following year.

Also in 1854, a second band of Norwegians set out with Cleng Peerson to investigate the possibility of settling in the vicinity of the new Canuteson homestead. Like the Canutesons, they were struck by the "abundance of wood and water . . . good building stone and [the] 'lay of the land' . . . altogether, an ensemble that strongly reminded them of the home valleys from which they came."[4] Within three years of this expedition, these Norwegians had preempted an additional ten homesteads in the southwestern section of the county. By 1860, there appear to have been 102 Norwegians in this area, living on fifteen separate farmsteads. The population had grown to over 350, and the number of homesteads had tripled to about forty-five by 1870.[5]

The majority of these early pioneers appear to have passed through the east Texas settlements of Brownsboro and Four Mile Prairie. Because of poor farming and health conditions, however, both of these eastern settlements had begun to stagnate by about 1870. Most of the later immigrants to Bosque County arrived directly from Norway. By 1890, when Norwegian immigration began to slow, there were about thirteen hundred Norwegians in Bosque County and only a few dozen left in east Texas.

According to tradition, the early settlers in Bosque County commonly erected small log shelters or dugouts in which to live immediately after their arrival. The only surviving examples of this type of structure, however, date to the middle of the 1870s (Fig. 1). All these log residences appear to have been small, single-pen buildings with side gables and central doorways. Some elements, including the plate logs that project beneath the gable ends of one example and the high stone cellar of another cabin, recall the

2. See Axel Arneson, "Norwegian Settlements in Texas," *The Southwestern Historical Quarterly* 45 (1941):125–35, and Lyder L. Unstad, "The First Norwegian Migration into Texas," *Norwegian-American Studies and Records* 8 (1934):39–57.

3. The standard histories for the area are Oris E. Pierson, *Norwegian Settlements in Bosque County, Texas* (Clifton, Tex.: Bosque Memorial Museum, 1947); and William C. Pool, *Bosque County, Texas* (San Marcos, Tex.: San Marcos Record Press, 1954).

4. Arneson, "Norwegian Settlements," p. 128.

5. See State Patent Records and the U.S. Census and Special Farm Schedule for Bosque County for 1860 and 1870.

Fig. 1. Adolf and Christine Godager cabin, erected about 1874 in Bosque County, Texas. (David Moore; all photos for this essay appear courtesy of Texas Historical Commission)

Norwegian log building tradition.[6] Characteristically, however, the Bosque County structures—in contrast to their Norwegian and east Texas counterparts—were much cruder in construction, with heavy stone and mortar chinking and makeshift corner notching. This probably reflects the type of timber that these immigrants found in their new home. A lack of wood adequate for construction is suggested by the fact that additions to these log buildings were usually undertaken in stone. Of the three surviving log structures, two have rear stone sheds. The third dwelling was extended with the construction of a stone pen that was connected to the log unit by an open hyphen. In other cases, early log houses appear to have been demolished and replaced with stone—or rock—houses.

As would have been common in a pre-industrial, pioneer community, these stone houses appear to have been erected largely by their owners, with the help and guidance of part-time Norwegian masons. At least one of these skilled workmen is said to have been trained in his homeland. Almost all the stone buildings were constructed over a thirty-year period, between 1855 and 1885. In spite of this, there is little distinction between those known to have been built before the Civil War and those erected later.

One of the most imposing and earliest of these stone houses was the Jens and Kari Ringness house (Figs. 2 and 3), which was probably erected in the late 1850s. Its symmetrical facade once displayed a small gable-roofed porch set over a wide entryway.[7] Some half-dozen other Norwegian houses constructed before 1885 exhibit similar facade configurations (Figs. 4 and 5). They can also be identified by their central-passage plan, which has one or two rooms set to either side of a wide circulation space. The half-story attic immediately beneath the gable roof was normally undivided and re-

6. See John Lloyd, "The Norwegian Laftehus," in *Shelter and Society*, ed. Paul Oliver, (New York: Praeger Publishers, 1969), pp. 33–48.

7. This is indicated in an old photograph published in the *Clifton Record*, 30 April 1954, n.p.

Fig. 2. Jens and Kari Ringness house with blacksmith shop in the background. The house was built about 1860 in Bosque County, Texas. (Kenneth Breisch)

Fig. 3. Plan of the Jens and Kari Ringness house in Bosque County, Texas. (Judy Mataya)

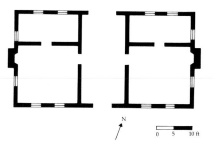

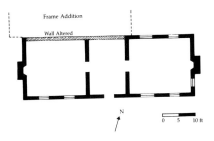

Fig. 4. Plan of the Keddel and Liv Grimland house in Bosque County, Texas. (Judy Mataya)

Fig. 5. Keddel and Liv Grimland house, constructed in Bosque County, Texas, between 1870 and 1875. (Daniel Hardy)

served as a sleeping room for the children. Stairways to these attics were typically located in the central passage. Large hearths were disposed at the ends of the buildings to heat the two main rooms during the short winters. Presumably, the placement of these hearths against the outside walls helped to dissipate cooking heat, if they were used during the summer months.

In addition to the big symmetrical houses such as the Ringness structure, there were constructed an equal number of smaller stone houses during the same period. These are composed of one room that is similar in dimensions and configuration to the main rooms of the symmetrical houses, and a second smaller room attached to the gable end opposite the hearth (Figs. 6–9). The chimney-end elevations of these houses are typically like those of the first group. The gable end opposite the chimney—where an external stairway often provided access to the loft—is usually pierced by a doorway or by windows. The long elevations indicate a flexible approach to design, with windows and doors placed in a great variety of tripartite configurations, but always copiously enough to provide for ample ventilation in the summer.

Fourteen rock houses constructed in these two forms have been identified. In construction date, the houses seem to be distributed evenly between 1855 and 1885. There are also a half-dozen other Norwegian stone residences that defy such neat categorization. For the most part, these are smaller, single-room structures scattered geographically and chronologically throughout the settlement. Many of these buildings, however, share characteristics among themselves and with the other Norwegian rock houses that serve to set them apart from contemporary dwellings erected by other pioneers in Texas. These features include the pitched roofs and massive chimneys flanked by small, square attic windows. Most characteristic is the ubiquitous first-floor living space, measuring somewhere between seventeen and twenty feet on a side, with a single hearth set into an outside wall.

The form and plan of many of these rock houses appear to be related, at least in part, to traditional Scandinavian house types. The central-passage dwellings (Figs. 2–5) in particular appear to be descended from the Scandinavian *Dobbelthus* (double-house or pair-house) tradition.[8] By the mid-nineteenth century, these double-houses had become a common type of residence for upper-middle-class land owners in all parts of Scandinavia. It was thus natural that variations of this imposing, symmetrical form should have been adopted by the new immigrant landowners in Bosque County—they had similar middle-class pretensions.

In Texas, however, this traditional form was adapted to local building materials. With its wide, dogtrot breezeways, multiple windows and doors, and hearths set at the far ends of the house, the form also seems to be related to the traditional Southern dogtrot dwellings and I houses, which the earlier immigrants would have seen in east Texas. They thus may have adapted a traditional Scan-

8. See Gunnar Jahn, *Byggeskikker på den Norske Landsbygd* (Oslo: Haschehoug, 1925). Similar three-room houses, constructed in the nineteenth century by Scandinavian settlers in Utah, have been identified by Tom Carter. See his National Register nomination, "The Scandinavian-American Pair-House in Utah," prepared in 1981.

Fig. 6. Bersvend and Kari Swenson house in Bosque County, Texas. The original two-room rock dwelling, constructed about 1865, forms the rear ell. The frame addition and the entire roof were added by a son, B. B. Swenson, in 1910. (Kenneth Breisch)

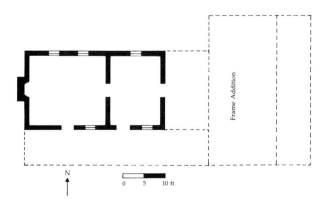

Fig. 7. Plan of the Bersvend and Kari Swenson house in Bosque County, Texas. (Judy Mataya)

Fig. 8. Gunsten and Lofise Grimland house, constructed in Bosque County, Texas, between 1870 and 1875. The original two-room stone dwelling is in the foreground, with a later frame addition behind. (Daniel Hardy)

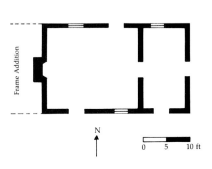

Fig. 9. Plan of the Gunsten and Lofise Grimland house in Bosque County, Texas. (Judy Mataya)

9. See Darrell D. Henning, "The Norwegian Two- and Three-Room Traditional House Type in America," abstracted elsewhere in this volume.

dinavian house form to a harsh local climate: intense summer heat must have been a trial for these pioneers from the north.

The two-room houses of Bosque County may be related by tradition to the two-room Norwegian houses identified by Darrell Henning in the Midwest.[9] There was, of course, also a common precedent for this form in east Texas, in the Anglo-American hall-parlor house. Likewise, models for the single-room plan can be found in both the Anglo-American and Norwegian building traditions. Additional research may clarify the origin of all these house forms in Bosque County.

In any case, the overall tendency to site the homestead on the slope of a valley wall or on the top of a small hill also distinguishes these buildings and may reflect the Nordic building heritage (Fig. 10). Siting, in fact, appears to have played a significant role in the development of the settlement as a whole. Several of the first pioneers, such as the Canutesons and the Swensons (Fig. 6), chose extremely prominent locations for their homesteads. These farms, in turn, served as focal points for the development of small rural communities that usually consisted of five or six closely grouped farmsteads. In Norway, farms such as these had long been organized into similar rural settlements that served, as they did in

Fig. 10. Kari and Sedsel Questad farm, constructed between 1855 and 1870 in Bosque County, Texas. The house is in the center background, with a spring-house and detached kitchen to the far left, and a blacksmith house on the right. (David Moore)

Bosque County, as centers of local social, economic, and religious activities.[10]

The Norwegian-Texan farm complex is commonly composed of the main house and a closely knit group of smaller stone outbuildings. These include such European types as bank barns and springhouses, as well as detached kitchens, smokehouses, and blacksmith shops. High stone fences of exceptional size and quality surround many of the farmsteads and enclose pens and pastures (Fig. 10). Ensembles of these structures not only give the impression of prosperity but also preserve the character of a Nordic mountain farmstead.

10. See, for example, Guthorm Kavli, *Norwegian Architecture Past and Present* (Oslo: Dreyers Forlag, n.d.), or Lloyd, "Norwegian Laftehus," pp. 33–48.

8

PAUL B. TOUART

The Acculturation of German-American Building Practices of Davidson County, North Carolina

1. A detailed analysis of the various schools of stonecutting, along with a discussion of the location and description of this German-American folk art tradition, is presented in the National Register Multiple Resources Nomination of Davidson County (1983). The tombstone research for the nomination was completed by Ruth Little in preparation for her doctoral dissertation. The only other printed material on the tombstones of Davidson County is found in Bradford L. Rauschenberg, "A Study of Baroque- and Gothic-Style Gravestones in Davidson County, North Carolina," *Journal of Early Southern Decorative Arts* 3 (1977):24–50.

Beginning in the 1740s, the central Piedmont and the Yadkin River Valley of North Carolina were settled by mixed groups of German, Scots-Irish, and English immigrants. Major waves of settlement by these groups occurred in the 1750s and 1760s. During the same period, German-Americans in search of cheap frontier land left Pennsylvania, Maryland, and Virginia and settled a large portion of what later became Davidson County, North Carolina. This essay considers the acculturation of German-American building forms and practices that were identified during a comprehensive architectural survey of Davidson County. The ethnic architectural traditions found in the county follow a general pattern of assimilation common to most of German-American culture.

The German-American cultural history of the region is vividly expressed by local *Fraktur* as well as by an incomparable collection of carved and pierced soapstone grave markers (Fig. 1).[1] These long-recognized and well-researched artifacts range in date from the late eighteenth century to the mid-nineteenth century and represent the clearest links between Davidson County settlers and their European ancestors. The decorative motifs used in *Fraktur* and tombstone carving, in addition to the German language, faded from popular use during the second half of the nineteenth century.

Paralleling the slow acculturation of *Fraktur* and tombstone art is the disappearance of an architectural tradition rooted in central Europe. An analysis of the acculturation of the German-American architecture in Davidson County makes it clear that assimilation occurred at different rates for different traditions. For various reasons, certain building forms and construction techniques were discarded, while others remained recognizable until the early twentieth century.

In the late eighteenth century, Valentin Leonardt, who emigrated from Katzenbach in Germany, raised a sturdy two-story log house in the Pilgrim vicinity of Davidson County. The house has disappeared, but in 1910 it was described by county historian J. C. Leonard:

Mansion House . . . [was built] . . . of immense logs. Its dimensions were forty and thirty feet, two stories. Two long beams, twelve by fourteen inches, ran through the whole length of the house to support the joists of the upper floor. They were hewn with a "broad axe" almost to perfect smoothness, and the lower edges nicely chamfered. The logs of the walls were very large, the two bottom ones being twelve by twenty inches, these bottom logs were rabetted on the inner side to receive the joists for the first floor. The joists themselves were worked out of logs with the "broad axe" and are much larger than carpenters now consider necessary. All the nails used in the house were made by hand, "wrought-iron" as were also the hinges of the doors and the window shutters. . . . Under the west end of the house was the great cellar, walled with large rough stones. This cellar was entered by a heavy slanting door on the south side of the house. The immense chimney stood near the middle of the house with a fireplace on either side below, but with none on the upper floor. The chimney was wide enough to receive wood eight feet long.[2]

Fig. 1. Tombstone with fylfot cross, Abbot's Creek Cemetery, Davidson County. (author, courtesy of North Carolina Division of Archives and History)

Houses fitting this description are found in the Valley of Virginia, northern Maryland, and southeastern Pennsylvania and point to the movement of Germanic people, as well as their preferred architectural forms and cultural heritage, down the "Great Wagon Road" to the Yadkin River Valley.[3] These one-and-a-half-story or two-story log or stone houses with a two-, three-, or four-room plan were traditionally built around a central chimney stack, as was described in the Leonard passage. This Germanic house, the *Flurkuchenhaus*, or hall-kitchen house, is a well-documented European form that was altered during the late eighteenth and early nineteenth centuries.

It is evident from J. C. Leonard's description that the *Flurkuchenhaus* plan of the Valentin Leonardt house consisted of two or perhaps three unequal-sized rooms divided by an off-center chimney pile. The larger of the two rooms, known in German as the *Kuche*, or kitchen, was heated by a large cooking fireplace that, according to Leonard, "was wide enough to receive wood eight feet long." This room traditionally extended the full depth of the house and was the main living and working space of the dwelling. Two doors, located opposite each other on the front and rear walls, served as the main access to the dwelling. The remaining room of the first floor, used in a more formal manner, was known in German as the *Stube*. It was similar to the Anglo-American parlor. A third room might be divided from the *Stube*. Known as the *Kammer*, it was often used as a first-floor bedroom. Leonard's description of an excavated cellar agrees with the accommodation of work spaces in other contemporary Germanic houses, and, in this respect, the Leonardt house resembles the Adam Spach house, the second pre-Revolutionary dwelling known to have stood in Davidson County (Fig. 2).

Built in 1774 for Adam and Maria Spach by Moravian masons, this bank-sited rubble fieldstone house was marked by an asym-

2. J. C. Leonard, "Valentin Leonardt, the Revolutionary War Patriot of North Carolina," *Pennsylvania-German* (1910):10–20

3. Edward Chappell's significant contribution to the understanding of the acculturation of German-American house forms was published in his "Acculturation in the Shenandoah Valley: Rhenish Houses in the Massanutten Settlement," *Proceedings of the American Philosophical Society* 124 (1980):55–89. Orlando Ridout supplied other examples of German-American house forms and construction techniques in the Valley of Virginia, western Maryland, and Pennsylvania. Personal communication, April 1983.

Fig. 2. Adam Spach house, built in Davidson County about 1774. This view dates from about 1939. (courtesy of Old Salem Restoration)

metrical placement of arched window and door openings on the principal facade. In contrast to the Leonardt house, the four rooms of the Spach house were heated by internal gable-end chimney stacks, a feature that became common by the turn of the nineteenth century.[4] The rear wall was also distinguished by an asymmetrical fenestration with segmental brick arches covering seven openings. A large doorway permitted access to a two-room cellar, where three windows provided light. An off-center main entrance was highlighted by a diamond-panel door.

These two houses have not survived, but their descriptions indicate a modified architectural tradition rooted in a Rhenish culture. The extant early nineteenth-century houses of Davidson County show a noteworthy mix of Anglo- and German-American traditions—they represent acculturation in midstream. Although house owners made the decisions to discard favored Germanic floor plans, the issues of house raising and finishing appear to have remained largely in the hands of the carpenters. As a result, a mixture of Anglo-American plans and German-American construction characterizes a portion of the early nineteenth-century domestic architecture in Davidson County.

This duality of form and construction is well illustrated by two early nineteenth-century log houses in the Lexington vicinity. The essential appearance and form of the A. N. Sink log house, built between 1810 and 1820, is similar to contemporary Anglo-American

4. John Larson, Old Salem, Inc., personal communication, May 1982.

examples of a three-room plan (Fig. 3). The main elevation has symmetrical fenestration. An exterior double-shouldered chimney was constructed instead of an internal stack. Originally, only the principal room of the first floor was heated by the large fireplace; the two equal-sized rooms were not equipped with a direct source of heat. The interior was finished with vertical board paneling trimmed with cornice moldings. Inch-thick vertical board partitions separate the three rooms, and flush six-panel doors provide movement between spaces.

At first glance, there is nothing about the A. N. Sink house that is clearly Germanic. The three-room plan follows closely the dimensions and relationship of spaces popularly used by Anglo-American builders, and the interior finish was completed along standard late Federal-period practices. However, closer inspection reveals that the detached log kitchen has a tapered batten door, an identifiable German-American construction practice.

The two-story Jacob Sink house was built between 1820 and 1840 with a symmetrical elevation and a hall-parlor plan (Fig. 4). The basic working elements of this two-room house are no different than those of an Anglo-American hall-parlor house. However, the interior finish of the house, unlike the A. N. Sink dwelling, has been attributed to Jesse Clodfelter, a documented German-American craftsman working during this period in the cabinetmaking trade. His most significant contribution to Davidson County was in furniture construction and tombstone carving. This house is the only known case in which his skills were applied to the interior finish of a dwelling. Like the A. N. Sink house, the first floor was divided by a vertical board partition, and access to the second floor was provided by a winder stair. The most skillful application of Clodfelter's expertise was in the construction of a dovetailed, tapered batten attic door.

The European technique of dovetailing battens into board doors appears in Virginia at Fort Egypt, as well as in Pennsylvania and Maryland houses.[5] In Davidson County, dovetailed battens were found in both the A. N. Sink kitchen and the Jacob Sink house (Fig. 5). Each batten was cut in a tapered shape and driven into a dovetailed trench to give the board door rigidity. The batten was then pinned or nailed in place. In post–Civil War houses in Davidson County, craftsmen discontinued the practice of cutting a dovetailed trench. Instead, the tapered battens were simply screwed or nailed onto the boards. This modification defeated the purpose of shaping the battens in the first place.

Another building tradition that has been identified as belonging to a German-American construction repertoire in Davidson County is sill-to-plate bracing of frame houses, a technique distinct from the Anglo-American practice of tying braces into sills and corner posts. At the John Peter Hedrick house, the braces extend from sill to girt or from girt to tie beam.[6] Raised during the first or second decade of the nineteenth century, the Hedrick house was planned

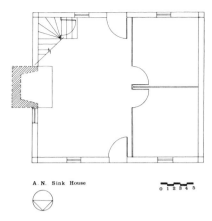

Fig. 3. First-floor plan of the A. N. Sink house, Lexington vicinity of Davidson County. (author)

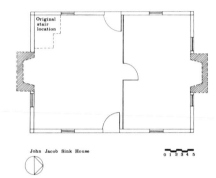

Fig. 4. First-floor plan of the John Jacob Sink house, Bethesda Church vicinity of Davidson County. (author)

5. Fort Egypt is a house cited in Chappell's "Acculturation in the Shenandoah Valley."

6. Earlier and contemporary examples of this construction technique appear in houses of Salem and in other German communities of North Carolina.

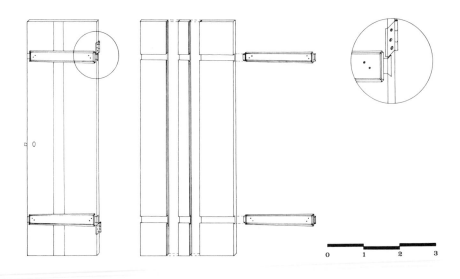

Fig. 5. Tapered batten door from the John Jacob Sink house in Davidson County. (author)

with a hall-parlor room arrangement and two exterior brick chimneys (Fig. 6). As in the Sink family houses, the stair is located in the corner of the principal room. Sill-to-plate bracing appears to have been dropped from general building practice by 1850.

One last construction feature associated with the Germanic domestic architecture of Davidson County is the manipulation of glazed header bricks to form a favorite German motif. Glazed bricks were widely used throughout the mid-Atlantic region as decorative highlights in Flemish-bond brickwork. During the construction of the Alexander Caldcleugh house around 1800, a heart, perhaps the most recognized German decorative motif, was laid in glazed headers in the Flemish-bond brick chimney.[7]

German-American building forms and construction techniques are not confined to the domestic architecture of Davidson County. Agricultural buildings also display German-American characteristics, but farm buildings have a history of standardization and acculturation that differs slightly from that of houses. The earliest barn form to survive in Davidson County is represented by the A. N. Sink barn, erected between 1810 and 1830 (Fig. 7). Its double-pen log form was brought to North Carolina by German-American immigrants and appears to combine construction techniques found in both German- and Anglo-American building vocabularies. In the earliest examples, two V-notched log pens are separated by a central passage and are covered by a continuous heavy-dimensioned, principal-rafter roof. Pent eaves or sheds normally surround the double-pen structure to insure proper water drainage away from the log walls.

A variety of roof-framing practices was used for barn construction. These include the Anglo-American principal-rafter system, the butt-purlin system, queen-post trusses, and the common-rafter system. The Shoaf barn, a contemporary of the Sink structure, has a

7. Tradition holds that a 1796 construction date was crudely etched into the Flemish-bond brick chimney on the southeast gable end. Despite a thorough search, this date could not be located. The chimney on the opposite end is initialed J. E. C. and dated 1896, probably recording the construction of the second chimney. Another early eighteenth-century date is carved in this stack, but it predates colonial settlement in this region.

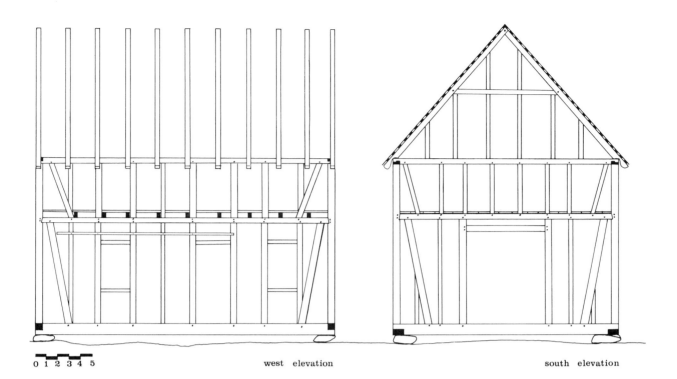

```
0 1 2 3 4 5
```
west elevation   south elevation

Fig. 6. Framing elevations of the John
Peter Hedrick house, Pilgrim Church
vicinity of Davidson County. (author)

Fig. 7. A. N. Sink barn, Lexington vicinity of Davidson County. (author,
courtesy of North Carolina Division of
Archives and History)

Buildings in Their Geographic Contexts / 77

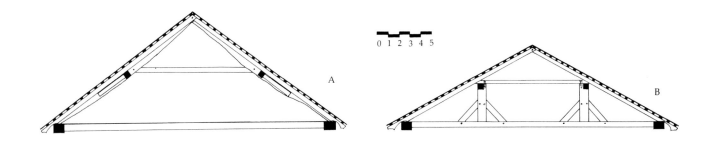

Fig. 8. Roof framing systems in Davidson County. A. Principal-rafter, butt-
purlin frame, Shoaf barn, Lexington
vicinity. B. Queen-post roof system,
Palmer barn, Silver Hill vicinity. (author)

roof frame consisting of four principal rafters that are separated and stabilized by three sections of butt purlins. The center section of the principal rafter is thicker, and the ends taper. The thicker section of the principal rafters provides a seat for the purlins, and the common rafters rest evenly on the purlins so that they are in the same plane as the principal rafters. Standard collars extend between each pair of principal rafters, and short braces help support the purlins. The rafters are joined at the peak with pinned open mortises (Fig. 8A).

A modified version of a Germanic roof frame is found on the Paul Palmer farm southeast of Lexington. In the Palmer barn, the continuous purlins rest on four pairs of queen posts. Collars extend across the top of each pair of posts, and each post is braced at its base (Fig. 8B). A series of common rafters with scalloped feet and open-mortise peak joints rests on the supportive truss.

Another common feature for double-pen log barns in Davidson County is a har-hung door system, a building technique that was shared by both German- and Anglo-American groups. Due to the scarcity and expense of iron fittings, Davidson County barn build-ers fashioned wooden hinges and door systems that precluded an extensive need for iron. Wooden posts or stiles supported a mortise-and-tenon frame to which exterior boards were nailed. The tops of the stiles were fastened in a cutout section of the header log and would swing on shaped stones or hollowed-out spots in a wooden floor (Fig. 9). Wooden strap hinges were fashioned for smaller doors that opened into the pens.

Around the middle of the nineteenth century, double-pen log barns achieved a standardization that continued for the next fifty years. The mid-century form, represented by the Sowers barn, re-mained essentially the same, but framing members were scaled down (Fig. 10). Instead of the heavy roof framing systems, a simple pole-rafter roof frame with slender collar beams was employed. The pent eave survived as a vital feature through the early twentieth century. Although improvements in construction technology revo-

Fig. 9. Detail of a wooden door system, Hamilton Everhart barn, Midway vicinity of Davidson County. (author, courtesy of North Carolina Division of Archives and History)

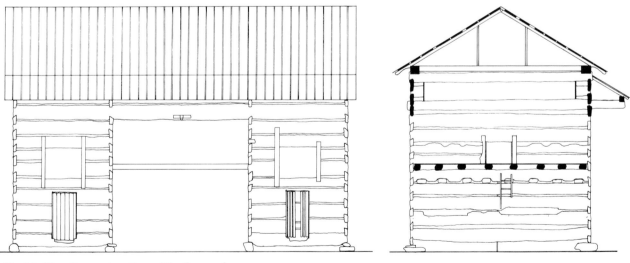

Fig. 10. Elevation and section of the Sowers barn, Churchland vicinity, Davidson County. (Carl Lounsbury)

Section A-A'

0 1 2 3 4 5

Fig. 11. D. T. Fritts barn, Lexington vicinity of Davidson County, about 1900. (Fritts family collection, courtesy of North Carolina Division of Archives and History)

lutionized barn building in the last decades of the nineteenth century, the double-pen central-passage barn was built on county farms until the first decades of this century (Fig. 11).

Standing on Davidson County farms are countless single-story or two-level outbuildings with cantilevered gable front roofs. This distinctive feature was used in springhouses, smokehouses, well houses, granaries, and potato houses. Even though these domestic and agricultural outbuildings were routinely built with log or, later, frame walls, the cantilevered roof continued to be a common feature through the late nineteenth century. Antecedents for outbuildings with bank sites and/or cantilevered roofs are found in eastern Pennsylvania as well as in central Europe.[8]

An examination of the acculturation of the German-American architecture in Davidson County, North Carolina, makes it clear that certain building forms and construction techniques were maintained as useful or symbolic traditions, while other techniques were abandoned in favor of alternative methods. In the case of the dichotomy apparent in many Davidson County houses between an Anglo-American form and German-American construction, the explanation appears to lie in a clear separation of decisionmaking processes.

Despite the continued use of certain building practices through the second half of the nineteenth century, external pressures from the dominant Anglo-American culture finally suppressed all traces of an architectural tradition rooted in central Europe. Just as the English language replaced German and popular mass-produced grave markers were substituted for elaborately carved tombstones, so German-American builders in Davidson County eventually discarded all ethnic traditions in favor of standardized construction practices common to the rest of the country.

8. Henry Glassie, *Pattern in the Material Folk Culture of the Eastern United States* (Philadelphia: University of Pennsylvania Press, 1968), p. 86.

9

HOWARD WIGHT MARSHALL

A Good Gridiron: The Vernacular Design
of a Western Cow Town

The nature of the small town is more and more the concern of ethnographic projects and field studies in folklife, architectural history, cultural geography, and anthropology. The town is a patterned yet pliant landscape. Studies of how towns function as organizers of communication and human interaction and as signifiers of shared cultural values can add useful dimensions to such subjects as settlement history, house types, archaeological remains, adjudicated property boundaries, social behavior, and legend cycles. As a case study in vernacular design, Paradise Valley, Nevada, can help explain something about the processes in which people create environment out of wilderness (Fig. 1).[1]

It is that terrain between big towns and county seats, located on lifelines such as rivers, railroads, and—most recently—interstate highways, that interests the material culture researcher. Paradise Valley is off the beaten path at the end of the road. While towns like Paradise seem isolated, they are not cut off from the rest of the world and never were. They are insulated by preference. The once-acclaimed thesis of Frederick Jackson Turner does not apply to places like Paradise Valley.[2] The town was not the last event in some ideal evolutionary progression of phases from hunters-trappers-explorers to settlers to civic society and commerce. It all occurred roughly at once, and the early establishment of towns—often on hopeful speculation—stimulated settlement.[3]

The region is the high sagebrush desert of northern Nevada, a terrain travelers know from high-speed automobile trips across the hard distance between Salt Lake City and Reno. It is a landscape where distant hazy mountains seem like mirages and yet contain cattle ranching valleys. Paradise Valley was found by prospecting hardrock miners in the early 1860s. They thought it was "a paradise," and, with the construction of railroads across the Great Basin, they recognized its opportunity for permanence and prosperity. In the wake of the gold rush in the Sierra, the pioneers saw a more practical future in providing beef to the Nevada mines than in grubbing after high-grade ore in the glory holes. As in countless other instances, the fast times of the gold and silver boom and the prox-

1. From 1978 to 1981, the author supervised a multidisciplinary field research project in Paradise Valley, Nevada, for the American Folklife Center in the Library of Congress. In addition to work in oral history and documentation of the valley's architectural environment, there was accumulated an elementary body of information on the personality of the town of Paradise itself. The broader project led to a joint exhibition with the Smithsonian Institution, a book-catalog, community programs, a motion picture, a videodisc, a research archive, and other products. See Howard Wight Marshall and Richard E. Ahlborn, *Buckaroos in Paradise: Cowboy Life in Northern Nevada* (Washington, D.C.: Library of Congress, 1980; rpt. Lincoln: University of Nebraska Press, 1981), p. 6; Marshall, "Jottings from the Circle A Line Camp," *Folklife Center News* 1, no. 3 (1978):6; Marshall, "Jottings from a Nevada Cattle Drive," *Folklife Center News* 2, no. 1 (1979):4–5; Marshall, "Chinks, Dallies, Sougans, and Grass Beef: A Cow Camp Lexicon," *Kansas Quarterly* 13, no. 2 (1981):57–71; Marshall, "The Land and Its People: Cultural Landscapes and Folklife Studies," in *Proceedings from the Clearing and Williamsburg*, ed. William H. Tishler and Susan Buggey (Madison, Wis.: Alliance for Historic Landscape Preservation, 1983), pp. 43–61; and Marshall, "Life and Work: Thoughts on the Cadence of the Cattle Rancher's Year," in *American Folk Custom*, ed. Wayland D. Hand (Washington, D.C.: Library of Congress, in press). The author also read a

Fig. 1. Paradise Valley, Nevada, and the Santa Rosa Range,
looking northwest from the Mill Ranch. (Carl Fleischhauer)

paper entitled "Bunkhouse Basics" at
the Home Sweet Home Vernacular Architecture Symposium at the University of California, Los Angeles, 1983.
The most promising extension by others of the Paradise Valley project is a
dissertation on the town by Margaret
Purser, a doctoral candidate in anthropology working with James Deetz at

the University of California at Berkeley.
    2. Turner's work has undergone stiff
analysis and bears revision in part due
to the extensive ethnography of the
twentieth century. For the basics on
the Turner thesis, see George R. Tayler, ed., *The Turner Thesis* (Lexington,
Mass.: D. C. Heath, 1956).

3. See John W. Reps, *Cities of the
American West: A History of Frontier Ur-
ban Planning* (Princeton: Princeton Uni-
versity Press, 1979), p. ix; Wilbur Ze-
linsky, *The Cultural Geography of the
United States* (Englewood Cliffs, N.J.:
Prentice-Hall, 1973), pp. 33–35; and
Tayler, *The Turner Thesis.*

Fig. 2. Old photographs of Paradise Valley, Nevada, printed as postcards about 1910. These images make it possible to visualize the town during its early stages. (private collections, Paradise Valley)

imity of a railroad shipping point encouraged establishment of Paradise Valley as a cow town (Fig. 2).

Following several years of settlement and the initiation of family ranching in the valley, the crossroads village of Paradise City—later renamed Paradise Valley—was situated near the U.S. Army's Camp Winfield Scott to meet the pioneers' concern for personal safety. Camp Scott was established in 1864 to enforce treaties with Paiute and Shoshone Indians who were still threatening settlement through occasional and largely symbolic shows of anger.

The town was laid out according to an orthogonal plan, a system of rectangles in which streets are parallel or normal to each other (Fig. 3). It is an ancient system, but not one that springs automatically into being.[4] The gridiron appeared in different periods and places. Indeed, remains of checkerboard towns in the Middle East date to about 3000 B.C.[5] The common grid, then, was the result of a long process of vernacularization and standardization of older and often fancier plans. America's first city with a specific grid plan seems to have been Philadelphia, laid out in 1682 at about the same time the French used the grid in the Mississippi Valley.[6]

4. An overview of the subject is contained in Dan Stanislawski, "The Origin and Spread of the Grid-Pattern Town," *Geographical Review* 36 (1946), reprinted in *Readings in Cultural Geography*, ed. Philip L. Wagner and Marvin W. Mikesell (Chicago: University of Chicago Press, 1962), pp. 318–29.

5. Ibid.

6. See David Denman's abstract elsewhere in this volume.

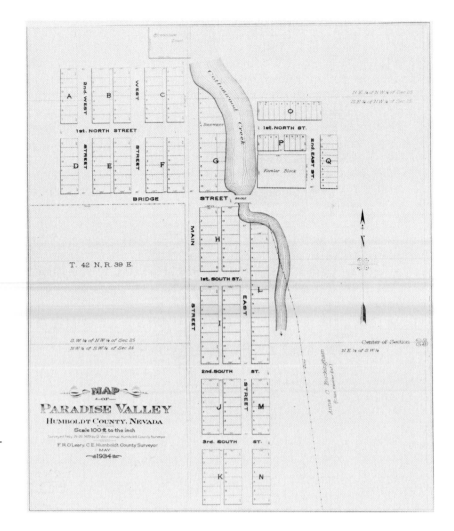

Fig. 3. The official 1934 survey of Paradise Valley by the Humboldt County surveyor was based on the original 1879 survey. It indicates a tidy, crisp plan and not the actual situation. (Humboldt County records)

The gridiron has disadvantages. It loses something in efficiency and it really has no central plaza to anchor action. In a grid town, the main street becomes the functional center. The grid also lacks the curvaceous and serendipitous boundaries and spaces that often lead to cozy neighborhoods and appealing views. Moreover, the grid is difficult to establish in topography that is not reasonably flat and wide.

Nevertheless, the gridiron has its attractions—especially for a townsite like that of Paradise Valley, distinguished by only modest undulations of land and river. The system seems quite American. It suits America's love for mechanical systems that can be cleanly extended with still more order the result. It is a movable system, too, transferrable to almost any locality with only minor alterations. It brings to mind interchangeable parts and the endless assembly of matchable units.

The gridiron offers more administrative or military control over the daily comings and goings of citizens than perhaps any other plan. It is an open system. The checkerboard can be infinitely expanded, and this optimistic flexibility was appealing to builders in the American West. These ambitious pioneers liked the order and logic of the checkerboard, admired its clarity and sense of strength and purpose. They had vigorous, urban futures in mind and wanted to build towns that would accrue the mechanics of communication, transportation, and commerce. The orthogonal plan is a good concept that services all strata of society and all designers. It has been used in town organization by elite or academic designers as well as by vernacular and folk builders.

Many gridiron towns in frontier situations were the result of a military, governmental, or industrial influence. In the case of Paradise Valley, it may be that the military personnel at Camp Scott offered advice and aid as the pioneers staked out the townsite. On the other hand, the average farmer and rancher of the time possessed the basic tools for plane surveying, including a surveyor's level, measuring devices, a spirit level, and a compass. The settlers also usually had the skills and experience necessary to determine boundaries, dimensional relationships, distances, angles, and directions. Pioneers could themselves locate property boundaries, create basic property maps, lay out building sites, and conduct effective surveys. In Paradise Valley, it is probable that the Italian immigrant stonemasons Batiste Recanzone and Angelo Forgnone played an important role in laying out the town. Recanzone and Forgnone were masters in the guild-like clan of north Italian builders who were active in the evolution of the Nevada vernacular environment, and they had previously secured a contract to design and erect the major adobe buildings at Camp Winfield Scott. Another Italian builder, Steve Boggio, is credited with the construction of a commercial building in Paradise Valley (Fig. 4).

The town's location conforms to the geographers' central-place theory that, given uniform environment and right conditions, a city will develop at the center of an area. Camp Scott was already situated on the northwestern edge of the valley's center, located on upward-sloping ground with the Santa Rosa Mountains behind it. Moreover, the center of the valley was an excellent environment with fresh water from the Cottonwood Creek and natural rye grass meadows that could be converted into productive fields. Concentric rings—or squares and rectangles—of use could develop around the valley center.

It is notable that there was village life in this spot beside Cottonwood Creek before the establishment of the army post. Paiute and Shoshone bands had used the site as a temporary dwelling place. Their encampment along the banks of the creek later became the location for earthen "dugouts" built by Chinese who performed basic services and cooked for ranchers.[7] The network of factors affecting the location of the town—the army garrison, the creek, the

7. As part of the American Folklife Center's Paradise Valley project, archaeological study of this intriguing site combining Indian, Chinese, and Anglo-American material culture was carried out by a team of researchers under the direction of James Deetz from the University of California at Berkeley.

Fig. 4. Case's Store, built in 1910 by Italian stonemason Steve Boggio. The structure now houses the town's only bar, store, and gasoline pump. With the post office and the Odd Fellows' Hall across the street, Case's anchors the present Paradise Valley townscape. (Carl Fleischhauer)

Indians, the coming of a mainline railroad forty miles away, and a livable mix of ranchers and businessmen eager to make a go of it—provided a recipe for endless tension. But it was tension that worked.

In this western region, all the mythical and urgent threats to the European-Americans were close at hand: the Indian, the rattlesnake, the coyote, the wilderness. These forces had to be subdued. What better way to mark the space with conquering order than to lay out a town of rational perfection. In this way, an anchoring "place" with symbolic identity and real power was created out of the challenging and alien space.

Paradise Valley's grid plan is like countless other small pioneer town plans throughout the western American frontier. The four-square gridiron was comfortable and familiar as well as practical for these European-Americans. Once in place and furnished with a good creek, the form helped the emporium invent itself. Despite its rigid appearance, the checkerboard is quite flexible. Endless variation can occur once the essential grid is set up. As elsewhere, the plan evolved through alterations and slight reorderings over generations of wear, and in the accumulation of a special identity. One of the grid's most interesting features is its very incompleteness. It is a pattern of ambition, pride, and Spartan idealism in its anticipation of rapid growth. Because of the vagaries of history, the pattern was seldom filled up in the typical small cattle town.

The development of Paradise Valley is not one of transformation from chaos to civil order. It began in order and now seems disheveled. The frayed town records the loss of businesses and services to Winnemucca, the county seat located an hour's automobile drive to the south. Today, the town is a ragged, pewter-brown hamlet full of holes and spotted with the ruins of old buildings. Its appearance belies the excellence of the cattle rancher's economic performance. Moreover, the present condition of the village embodies a winding down of the settlers' expectations and dreams of a city born in the nineteenth-century sagebrush wilderness.

The gridiron is a simple rectangle or square spread out to the right of a fixed datum point that could be located easily and recognized in the community as a permanent landmark. The job of laying the gridiron is technical but not exceedingly demanding: drive a stake in the ground, find north, and begin. The referent in Paradise Valley was a huge cottonwood tree, a sentinel that, dead and cropped, still stands imperially in front of the little post office on Main Street.

Cottonwood Creek is near the reliable datum point. Main Street was put alongside but not too near the creek. It followed the original wagon road from Winnemucca, forking off toward the fort and mining camps in the northwest and toward other mining camps and the Owyhee Desert to the northeast. An avenue eventually named Bridge Street was added to intersect with Main Street at ninety degrees. The rectangular blocks with their dividing alleys and rows of lots were then set off, creating a checkerboard awaiting players.

In Paradise Valley, an informal committee of experienced builders acting in concert with other ranchers and businessmen simply assumed leadership and devised the plan. It was accepted without question by the pioneers. The influential ethnic and national segments of this frontier Nevada community—Americans, Germans, British, Italians—were already familiar with the orthogonal plan. Furthermore, the land division system mandated by the Ordinance of 1787 and employed in the West was based on thirty-six-square-mile townships divided into a checkerboard. This factor also strongly predisposed the Nevada pioneers to their gridiron.

In a Nevada frontier gridiron, it is possible to track the process of evolution by which towns are created, used, and changed through time and shifting community requirements. How logical and useful is the ancient checkerboard plan? How well did it function as the framework for everyday life? How well did the plan embrace the shared notions of worth in the community? Did it adequately respond to the intentions of the pioneer ranchers, entrepreneurs, and builders who controlled the landscape and invented a center for the satisfaction of commerce and society?

Today's Paradise Valley indicates a shift away from the original gridiron (Fig. 5). Contemporary values tend toward the siting of a new house at the margin of town, rather than in one of the old town blocks. Ideas change. The community leaders recognize that the original gridiron town plan will never be completed. The town's importance as a commercial center has almost been lost. No signif-

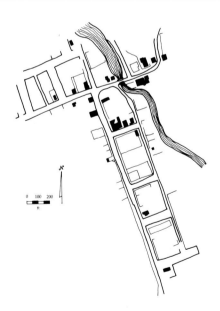

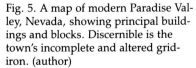

Fig. 5. A map of modern Paradise Valley, Nevada, showing principal buildings and blocks. Discernible is the town's incomplete and altered gridiron. (author)

8. In approaching the subject of town planning and town study, see Fernando Castagnoli, *Orthogonal Town Planning in Antiquity* (Cambridge: MIT Press, 1981); the writings of Lewis Mumford, especially *The City in History: Its Origins, Its Transformations, and Its Prospects* (New York: Harcourt Brace and World, 1961), pp. 87, 421–25; Arthur Smailes, *The Geography of Towns* (London: Hutchinson University Library, 1964); Emrys Jones, *Towns and Cities* (New York: Oxford University Press, 1966); Henri Pirenne, *Medieval Cities* (Princeton: Princeton University Press, 1925); Patrick Geddes, *Cities in Evolution* (London, 1915); Gideon Sjoberg, *The Preindustrial City* (New York: Free Press, 1960); Robert Redfield, *The Little Community* (Chicago: University of Chicago Press, 1956); and Elvin Hatch, *Biography of a Small Town* (New York: Columbia University Press, 1979). Among other inviting works are Kevin Lynch, *What Time Is This Place?* (Cambridge: MIT Press, 1972); Paul Zuker, *Town and Square: From the Agora to the Village Green* (Cambridge: MIT Press, 1959); Dora P. Crouch et al., *Spanish City Planning in North America* (Cambridge: MIT Press, 1982); Ronald Blythe, *Akenfield: Portrait of an English Village* (New York: Delta Books, 1969); Lawrence Wylie, *Village in the Vaucluse: An Account of Life in a French Village* (New York: Harper and Row, 1964); Christopher Tunnard, *The Modern American City* (Princeton: D. Van Nostrand, 1968); Sam Bass Warner, *The Urban Wilderness: A History of the American City* (New York: Harper and Row, 1972); Ervin H. Zube and Margaret J. Zube, eds., *Changing Rural Landscapes* (Amherst: University of Massachusetts Press, 1977); Henry Glassie, *Passing the Time in Balleymenone: Culture and History of an Ulster Community* (Philadelphia: University of Pennsylvania Press, 1982); and John Fraser Hart, *The Look of the Land* (Englewood Cliffs, N.J.: Prentice-Hall, 1975).

9. See J. B. Jackson, "The Public Landscape," in *Landscapes: Selected Writings of J. B. Jackson*, ed. Ervin Zube (Amherst: University of Massachusetts Press, 1970), p. 153.

icant new businesses have located in Paradise Valley for a generation or more. Though the town now looks more linear than orthogonal, it is not. It has merely been rounded off and left unfinished. But however limited the town's economic functions may be, its social functions are as vital as ever.

The planning and personality of towns is an area of increasing interest to students of vernacular architecture and material culture. The formal geometry of townscape and the replication of traditional patterns of movement are important factors in the cultural landscape—they are just as interesting as architectural styles or small-group behavior. A townscape like Paradise Valley is the creation of particular and usually unnamed designers following and modifying tradition—here, the classic orthogonal plan.[8] Each ingredient in the jumble of pathways, streets, monuments, gardens, ruins, wells, public spaces, boundaries, dumps, cemeteries, and structures called a "town" can be recorded and explained. Some are private things, while some constitute the public landscape of shared experience and social interchange.[9] All are vital to the total visual personality and the rich sense of place that accrue anywhere. Obsolete structures that help bolt a town together often persist despite changing functions, values, and economies. They sometimes remain—the old water tower, the stone hitching post—in new roles as memorials to the common and generally unspoken community past. For all their apparent simplicity, innocence, and accidental quality, these collected artifacts help explain the power of custom in dynamic interchange between old and new, conservative and fashionable, persistence and demise.

It is sometimes said that the small town is on its way out as a viable artifact, that the colorful hamlets are just oddities, even museums. Urban areas are gradually spreading out and engulfing hamlets, yet there are thousands surviving in differing degrees of health. In the western states, the small town has managed to maintain much of its importance over the years, partially as a result of the scattered population in the cattle-ranching regions. Notwithstanding the problems of loss and decay, the small-town way of life continues to work as the common way of life in northern Nevada and throughout the Great Basin. Paradise Valley is not an isolated "kiwi." It is a fair representative at the base of the pyramid of community life in the American West.

III. Types of Vernacular Buildings

10

DELL UPTON

Anglican Parish Churches in Eighteenth-Century Virginia

When scholars of the early Chesapeake have treated objects as evidence for the history of social life, they have preferred to examine artifacts of the personal and domestic realms—houses and their contents. Studies of public artifacts have so far been confined to art-historical inquiries that focus less on the relation of the object to its community than on its relation to European aesthetic currents. At the same time, scholars of domestic artifacts have preferred to ask about wealth distribution and the social relations of the family. Little attention has been given, as yet, to the ideological functions of artifacts.

This paper considers an assemblage of publicly owned and used objects: the buildings and fittings of the Anglican parish church in eighteenth-century Virginia. It is an attempt both to understand what have seemed to be transparently simple and self-evident artifacts and to probe the ways that artifacts play a direct role in reproducing social structure and ideology in one group of colonial communities. Such an undertaking has two aspects. First, the system must be described and the principles of its functioning must be outlined. Then the system must be observed in operation in a specific historical context. In this brief essay, only the first of these aspects will be considered.[1]

The Anglican Church in eighteenth-century Virginia was a state church, established by law as an official religion and supported by public taxation.[2] In addition to its ritual functions, the Church provided a variety of social services including support of the poor and maintenance of public morality. Officially, the church in Virginia was ruled by the governor of the colony and by the commissary, a representative of the bishop of London, under whose jurisdiction the colonial Church was placed. The governor and the commissary claimed overlapping and occasionally conflicting powers over the appointment of the local clergy and the oversight of the day-to-day operation of the parishes. Except in extraordinary circumstances, however, their intervention in local affairs was minimal. The life of the colonial Church lay in the parish, a geographical unit with boundaries that often coincided with, but never exceeded, those of

1. Ideas and data cited here but not noted are drawn from the author's longer work, *Holy Things and Profane: Anglican Parish Churches in Colonial Virginia* (New York and Cambridge: Architectural History Foundation/MIT Press, 1986).

2. Throughout the text, *church* will refer to the building and *Church* to the institution.

the county. In populous counties there might be more than one parish; Gloucester County had four. The parish was governed by its vestry, a self-perpetuating group of local gentry. In a colony lacking significant urban development until the third quarter of the eighteenth century, the Anglican parish was the smallest official community in which Virginians participated. Its churches were the largest public buildings in the colony. Since there were between one and four churches in each of a hundred parishes at the time of the Revolution, they were the most numerous public buildings as well.

The position of the Anglican parish church in colonial life presents interesting problems. Aside from its official role, the church performed an integrative social function that cannot immediately be understood. While most parishioners attended ostensibly to hear the sermons, many eighteenth-century observers found Anglican services perfunctory and the sermons particularly unsatisfying and dull. Devereux Jarratt, an Anglican clergyman later active in the Methodist movement, described the minister of his native St. Peter's Parish as "but a poor preacher—very unapt to teach or even gain the attention of an audience."[3] Philip Fithian, a Princeton-trained Presbyterian working as a tutor on the Northern Neck, allowed that sermons in the Cople Parish churches were "always made up of sound morality, or deep studied Metaphysicks," but thought them at best "cool, spiritless harangues."[4] While both men were writing from the perspective of the evangelical opponents of Anglicanism, their comments demonstrate that some attenders of Virginia's Anglican churches were aware of a different, more impassioned standard. Even committed Anglicans, like the planter Landon Carter and the traveler Nicholas Cresswell, noted the indifferent attitude of some Anglican clergy, their tendency to rush the service, and their failure to preach or even to go to church when they did not feel like it.[5]

Despite the negative reports, there are indications that the churches held an attraction for parishioners that transcended the vapidity of the service. While attendance figures are not available, many qualitative sources suggest the popularity of churchgoing among many segments of the population. Travelers like the Rhode Island Anglican cleric Alexander MacSparran commented on the numbers who attended and on the distance some parishioners traveled to get to church.[6] Large sums were spent on lavish church buildings, with little dissent other than occasional complaints that new churches were sited too far away for easy attendance. In St. George's Parish, Spotsylvania County, residents burned down a standing church to force the vestry to build a new one in their own neighborhood. Churches were regularly enlarged, or were replaced by larger buildings because they could not hold the number of people who attended. Even dissenters participated in parish life. The Presbyterian James Gordon of Lancaster County attended the Anglican church when there were no Presbyterian services available, until he was offended by one too many anti-Presbyterian ser-

3. Devereux Jarratt, "The Autobiography of the Reverend Devereux Jarratt, 1732–1763," ed. Douglass Adair, *William and Mary Quarterly*, ser. 3, 9 (1952):364.

4. Philip Fithian, *Journal and Letters of Philip Vickers Fithian, a Plantation Tutor in the Old Dominion, 1773–1774*, ed. Hunter Dickinson Farish (Charlottesville: Dominion Books, 1968), pp. 29, 100.

5. Landon Carter, *The Diary of Colonel Landon Carter of Sabine Hall, 1752–1778*, ed. Jack P. Greene (Charlottesville: University Press of Virginia, 1965), pp. 563, 743–44; Nicholas Cresswell, *Journal of Nicholas Cresswell, 1774–1777*, ed. Samuel Thornley (New York: Dial Press, 1924), p. 46.

6. Wilkins Updike, *A History of the Episcopal Church in Narragansett, Rhode Island*, ed. Daniel Goodwin, 3 vols. (Boston: Merrymount Press, 1907), 3:12.

Types of Vernacular Buildings / 91

Fig. 1. Lower chapel, Christ Church Parish, Middlesex County, built between 1714 and 1717. This is the first Virginia church known to have all the elements of the rectangular church plan. The oval window in the gable lights a gallery. (author)

mons. Although he stopped attending, Gordon continued to serve on the Anglican vestry of Christ Church Parish.[7]

A close look at the Anglican parish churches and their contents makes it easier to understand the church's appeal. The key is contained in the legend engraved on a communion cup made in London about 1660 and presented to James City Parish. The cup is inscribed *Mixe not holy thinges with profane* and *Ex Dono Francisci Morrisson Armigeri Anno Dom. 1661.*[8] Taken together, the form of the object, the sentiment expressed, and the donor identification neatly sum up the reason for the success of the Anglican Church in Virginia. The Church very effectively melded holy things with profane ones in a way that allowed a specific social order and an idealized religious one to buttress each other's legitimacy. It did so in large part by assembling architectural elements and ritual objects that presented in vivid, concrete form a proposition about the relationship between the sacred order and the social order of eighteenth-century Tidewater Virginia.

7. James Gordon, "The Journal of Colonel James Gordon of Lancaster County, Va.," *William and Mary Quarterly*, ser. 1, 11 (1903):98–112, 195–205, 217–36; 12 (1903):1–12.

8. The James City Parish communion cup is illustrated and described in *Church Silver in Colonial Virginia* (Richmond: Virginia Museum, 1970), pp. 26–27.

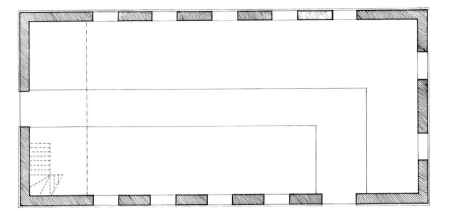

Fig. 2. Plan of Lower church, Southwark Parish, Surry County, built about 1751 to 1754. Although the church is now a ruin, the location of the original aisles, gallery, and stairs is revealed in the brick walls. (author)

The standard eighteenth-century vernacular Anglican church in Virginia was a rectangular building without exterior embellishments beyond its compass-head windows and, on many brick buildings, its classical doorways (Fig. 1). Usually disposed in a single story, the regular fenestration was interrupted only by a principal door in one short end and a chancel door on the long side near the other end. Since all churches were "oriented," that is, set east-west, these doors were at the west and south sides, respectively. When a building larger than a rectangular one was required, churches were built on cruciform plans. Rectangular churches might be enlarged with the addition of a perpendicular wing on one long side, creating a T-shaped plan. On the interior, a single central aisle leading from the west door intersected another aisle that led from the south door to the pulpit on the north wall (Fig. 2). Beyond the cross aisle at the east was the chancel, undifferentiated from the rest of the building except for the presence of a raised platform, surrounded by a low rail enclosing the communion table.

Many of the fittings of the church served the Anglican liturgy and were required by civil and ecclesiastical law to be present. These included the table and rail, along with the pulpit and an altarpiece that displayed the Ten Commandments (Figs. 3 and 4). Altarpieces could be as simple as a pair of boards standing on the back of the table, or they could be elaborately decorated architectural installations as large as sixteen by twenty feet that dominated the interior of the church. Many of them were lettered with the Lord's Prayer and the Apostles' Creed in addition to the required Ten Commandments. Also required by law were the church "ornaments," which included an altar and pulpit cloth, a cushion for the pulpit, a Bible and two large copies of the *Book of Common Prayer*. Finally, somewhere in the church, usually above the altarpiece, hung the royal arms, also a legally prescribed feature after 1660.

These fittings were the products of the dual, sometimes contradictory, religious characteristics of the eighteenth-century An-

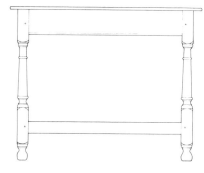

Fig. 3. Communion table, made about 1740, at Fork church, Hanover County. (author)

Fig. 4. Altarpiece, St. Mary White Chapel church, Lancaster County. The tablets containing the Ten Commandments were bequeathed by David Fox in 1702, while the flanking tablets were left by his son in 1718. The painting was restored in 1882. (author)

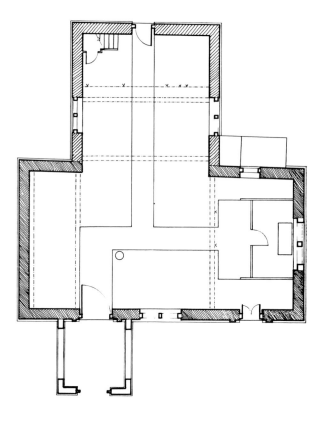

Fig. 5. Plan of Yeocomico church, Westmoreland County. The original church was built about 1706, and the north wing was probably added in the second quarter of the eighteenth century. The chancel is in its original location, but the pulpit and font (indicated on the plan by a small circle) have been moved. The notches (<) in the east tie beam probably reveal the former presence of a chancel screen, while those in the north gallery indicate the location of pew walls. (author)

glican church. The communion table, surrounded by its rail, embodied the mystical elements of the mass surviving from the pre-Reformation era. But while the table stood against the east wall in emulation of a medieval altar, and while churches continued to be oriented, the mystical nature of Anglicanism was deemphasized. Pulpit and altarpiece served to convey the verbal and moral tone that dominated the Church of England in the eighteenth century.

The tablet form of the altarpiece alluded to the tablets on which the Ten Commandments were originally given to Moses. In at least two instances, the reference was made explicit by large figures of Moses and Aaron painted on either side of the tablets.[9] At the same time, large altarpieces were also enclosed in classical frames with large pediments, which, since antiquity, had been architectural signs of earthly dignity. These huge installations dwarfed the communion tables below them. Similarly, pulpits were often surmounted by large canopies. These are now called sounding boards, but their acoustical function was minimal and unintended by Virginia church builders. To them, the canopies were "tops" or "types." They stand squarely in the tradition of furniture of state—chairs, beds, even cupboards with canopies above them to convey their owners' great status.[10] According to the *Oxford English Dictionary*, the word *type* signifies both a small cupola or dome and, figuratively, "the summit, acme, or highest point (of honour, dignity, or other state)."

Churches were planned to facilitate hearing the service read from the pulpit and the attached reading desks. The pulpit and desks were placed to one side of the church, a third to a half of the way down the church from the east, further drawing the focus away from the chancel and communion table. In cruciform and T-plan churches, the pulpit stood on one of the interior corners, visible to all (Figs. 5, 6, and 7). Yet many parishioners could not even see the chancel in such a church.

The arrangement and decoration of the church served to convey a variety of messages to the parishioners. To present the Ten Commandments on the altarpiece in elaborate script gave them a force and reality that drew on what Rhys Isaac has called the "dramaturgical possibilities available through the display of formal documents in a society where the written word was not yet commonplace."[11] That is, the very fact of the display of texts above the communion table, in great gold or black letters, gave them power. One only had to know what they were about. If one could actually read them, so much the better. To frame the altarpiece in an elaborate—often gilded, sometimes japanned—architectural tabernacle, and to place the altarpiece in a building where the only other significant decoration was on the pulpit from which the same doctrines were orally proclaimed, was to reinforce the inherent drama of the gold letters themselves. Similarly, what mattered was the act of proclaiming familiar doctrines from a pulpit dignified by the traditional material trappings of state—not the specific contents of any par-

9. The two churches were the Lower Southwark Parish church in Surry County and the Newport Parish (St. Luke's) church in Isle of Wight County. See "Will of Mrs. Elizabeth Stith," *William and Mary Quarterly*, ser. 1, 5 (1896):115; Lewis P. Clover, "Colonial Churches in Virginia: Old Smithfield Church," *Church Review* 5 (1853):572.

10. Henry Havard, *Dictionnaire de l'ameublement et de la décoration depuis le XIIIe siècle jusqu'à nos jours* (Paris: Maison Quantin, 1887–1890), 2:7–11, "Dais."

11. Rhys Isaac, "Dramatizing the Ideology of Revolution: Popular Mobilization in Virginia, 1774 to 1776," *William and Mary Quarterly*, ser. 3, 33 (1976):372.

Fig. 6. Blandford church, Petersburg, built 1734 to 1737, enlarged 1752 to 1770. This view of the church shows the original building surrounded by its colonial wall. Beyond the main structure can be seen the north addition. (author)

ticular sermon. Eighteenth-century commentators frequently remarked on the difficulty of hearing what was actually said from the high-sided pulpit. It was often too high for the parson to see the congregation or to be seen by it. Placed at the end of the cross aisle, the pulpit faced the south door rather than the pews. The nineteenth-century historian William Meade noted that the sermon was commonly written in a tiny hand, and the minister was constrained to bury his face in the pulpit cushion to read it.[12] Jarratt wrote that in consequence the sermons were "addrest rather to the cushion than to the congregation."[13]

The royal coat of arms was another significant visual feature. Just as the prominent display of the Ten Commandments gave evidence of a commitment to biblical morality, so the arms made the abstract concept of royal authority real in a way that words could not. Furthermore, the juxtaposition of arms and commandments made an implicit argument about the nature of religion and the state. It served, in the words of one eighteenth-century observer, "to satisfy all those who tread the courts of the Lord's House and are diligent in the performance of their duty according to the contents of these grand rules of the Christian religion that they shall meet with encouragement and protection from the state."[14]

The Anglican parish church is a discourse about power, to use anthropologist Clifford Geertz's term. Specifically, it is about the relationship between divine and earthly power.[15] But this is the concern of most religions, and more important things are going on in

12. William Meade, *Old Churches, Ministers and Families of Virginia*, 2 vols. (1857; rpt. Baltimore: Genealogical Publishing Company, 1966), 1:399–400.

13. Jarratt, *Autobiography*, p. 364.

14. Quoted in Marcus Whiffen, *Stuart and Georgian Churches Outside London, 1603–1837* (London: B. T. Batsford, 1947), p. 6.

15. Clifford Geertz, *The Interpretation of Cultures* (New York: Basic Books, 1973), pp. 87–143.

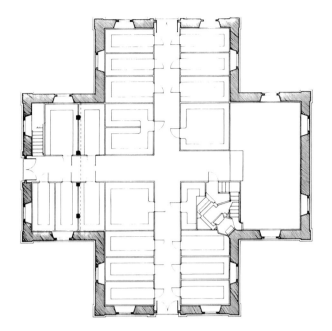

Fig. 7. Plan of Aquia church, Stafford County, built between 1751 and 1754, rebuilt between 1754 and 1757. Aquia church burned just after it had been completed and was reconstructed immediately. Like all other cruciform churches, it was built in one piece, in contrast to the T-plan churches like Yeocomico and Blandford, which were the result of enlargement. (author)

Virginia's Anglican parish churches. The parish church was above all a local institution, and local relationships were most important in it. If the royal arms and the altarpiece made an argument about religion and the state, the seating patterns established by the parish vestry and manifested in the construction of pews and benches made another argument about local society.

Seating varied by kind, by elaboration, and by placement. Of highest quality and prestige were the pews, classed as great pews, with seats on three or four sides; double pews, with seats on two sides; and single pews, with one long bench in each. Lesser seating was on open benches with backs and on backless forms. Churches used these in varying combinations. Some had pews throughout, some had pews on the main floor and benches or forms in the galleries, and others contained only three or four pews while the rest of the church was fitted with benches and forms. There was also a range of decorative detailing. At Christ church, Lancaster County, there is raised paneling inside and outside the great pews, raised paneling outside and recessed panels inside the double and single pews, and only recessed-panel backs on the benches.

Seating order was determined by the vestry. Some parishioners were given preferred seating according to their rank—as magistrates, vestrymen, or, in one case, merchants. There was segregation by age in some parishes—often schoolboys were seated separately—and many parishes placed men and women on opposite sides of the building. The assignment of seats to individuals who were not distinguished by formal rank was a delicate negotiated process. There was rarely any standard for ranking parishioners.

As a result the vestry's decisions were sometimes disputed and occasionally overturned.

It is also important to note that there was no regularity from parish to parish in determining which were the best seats in the building. At first, following English precedent, the chancel was preferred. This was the case at Christ church, Lancaster County, where Robert Carter, donor of a large sum toward the church's construction, reserved a pew in the chancel for his family.[16] By the mid-eighteenth century, galleries were the favored seating of the dominant parishioners (Fig. 8). Yet galleries could also be used to seat the general public, schoolboys, or, less often than in the nineteenth century, blacks. The point is that while some seats were better than others in any parish, convention rather than any uniform spatial hierarchy determined which those were. Within the bounds of convention, a seating order was ultimately established, and in it the local hierarchy was visible.

Clifford Geertz has described the function of religion as the rendering of

> a group's ethos . . . intellectually reasonable by being shown to represent a way of life ideally adapted to the actual state of affairs the world view describes, while the world view is rendered emotionally convincing by being presented as an image of an actual state of affairs peculiarly well arranged to accommodate such a way of life. The confrontation . . . objectivizes moral and aesthetic preferences by depicting them as the imposed conditions of life implicit in a world with a particular structure, as mere common sense given the unalterable state of reality. . . . Religious symbols formulate a basic congruence between a particular style of life and a specific . . . metaphysic, and in so doing sustain each with the borrowed authority of the other.[17]

Religious ideology, in other words, describes an ideal that is very like the existing order.

This mutual reinforcement was effected most convincingly in the material form of the eighteenth-century Anglican church and its fittings. On the one hand, the church argued visually that within its walls a separate reality existed. The building was much larger and more elaborate than the other buildings eighteenth-century Virginians knew. Its compass, or barrel-vaulted, ceiling represented the sky, containing the space beneath it and by implication shutting out everything outside it. The reference was often made explicit by painting the cornice or the whole ceiling "sky color," with clouds. This separate world was ostensibly a universal one, with the entire community gathered together within it, their attention drawn to the dual focal points of pulpit and altarpiece.

Yet within this microcosm, the facts of the larger world were reproduced. The space was divided into smaller, private spaces that mirrored the divisions among men and women in the secular world. Elaborate architectural decoration was applied selectively. The pulpit and the altarpiece—the points at which Anglican ideology was

16. "Carter Papers," *Virginia Magazine of History and Biography* 6 (1898):3.
17. Geertz, *Interpretation*, pp. 89–90.

Fig. 8. Gallery of St. John's church, King William County. This gallery is in the north wing, which was added about 1750. The original portion of the church, built between about 1731 and 1734, also has a gallery. (author)

transferred to its audience—and the doorways that marked the boundaries between the world of the church and the world outside received most embellishment. This decoration was cast in the forms used by a specific, elite group within the parish. They were motifs that could be found in the houses of great planters and their greater European allies, hardly ever in the houses of ordinary planters and slaves. By clothing an ostensibly universal message in the specific artifactual language of one group, the critical fusion of holy and profane was effected.

The social discourse of the Anglican parish church in Virginia had a specific historical content. The subject was power and social structure in a specific place. Throughout Christian history, the church has been described as the house of God. The communion was served as a meal in the house of God, from a domestic-sized and -styled table, covered with a tablecloth and napkins. The bread and wine were dispensed from communion vessels of domestic form and shape. Their forms were those used in the homes of the elite. A few had been the personal possessions of wealthy planters who bequeathed them to the Church.

The employment of the elite style in the church and its fittings thus went beyond mere taste and power to do two things. It mystified the physical embodiment of religious ideology by setting it dramatically apart from ordinary people's experience. At the same time, it identified religious order with the gentry style. The identification was made not only visually but also in the names of the objects and in the method of acquiring them. The communion, for example, was served from "plate." *Plate* had a double meaning in the eighteenth century. It referred specifically to the communion vessels, whatever their material. *Plate* also designated wrought-silver objects in general, and it was the form in which many wealthy people stored their surplus capital. Furthermore, despite the fact that there were silversmiths in Virginia, plate was in every recorded instance "sent for" from England, as the church ornaments commonly were. That is, they were obtained through the same trade channels by which the gentry dominated economic life. Access to an alien artifactual style melded with and emphasized other arcane abilities.

The end result was a resonant ambiguity. Ostensibly within the house of God, parishioners were surrounded by liturgical artifacts cast in the form of household objects, often engraved with planters' names or monograms. Even the tablets of the altarpiece, given by God to Moses, frequently bore the name of an earthly donor as well (Fig. 4). The domestic reference and the divine/earthly ambiguity provide the metaphor by which the specific form of cultural hegemony in eighteenth-century Virginia can be described. The relationship of church to parishioner, of gentry to church, of vestry to parishioners, was that of *hospitality*.

Hospitality was a peculiar form of social relationship for which Virginia was renowned in the eighteenth century. It was a boon freely given by a great planter at his house to those who needed it, as salvation was freely given by God to sinners. It was dispensed by the planter to great and small, but in a form befitting each recipient's status. It placed the beneficiary under a real, but unspecific, obligation that might or might not be repaid, but that served a cohesive purpose in any case. To the elite planter, the church was the house of another, greater planter, and he expected appropriate treatment from the servants in the house of God.

At the same time, as a potential or actual member of the vestry, the elite planter was in a sense in his own house while at church. Church was a place for the gentry to exercise hospitality toward one another by opening their private pews to guests. Hospitality also describes the relationship of the great planter/vestryman to the ordinary parishioners. In return for real service—the boon freely given in the form of work for the parish or gifts of plate, ornaments, Bibles, money—the planter expected the prerogatives of ownership: respect from his guests and acceptance of his precedence and discretion. Parishioners reserved the right to withhold their respect and obedience when the gentlemen seemed not to have fulfilled the obligations of hospitality, for if hospitality, like salvation, was a boon freely given, it was paradoxically something that the recipient had a right to expect.

The success of the Anglican parish church in eighteenth-century Virginia, then, depended on its material forms. Virginians had created in their parish churches a physical world that synthesized religious ideology, traditional religious symbols, social ideology, local social customs, and the artifactual language of the upper class. By casting this mixture into physical form, Virginians transformed it from a proposition into a reality. Physical objects and visual images are always more powerful than mere words. In speaking of the word made flesh, Christian theology recognizes this. Because the word of eighteenth-century Virginian society was not flesh but bricks, mortar, silver, and velvet, the word seemed natural, commonsensical, indisputable—the only way things could be. This is the function of ideology and, for a while, Virginia's Anglican parish churches performed it.

11

WILLIAM TISHLER AND
CHRISTOPHER S. WITMER

The Housebarns of East-Central Wisconsin

Unlike other vernacular structures with Old World origins, the housebarn did not develop as a traditional form of shelter in America. Essentially a building that houses both humans and cattle under a single roof, it was a common dwelling type in Europe, but the American vernacular landscape is nearly devoid of such structures. Thus, when a number of housebarns were discovered in east-central Wisconsin, many questions arose regarding their significance, utilization, and origin.

Housebarns were an ancient form of shelter in continental Europe, as well as in England, where they are referred to as "long" or "hall" houses, and in Ireland, where they are called "byre dwellings."[1] Indeed, some scholars suggest possible prehistoric origins in portions of Scandinavia and Jutland, where very early traces of human and animal occupation have been found.[2] Utilization in Neolithic times was verified at the archaeological site of Trøldebjerg in Denmark, where carpenters and house builders with stone tools fashioned several houses with "one end for the owners and one for the beasts."[3] Archaeological investigations in Cornwall and other lowland areas of Britain have dated housebarns to at least early medieval times. After the fifteenth century, this shelter type was gradually abandoned in much of the British lowlands in favor of separate domestic and agricultural farm structures. However, in the uplands of the north and west, it continued as a common form of peasant shelter,[4] just as it remained a customary building type on the European mainland, particularly in Germany, the Netherlands, Belgium, Luxembourg, Denmark, Switzerland, and France.

Typically a rectangular structure, this "most simple and economical of all forms of the peasant house" was especially suitable in areas with a harsh winter climate.[5] In it, cattle could be more easily protected and tended—and they could also generate heat to warm the nearby human occupants. Early examples consisted of essentially a long, continuous, sheltered space with a common entrance permitting humans and beasts to intermingle freely. Later, there emerged a differentiation of interior use: the family occupied the upper end, and animals inhabited the lower end, thus permit-

1. See, for example, Iorwerth C. Peate, "The Welsh Long-House," in *Culture and Environment: Essays in Honour of Sir Cyril Fox*, ed. L. L. Foster and L. Alcock (London: Rutledge and Kegan Paul, 1963), pp. 440–42; Hugh Braun, *Old English Houses* (London: Faber and Faber, 1962), p. 91; Karl Baumgarten, "Some Notes on the History of the German Hall House," *Vernacular Architecture* 7 (1976):15; Caoimhin O'Danachair, "The Combined Byre-and-Dwelling in Ireland," *Folklife* 2 (1964):58–75.

2. Peate, "Welsh Long-House," p. 443.

3. Ibid., p. 444. Another useful discussion relating to the origin of housebarns can be found in Walter Horn, "On the Origins of the Mediaeval Bay System," *Journal of the Society of Architectural Historians* 17 (1958):5–6.

4. Nigel Harvey, *A History of Farm Buildings in England and Wales* (Newton Abbot: David and Charles, 1970), pp. 53–54.

5. W. G. Hoskins, *History from the Farm* (London: Faber and Faber, 1970), p. 16.

ting better interior drainage. "This extremely self-contained establishment, combining the whole farm-yard under one roof, would seem to us to have its disadvantages, but we are assured that . . . so long as the smoke of the great hearth fire, which had no chimney, permeated the whole building, insects and bad stench were driven away."[6]

Later, an interior wall between the house and barn became common, and a doorway in the interior wall was sometimes built to provide the householders with direct access to the cattle. Separate entrances for humans and beasts resulted from this arrangement. As housebarns continued to evolve, the house end was divided into separate rooms for sleeping, eating, and other living functions. The barn also might be partitioned off with various stall arrangements.

Since housebarns were widely accepted as a building tradition in Europe, it might be reasonable to expect some transfer of this ancient but effective dwelling type to the New World, especially in isolated rural areas of the northern states. Yet housebarns rarely appear on the American landscape, and there is little information in the literature concerning this type of habitation.

One early reference to housebarns in America appears in 1955 in *The Pennsylvania Barn*. Author Alfred Shoemaker notes,

> One of the great puzzles of Colonial Pennsylvania is why not more of the basic Continental folk-cultural patterns, especially the one of housing the animals under the same roof that sheltered the family, were not transferred to Pennsylvania. . . . Were there even no isolated instances of a barn and house under one roof in early Pennsylvania? [He concluded that] excepting for a casual reference by Levering in his history of Bethlehem that the first Moravian structure built in that city in 1741 served such a combination of purposes . . . no other evidence of the transfer of this folk-cultural pattern has been presented.[7]

Three years later, *Pennsylvania Folklife* published a sketch, executed by Charles Alexander Lesueur about 1822, of what was claimed as "the only known contemporary pictorial record of what definitely appears to be a combination house and barn."[8]

With the exception of Richard W. E. Perrin's work in Wisconsin, other substantive references to housebarns appear considerably later in the literature. One article, for instance, discusses examples built on the vast prairies of South Dakota.[9] Here, Mennonites, German-Russians, and Ukrainians constructed long, rammed-earth, mud-brick, and wood-frame housebarns that bear a striking resemblance to their counterparts in portions of east and south Russia. Built during the 1870s, several survive in Turner and Hutchinson counties near the community of Freeman, South Dakota.[10]

The survival of a housebarn in Missouri is documented somewhat later by Charles van Ravenswaay.[11] This *Fachwerk* structure was built in 1855 on a hillside setting in the "Rhineland" region, an area of Germanic settlement along the Missouri River. It is different from other American examples in that it consists of four levels, and

6. M. E. Seebohm, *The Evolution of the English Farm* (London: George Allen and Unwin, 1952), p. 74.

7. Alfred Shoemaker, *The Pennsylvania Barn* (Lancaster: Pennsylvania Dutch Folklore Center, 1955), p. 9.

8. *Pennsylvania Folklife* 9 (1958):8. Subsequent minor references to Pennsylvania housebarns include an example in Berks County cited in John Joseph Stoudt, *Sunbonnets and Shoofly Pies: A Pennsylvania Dutch Cultural History* (South Brunswick: A. S. Barnes and Company, 1973), p. 41. Log and stone housebarns are treated in *Der Reggeboge, Journal of the Pennsylvania German Society* 17 (1983):2–3.

9. Reuben Goertz, "German Russian Homes: Here and There, Now and Then," *Clues* (1976):32, 40–42, 46.

10. See Ludwig and Koop's abstract elsewhere in this volume.

11. Charles van Ravenswaay, *The Arts and Architecture of German Settlements in Missouri* (Columbia: University of Missouri Press, 1977), pp. 279–84.

Fig. 1. Map of Wisconsin, showing the locations of housebarns discussed in this essay. Stippled areas indicate counties where housebarns are said to have been built. (William Tishler)

12. This structure was recently the focus of extensive restoration efforts by the Missouri Heritage Trust and has been featured in an exhibit on the German housebarn in America, sponsored by the Missouri Cultural Heritage Center and the National Park Service.

13. T. Lindsay Baker, "Silesian Polish Folk Architecture in Texas," in *Built in Texas*, ed. Francis Abernathy (Waco: E-Heart Press, 1979), p. 133.

14. H. Wayne Price, "The Double-Crib Log Barns of Calhoun County," *Journal of the Illinois State Historical Society* 73 (1980):149–50.

15. LaVern J. Rippley, "Pattern and Marks of German Settlement in Minnesota," in *A Heritage Deferred: The German-Americans in Minnesota*, ed. Clarence A. Glasrud (Moorehead, Minn.: Concordia College, 1981), p. 61.

16. "Wiegend Name Plays Important Part in Agricultural Development of the Town of Centerville for 80 years," *Manitowoc Herald-News*, 23 September 1931, p. 9.

17. Richard W. E. Perrin, "German Timber Farmhouses in Wisconsin: Terminal Examples of a Thousand-Year Building Tradition," *Wisconsin Magazine of History* 44 (1961):199–202. See

the house portion is oriented away from the adjacent dirt access lane.[12]

Other scholars have commented briefly on housebarns in broader studies dealing with specific states, ethnic groups, or building types. *Built in Texas* describes a "Silesian Polish cottage . . . showing the traditional combination of home and stable under one roof."[13] Another source noted an unusual double-crib specimen in Calhoun County, Illinois, where "an emigré from Alsace-Lorraine built the barn in 1865 and boarded his family in one of the two cribs until about 1875."[14] *A Heritage Deferred: The German-Americans in Minnesota* indicates that "few of the Mennonite German-speaking settlers in the Mountain Lake area of Minnesota resorted to their traditional style by constructing the barn and the house into one continuous building."[15] To date, however, no definitive published work exists on the topic of the housebarn in America.

Despite their apparent rarity, an unusually large number of housebarns were built in Wisconsin by German and Bohemian immigrants—and possibly by Belgian, Polish, and Russian settlers as well. Several have survived, and information concerning demolished examples can be found in occasional written sources. Local folklore and recollections have noted the existence of other housebarns, but, in most cases, no physical or documentary evidence can be found to verify these claims.

The earliest published housebarn reference was found in a 1931 newspaper article commemorating a pioneer German farming family in Manitowoc County, Wisconsin. It provided an account of the construction, in 1848, of the family's initial shelter: "A small barn was built in connection with the house with a thresh floor between the dwelling part and the part where the livestock was housed."[16] Serious scholarly attention was finally given to the American housebarn in 1961, when Richard W. E. Perrin discussed the Langholf structure, the only house and barn combination then known in Wisconsin, in his pioneering article on the state's German timber farmhouses.[17]

In the 1970s, Old World Wisconsin, an outdoor museum, was established to preserve and interpret the state's diverse cultural heritage. During intensive fieldwork initiated by the museum, two additional standing housebarns were identified and recorded.[18] Others were discovered during surveys undertaken by the University of Wisconsin's Summer Historic Preservation Field Workshop. All these structures are located in Dodge and Manitowoc counties in east-central Wisconsin (Fig. 1).

The Stradall housebarn is the most recently built example (Fig. 2). It was erected about 1900 of large white cedar logs joined with full dovetail corner notches. It measures twenty-five by sixty-one feet. Situated on the south end and toward the nearest road, the house portion is nearly square in proportion. An interior log wall divides the house into two uneven rectangular spaces. The narrower room is adjacent to the barn and contains the exterior door.

Fig. 2. The Stradall housebarn in Franklin Township, Manitowoc County, was built about 1900 by a settler from Bohemia. The small detached structure to the right is not part of the housebarn. (William Tishler)

An unusual characteristic of this building is that direct access is not provided from the house to the barn through the adjoining wall. The structure is located on gently rolling terrain at the corner of two country roads within a large Bohemian settlement in Manitowoc County.

The Lutze housebarn, located in Centerville Township of Manitowoc County, is one of the largest and, in many respects, the most interesting of Wisconsin's housebarns (Fig. 3). Built in the early 1850s by Gottlieb Lutze, an immigrant from Saxony, this half-timber structure is nogged with mud in the traditional German *Fachwerk* manner and covered with sawn weatherboards. The original housebarn measures seventy-three by twenty-eight feet and includes a large stable area on the west end, while the east half of the building was used for human occupation. The house contains a living room, dining room, kitchen, and an entry space with stairways leading to both the second floor and cellar (Fig. 4). The second floor includes four bedrooms, a parlor, a storage area at the top of the stair, and a large room at the west and where grain was stored and where poultry and some small stock were sheltered. This building is in remarkably good condition and, with its scores of artifacts, is probably one of the best preserved housebarns in America.

Built to dimensions of thirty-three feet by fifty-three feet of random fieldstone, the Quandt housebarn was found in Herman Township in Dodge County (Fig. 5). It was constructed in the 1850s by Wilhelm Quandt, an *Oderbrücher* German from Pomerania. Sited perpendicular to the east-west road, the structure is oriented so that the house portion faces the road. Dwelling space is separated from the livestock area by a central passage, and the house, passage, and stable all have separate exterior doorways. In 1860, according to census information, twelve large stock animals were housed in the

also Perrin's *Wisconsin Architecture* (Washington, D.C.: United States Department of the Interior, 1965), pp. 16–17, 76.

18. These structures were called to the authors' attention by Alan C. Pape, former site manager for Old World Wisconsin.

Fig. 3. South elevation of the Lutze housebarn in Cleveland Township, Manitowoc County. Built by an immigrant from Saxony, it is one of the few surviving *Fachwerk* housebarns in America. (William Tishler)

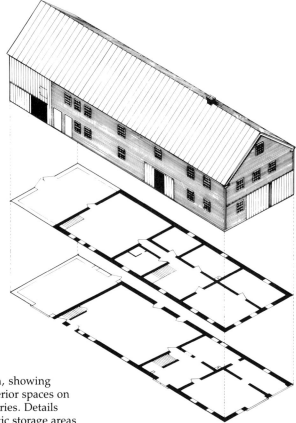

Fig. 4. Lutze housebarn, showing the arrangement of interior spaces on the first and second stories. Details of the basement and attic storage areas are not shown. (Ann Ziegelmaier)

Fig. 5. The Quandt housebarn in the Herman Township of Dodge County retains the chimney set into the interior wall that separates the barn from the house area on the right. (William Tishler)

Fig. 6. Demolished in 1983, the massive Oertwig housebarn was built of local fieldstone in Dodge County by an immigrant from the Oder River area of Germany. (William Tishler)

barn. The original chimney stack is situated in the central circulation space.

The Oertwig housebarn is located in Theresa Township of Dodge County, about six miles northwest of the Quandt structure (Fig. 6). Also of random fieldstone construction, and also built by an *Oderbrücher* German, the house unit faces north toward the road. Measuring twenty-six feet by seventy-five feet, the Oertwig building has exterior walls that are two feet thick. The layout of this example is distinct from that of other surviving housebarns: a third

Fig. 7. The Macksam housebarn in Theresa Township, Dodge County, is the smallest example that has been found in Wisconsin. Built in the 1850s by an immigrant from the Brandenburg area of Germany, it combines fieldstone construction with brick details. (William Tishler)

bay is partitioned off from the stable at the end of the structure opposite that occupied by the dwelling space. The original function of this area remains a mystery. Frederick Oertwig probably built this structure in the 1850s. By 1860, he owned twelve large stock animals and farmed 108 acres of land. Unfortunately, this structure was recently demolished and replaced with a larger pole barn.

Located three miles to the northeast and sited atop one of the many glacial drumlins scattered throughout Dodge County is the Macksam housebarn (Fig. 7). The smallest of the housebarns found in east-central Wisconsin, it measures twenty-three by thirty-three feet and is constructed of random fieldstone masonry. Brick is used at the corners and for the window and door lintels. It appears that this structure was built in the 1850s by Charles Macksam, an *Oderbrücher* from the Brandenburg area of Germany. The dwelling unit faces south toward the road and is subdivided into two rooms of equal size. This building has not been seriously altered, and its size is apparently the result of the owner's small original landholding of forty acres. According to the 1860 agricultural census, Macksam owned six large stock animals.

About five miles to the south, the *Fachwerk*, or half-timbered, Zimmel housebarn can be found (Fig. 8). Sited on a plot of land purchased in 1849 by Francis Grimmer, the structure was either built by him or by S. F. Zimmel, whose descendants currently own the property. Three interior spaces are defined, with the domestic portion situated at the west end. The roof framing system contains a rare example of a king-post and ridgepole structural system. No evidence of a chimney remains, and the nogging of mud and ver-

Fig. 8. The Zimmel housebarn, built about 1850, incorporates *Fachwerk* construction under a sheathing of vertical pine boards. The living quarters were converted to storage space when a new *Fachwerk* house was built nearby. (William Tishler)

tical staves has been covered with vertical board siding. The structure measures twenty-three by fifty-one feet and has a recent shed addition on the east end. It is in remarkably good condition, although little interior evidence remains from the period of human habitation.

The Langholf housebarn is the best-known and best-documented housebarn in Wisconsin (Fig. 9). Located near the community of Watertown in Dodge County, it was built in the 1850s—probably by a German named Frederick Kliese or by a subsequent property owner and native of Saxony, Gotlieb Vinde. The building is half-timbered with panel nogging of staves and mud daub. This original infill was later replaced by cream brick masonry. The building is two stories in height, and it measures thirty by sixty-five feet. The house, located in the east end, is important because it contains a chimney extending from a large brick-enclosed area with a barrel-vaulted ceiling. This unique space is thought to have been associated with food preparation, such as the smoking of meat or fish. The capacity of the Langholf housebarn is indicated by 1860 census information, which records that Gotlieb Vinde had fifteen large stock animals, including eight milk cows—nearly twice the number owned by most of his neighbors.

Initial attempts to shed light on the housebarns of east-central Wisconsin have answered only a few of the questions raised by their recent discovery in the rural countryside. However, some general conclusions are possible. It remains clear that this common northern European folk structure was seldom built in America but that, in the latter half of the nineteenth century, German and Bohemian immigrants to Wisconsin did bring the memory of this traditional form of shelter with them, and they built housebarns on their farm-

Fig. 9. The Langholf housebarn, located near Watertown in Dodge County, is still used for storage and livestock shelter. The house unit was located at the right end of the building. (William Tishler).

steads. It is also apparent that the housebarn was the first permanent structure built on these farmsteads, and that it was later abandoned by its human occupants when a detached house was constructed.

As is the case with many of their European antecedents, Wisconsin's housebarns were built as rectangular forms with the dwelling section located on the end closest to the road. The house units also typically exhibit refinements lacking on the barn section. These include more windows, better window trim, and often some form of interior finish, such as plaster, whitewash, or paint.

Clearly, more serious study must be given to the housebarn—an ancient and potentially informative dwelling type in both Europe and America. With additional scholarly work, more questions can be answered regarding this unusual European transplant to the American rural landscape.

12

CHRISTOPHER MARTIN

"Hope Deferred": The Origin and Development of Alexandria's Flounder House

The historic district of Alexandria, Virginia, contains seventeen surviving examples of a form known as the flounder house. Residents identify this visually arresting house by its shed roof and front-facing gable (Fig. 1). Since the 1930s, the flounder's odd shape has provoked much speculation concerning its origin and character. In 1938, novelist Frances Parkinson Keyes envisioned the flounder as an incomplete residence, resulting from unfulfilled expectations or "hope deferred."[1] The well-traveled Thomas Tileston Waterman endorsed this view in 1944, suggesting that the flounder was indigenous to Alexandria.[2] Tourist guidebooks, coffee-table architectural histories, and popular magazines have consistently repeated these early beliefs, which are currently circulated and reformulated in local oral tradition.[3]

By examining the artifact and the oral legends it has inspired, this paper will explore the past and present meanings of Alexandria's flounder house. The most frequently heard explanation for the flounder label has to do with the structure's tall, windowless side wall, which brings to mind the eyeless side of the flounder fish. Theories of origin may be grouped according to three legend cores that explain the flounder house's unique form as a result of an early restrictive building ordinance, the original owner's plan for future expansion, or a desire to reduce property taxes. Each legend core has a most popular version. The building-ordinance theory usually maintains that the flounder was conceived in response to a time stipulation in an Alexandria ordinance that was designed to discourage speculative land development. The quick-to-build flounder could be sited at the back of an urban lot, thus both fulfilling the building requirement and leaving room for the eventual construction of a more formal main house that the flounder would serve as a rear ell. The half-house theory explains that the tallest side of the flounder was left windowless because the structure was intended as only the first half of an eventual semidetached pair. Finally, the tax theory holds that the blank wall reduced the amount of glass tax that could be levied on the house.

An elaborate explanation incorporating familiar legend cores was collected from Roger DiGilio, a real estate agent who lives in a

1. Frances Parkinson Keyes, *Parts Unknown* (New York: Julian Messner, 1938), p. 157.

2. Thomas T. Waterman, "Flounder Houses," *Antiques* 47 (1945):92.

3. For examples, see Mary Lindsey, *Historic Homes and Landmarks of Alexandria, Virginia* (Alexandria: Newell-Cole Company, 1931), p. 33; Deering Davis, Stephen P. Dorsey, and Ralph Cole Hall, *Alexandria Houses 1750–1830* (New York: Bonanza Books, 1946), p. 17; Agnes Rothery, *Houses Virginians Have Loved* (New York: Rinehart and Company, 1954), p. 8; Mollie Sommerville, *Alexandria, Virginia: George Washington's Home Town* (Alexandria: Newell-Cole Company, 1966), p. 31; Ethelyn Cox, *Historical Alexandria, Virginia, Street by Street: A Survey of Existing Early Buildings* (Alexandria: Historic Alexandria Foundation, 1976), pp. x, 20; "The Flounder: Alexandria's Half-Houses," *Southern Living*, September 1981, pp. 164–65.

Fig. 1. Frame flounder house at 514 South Fairfax Street, Alexandria, built about 1795. The upper story of the porch was enclosed about 1920. (author)

frame flounder house. Mr. DiGilio retold the story during a tape-recorded interview.

> I'll start at the beginning with what I've heard about flounder houses. The reason people built flounder houses in Alexandria was that most of the people would come to Alexandria, they would buy a lot from the municipality, the municipal corporation, and you had to build on the lot within five years or it was forfeited back to the corporation, and this was done to curtail land speculation, therefore the people had to erect a building on the lot or they would lose it.
> Now most of the people who settled in Alexandria were city dwellers. They were merchants, traders, who needed their capital for their business, and if they spent their capital erecting a house, they would then have a shortage for their business. So the flounder house was a compromise to meet these conditions. They would erect, usually of frame construction, the back of their house on their lot, and they would erect it as cheaply as possible. This met the criteria of having a dwelling on the lot and gave them a place to live at very little expense without their capital tied up. Then, as they went along and prospered at their endeavors, they could buy enough so they could erect the front of the house, usually out of masonry. Then, a few years later, if they continued to prosper, they could tear down the wood flounder and erect a masonry flounder, making a complete house. And that is the story I've heard as to why one finds flounder houses.[4]

The rear-ell theory is the most popular description of flounder origin. House tours reinforce this belief by featuring flounder houses located relatively far back on their lots. However, of the seventeen inventoried examples, four front directly on the street, six are less than twenty feet from the street, and only seven are be-

4. Roger DiGilio, personal interview, 18 July 1984.

Fig. 2. Brick flounder house at 321 South Lee Street, Alexandria, built about 1824. This two-and-a-half-story example has a Flemish-bond facade. The first-story window on the porch side was originally a door. (author)

tween twenty and fifty feet from the street (Fig. 2). The survey group includes ten brick and seven frame houses. Many examples retain shed-roofed rear kitchen ells that are narrower than the main blocks. Some brick flounders, with Flemish-bond facades, sawtooth cornices, and walls three courses thick, are quite handsome and substantial dwellings.

The surviving flounder houses were initially owned by typical Alexandrians with such occupations as baker, grocer, carpenter, merchant, and mariner. The houses were erected between 1787 and 1877, during a period when most of the town's lots were subdivided and developed. Flounder houses are located on narrow, deep urban lots that measure approximately twenty-five by ninety feet. Ten examples remain in their original detached contexts, thus appearing to some residents as uncompleted half-houses. If this was the de-

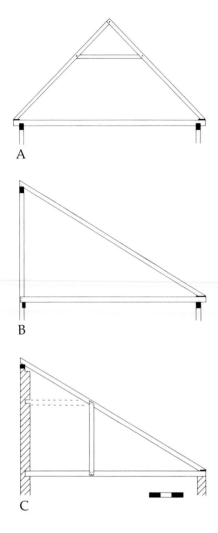

Fig. 4. Roof frames: A. A typical Tidewater roof. B. A typical Alexandria flounder roof. C. The roof of a brick flounder house at 511 Queen Street, Alexandria. (author)

5. Henry Glassie, *Pattern in the Material Folk Culture of the Eastern United States* (Philadelphia: University of Pennsylvania Press, 1968), pp. 7–8.

signers' intention, however, they might have left room on each lot for a mirror-like addition. But the tall, windowless wall of all except one example is located on a side lot line. Clearly, the flounder builder's intention was to maximize yard space and to prepare for a possible semidetached relationship with future neighboring houses.

Just as the folklorist searches for pattern among oral traditions, so the contemporary material culture scholar identifies degrees of conformity and creativity in traditional buildings through regional comparisons of core architectural features. The primary characteristics of folk housing are plan and height, features that dictate interior spatial organization.[5] Of seventeen surveyed flounder houses, fourteen are two stories tall, two are two and a half stories, and one is a story and a half. Relatively consistent main block height was combined with three floor plans. Thirteen examples have two-room or hall-parlor plans, two have one-room plans, and two have central-passage I-house plans. Through the alteration and modification of secondary formal characteristics and siting, the urban builder prepared some familiar rural types for close company in an urban context. In creating a flounder house, he turned the gable end of a traditional type to the street, altered the roof shape, relocated the chimneys, placed a windowless wall on the side lot line, and, in many cases, replaced a gable-end window with a front door (Fig. 3).

The flounder's asymmetrical roof is essentially a reoriented half-gable roof suitable for covering a single-pile space. Although building materials were not necessarily minimized in flounder roof construction, the elimination of rafter-to-rafter joinery streamlined the building process. When compared with the typical Tidewater gable roof frame, flounder roof joinery exhibits tendencies toward simplification and improvisation (Fig. 4A). Studs are attached to the eaves-wall plate and the ridge-wall plate with mortise-and-tenon joints. Joists are nailed to the eaves-wall plate and laid across a clamp that is recessed into channels cut in the tall ridge-wall studs (Fig. 4B). The monoplane flounder roof did not require stabilizing collars, but some builders constructed their half roofs with collars. In one unusual flounder roof, missing side-wall headers indicate an intention to use collars, but the carpenter converted collar lumber into struts that aid in supporting the roof load (Fig. 4C).

The flounder house, so different from surrounding urban house forms, was generated from elements familiar to both urban and rural traditional builders. In Alexandria, the designer's willingness to dissect and reassemble traditional plans and structures becomes more apparent when other building types are examined. The front-gable half-roof form caps a few remodeled brick carriage houses, as well as some one- and two-story warehouses located among Alexandria's narrow alleys. Regardless of function, each structure has a tall, windowless wall sited on a side lot line. Another variant in the urban builder's repertoire is the half-gambrel roof,

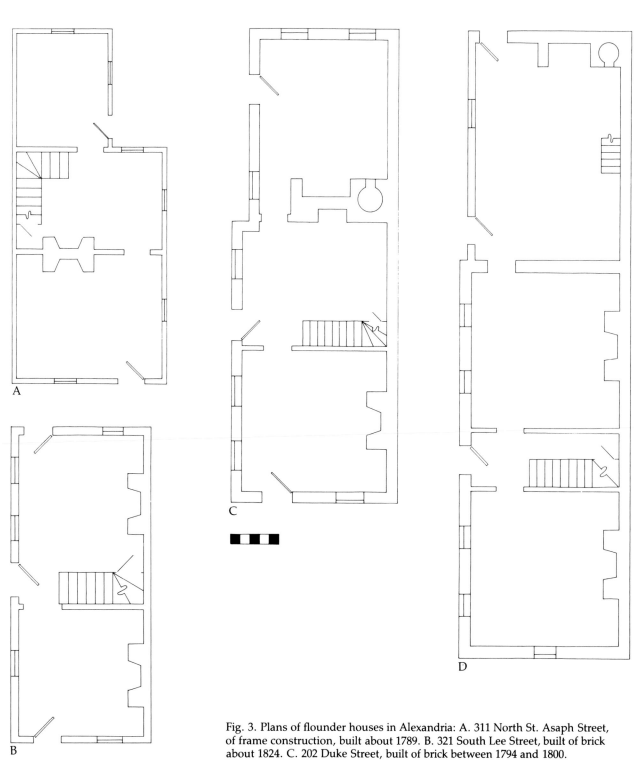

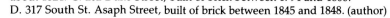

Fig. 3. Plans of flounder houses in Alexandria: A. 311 North St. Asaph Street, of frame construction, built about 1789. B. 321 South Lee Street, built of brick about 1824. C. 202 Duke Street, built of brick between 1794 and 1800. D. 317 South St. Asaph Street, built of brick between 1845 and 1848. (author)

Types of Vernacular Buildings / 115

Fig. 5. Deteriorating half-gambrel-roofed warehouse in Swift's Alley, Alexandria. (author)

6. Examined sources include Cox, *Historical Alexandria*; Davis, Dorsey, and Hall, *Alexandria Houses*; and *Historic Chart: Alexandria, Virginia* (Alexandria: Historic Alexandria Foundation, 1963).

which survives on a deteriorated Swift's Alley warehouse (Fig. 5). Further design flexibility is revealed in at least four single-pile side-hall-plan houses that are sheltered by side-gable half roofs (Fig. 6). Since these houses do not disturb the eye when viewed from the street, local residents do not refer to them as flounder houses.

Remodeled flounder houses, old photographs, and local architectural surveys are valuable sources for the assessment of a house form that is now rare. In addition to the seventeen measured examples, Alexandria has five flounders that are so heavily remodeled that their original room arrangements cannot be determined. Public and private photograph collections, as well as published sources, make it possible to enumerate a total of thirty known flounder houses (Fig. 7).[6] Before the initiation of urban renewal efforts, Alexandria may have contained as many as seventy-five flounders.

Fig. 6. Built about 1810, this house originally had a side-passage plan. The first-story window nearest the gate was once a door. Alexandria has several two- and three-story brick houses with similar side-gable half roofs. (author)

Fig. 7. Flounder houses once located in the 400–600 blocks of South Lee Street, Alexandria, photographed about 1863. These houses were demolished during a waterfront redevelopment project in the early 1900s. (National Archives)

Types of Vernacular Buildings / 117

Fig. 8. One-story frame house, built about 1925, in Pittsburgh's North Side. (author)

Even so, these projected numbers would represent a relatively small proportion—perhaps 5 percent—of the town's eighteenth- and nineteenth-century housing stock.

The geographic scope of this study was limited for practical reasons, but observations of housing patterns in other cities affirm the viability of the half roof in the urban environment. Although some scholars and many local residents claim that the flounder is unique to Alexandria, the form exists in other towns and cities, including: Fredericksburg, Virginia; New Castle, Delaware; Charleston, South Carolina; Cincinnati; and St. Louis. One- and two-story versions may be found in the early twentieth-century working-class neighborhoods of Pittsburgh's North Side (Fig. 8). Boston has some three-story flounders. The side-gable half roof was noted on some three-story rowhouses in both Baltimore and Philadelphia.[7]

These limited findings confirm the half roof as an urban characteristic and therefore support the views of cultural geographers and folklorists who have identified cities as complex entities with

7. For an illustration of some shed-roofed rowhouses in Baltimore, see Mary Ellen Hayward, "Urban Vernacular Architecture in Nineteenth-Century Baltimore," *Winterthur Portfolio* 16 (1981):62.

material culture patterns different from those in their surrounding folk regions.[8] The half roof may be viewed alone as an index of urban interaction, and it seems likely that Alexandria's populace of builders, merchants, and tradesmen influenced the cultural diffusion of the form. At the same time, this study suggests that urban-rural architectural distinctions are not always clear. In Alexandria's flounder house, an urban roof form was combined with the one- and two-room plans commonly found in the surrounding country-side of Virginia and Maryland.

The structures of Alexandria's flounder houses and flounder legends were altered to suit specific needs. A limited number of beliefs about early architectural design explain the existence of an asymmetrical house facade in a community that has historically embraced formal symmetry in many aspects of material culture, including architecture, gravestones, decorative arts, and costume. The printed page and widely circulated oral traditions have engendered such tremendous interest and pride in the flounder that the form has recently enjoyed a material revival. Since the late 1960s, a few residents have built copies of historic flounder houses. While conforming to the contemporary preference for individualized asymmetrical house forms, occasional facade renovations create the fashionable flounder look for other residents. This vigorous flounder renaissance will probably continue as the Old Town section of Alexandria becomes a thoroughly upper-middle-class suburb of Washington, D.C.

8. Fred Kniffen, "Folk Housing: Key to Diffusion," *Annals of the Association of American Geographers* 55 (1965):552; Glassie, *Pattern*, p. 216.

13

WILLARD B. MOORE

The Preferred and Remembered Image: Cultural Change and Artifactual Adjustment in Quaker Meetinghouses

The architectural traditions of the Society of Friends, commonly referred to as "Quakers," are widely recognized. While their culture and theology are unfamiliar to the extent that the Quakers are sometimes confused with the Amish and the Shakers, their meetinghouses often serve as historic landmarks, recognized even by those without Quaker affiliation. Clearly, these graceful and simple meetinghouses not only embody important aesthetic qualities but also symbolize a vital social and historical heritage. A closer look at meetinghouse architectural forms in the context of Quaker culture makes it clear also that meeting members have consciously perpetrated an identity that is distinct, practical, and reflective of their spiritual position. Using Quaker meetinghouses as source material, this essay focuses on two related phenomena found in all changing culture groups: ambiguity in group identity and cognitive control of the expression of that identity.[1]

Though subtle and complex, group identity in the sect is durable, both among members of the Society of Friends and between Quakers and non-Quakers. Problems of ambiguous identity are related to cultural symbol systems, metaphors, and the manipulation of expressive forms.[2] The process of selection and manipulation of forms from both the past and the present, turning image to reality, is one that anthropologist George Spindler sees linked to culture as "an organization of things and processes, people, and their behavior and emotions."[3] What begins as divergent and segmented perceptions of a problem—in this case, how to design and build a place of worship—requires cognitive control, if the effort is to be successful. In this process, group members react to divergent or "outside" confrontation with other cultural norms and, with varying degrees of intensity, "establish a new identity commensurate with new conditions of life, or assert the validity of the old identity."[4] In brief, this process selects appropriate materials and forms by confronting those areas of adaptation, striving toward order and a reduction of complexity and ambiguity.

An examination of published sources and extant buildings suggests that a convention in meetinghouse form had emerged by 1800.

1. One of the best comments on cognition is M. Estelle Smith, "The Process of Sociocultural Continuity," *Current Anthropology* 23 (1982):127–35. For an overview of the subject, see special issues of *American Ethnologist* 8 (1981) and 9 (1982), edited by Janet W. D. Dougherty et al.

2. Miles Richardson, *The Human Mirror* (Baton Rouge: Louisiana State University, 1974), p. 12. See also James P. Spradley, ed., *Culture and Cognition* (San Francisco: Chandler Publishing, 1927), especially Kenneth Boulding's remarks, pp. 41–51.

3. George D. Spindler, "Psychocultural Adaptation," in *The Study of Personality*, ed. Edward Norbeck et al. (New York: Holt Rinehart, 1968), pp. 326–47.

4. Ibid., p. 343.

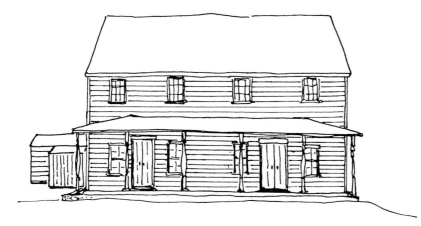

Fig. 1. A frame meetinghouse built in eastern New York about 1740. The original structure is the left, or western, half of the building. The meeting is now "laid down," and this structure is only used for annual commemorative gatherings by Friends in the area. (author)

Most of these examples can still be found on the Atlantic seaboard and in Canada, with antecedents of some elements in English meetinghouses and in American regional architecture.[5] This preferred form was built of wood, brick, or stone. It was rectangular and barnlike, distinguished by twin entrances. It was furnished with plain wooden benches. Seating was oriented not toward an altar, but rather toward a facing bench for elders and gifted speakers or ministers (Figs. 1 and 2).[6] Symmetrical fenestration lighted stairways to upper galleries used by youths and servants. Natural light and artificial light were accommodated in the essential structure of the building so as to contribute to meditation and spiritual growth. Minor embellishments included paneled shutters, projecting door hoods, and pent roofs, all elements that meetinghouses shared with Quaker domestic housing.[7]

Most commentators on Quaker architecture show that form and function are influenced by Quaker concepts of ministry, worship, church governance, egalitarianism, and simplicity. For example, while male and female Quakers usually worshiped together, they held separate business meetings. Therefore, most eighteenth- and early nineteenth-century meetinghouses in America had counterbalanced sliding partitions or hinged panels for the purpose of creating two separate compartments.

The factors influencing meetinghouse architecture after the 1850s include changes in regional vernacular architecture, doctrinal changes within the Society of Friends, and confrontation with both the theology and the architectural traditions of other denominations.[8] For those Quakers who retained eighteenth-century polity into the late nineteenth century, the traditional meetinghouse remained the remembered image. But for those who sought a more active role in social and spiritual reform and a wider contact with "the world's people," the preferred image was sometimes less severe and more in keeping with other styles of American religious architecture.[9]

5. Dorothy G. Harris, "Factors Influencing the Architecture of Nineteenth Century Quaker Meeting Houses in America" (manuscript, University of Pennsylvania, 1955); Nancy L. Cary, "The Architecture of American Quaker Meeting Houses" (manuscript, University of Pennsylvania, 1949). I am grateful to Don Yoder for copies of these two essays. Other studies include Horace Mather Lippincott, *Quaker Meeting Houses and a Little Humor* (Jenkintown, Pa.: Old York Road Publishing Company, 1952), and F. Charles Thum, "Balanced Simplicity," *Journal of the American Institute of Architects* 19 (1953):195–200. For coverage of English meetinghouses, see David M. Butler, *Quaker Meeting Houses of the Lake Counties* (London: Friends Historical Society, 1979). Finally, there is the excellent model for meetinghouse research provided by Peter Benes, ed., *New England Meeting House and Church* (Boston: Boston University Press, 1980).

6. This facing bench or "ministers' stand" is well documented by David M. Butler in "The Making of Meeting Houses," *The Friends' Quarterly* (July 1980):316–24.

7. See Horvath's essay elsewhere in this volume.

8. In eastern states, Quaker meetings lost vast numbers of members to other churches, especially the Episcopalian, in the latter half of the nineteenth century. In the Midwest, particularly in Indiana, Methodism took its toll among Quaker meetings.

9. Harris, "Factors," pp. 9–11.

involved in determining this design, nor is it clear what role was played by members of the off-campus Quaker community who have attended the meeting longer than have Earlham College students and faculty. The meetinghouse announces the philosophy of the college: firm ties with a religious tradition that originated in the eastern United States, but an awareness of modern problems and modern solutions. The message is apparently aimed at two audiences: the families of potential students, many of whom have no Quaker affiliation but admire the tenets of the sect, and the evangelical Friends Church across town, which offers a program of worship closely resembling that of other protestant churches. The architecture of the Friends Church reflects the late nineteenth-century struggle toward conformity within mainstream American protestantism.

The second example was built in 1967 in Lake Forest, Illinois, by a meeting that was first organized in McNabb, Illinois, in 1876. In the early twentieth century, the meeting declined and was "put down," only to be reorganized in 1953. This new brick and open-beam meetinghouse is the result of extensive planning and subtle blending of traditional Quaker form and upper Midwest regional style (Fig. 4). The meeting consciously prefers to designate itself Hicksite, thus aligning itself with Quakers who gather in unprogrammed meetings, eschew the ritual of other protestants, and have, since the early nineteenth century, resisted assimilation with nonsectarian theology. This passage from a letter by architect Lewis B. Walton is pertinent:

> As the designing architect (and member of the meeting) with Quaker ancestors traceable for over three hundred years, I had acquired a liking for certain special Pennsylvania meeting houses (Newton, Abington, Horsham, and London Grove), and that influence was most certainly present when I conceived the design of the building. The seventeen hand-made benches, the gift of a skilled member, each with a capacity of five, are arranged in a three-row "U" with the view to the woods in the summer and with the open end of the "U" at the fireplace in the winter.

Walton goes on to describe his design negotiations with the meeting:

> The meeting was formed in 1953 by about a dozen people, some holding membership in eastern meetings, but there was never a strong influence to design a building that "looked like" a Quaker meeting house.[12]

12. Lewis B. Walton, personal interview, 4 October 1979.

After three years of study and consideration, the meeting rejected three early designs as being "too modern, too non-descript contemporary, and too big for our financial capability." The fourth design was clearly a comfortable and appropriate one. From the building's appearance, it would seem that eastern Quaker design prevailed unconsciously and the image of traditional worship space asserted itself.

In this building, the exterior is less traditional; the generous windows associated with Quaker meetinghouses are set in a manner reminiscent of Prairie School designs in the Midwest. The kitchen, library, and facilities for religious education are all arranged efficiently in line with the main worship area, thus reducing construction costs and simplifying the overall plan. The double-entry door is set between the main worship space and the auxiliary rooms. This acknowledged departure from older plans accommodates a modern vision of Quaker family worship and religious life.[13]

The interior space dramatically illustrates the modern Quaker view. Unlike their forebears, who testified that they wanted no distractions from meditative worship, contemporary Friends frequently incorporate the outdoors—preferably natural surroundings—into the contemplative setting. Windows are more accommodating to this view, as Walton's letter affirms. The older, traditional seating arrangement that Walton remembered from Pennsylvania's eighteenth-century meetinghouses has remained. However, the stern governance of elders has passed, and the elders' bench has been replaced by a less judgmental domain. The fireplace, used as a central and centering symbol, conveys warmth, unity, and egalitarianism (Fig. 5).

The final example shows still another and somewhat different attempt to capture both the preferred and the remembered image. The Orthodox Poughkeepsie Friends Meeting in eastern New York state gathered for several decades in "adopted" buildings and fi-

13. Many older meetinghouses have added-on kitchens and education offices to accommodate a modern outreach program, yet some of the most historically significant buildings, such as the Jericho meetinghouse on Long Island, have no such facilities.

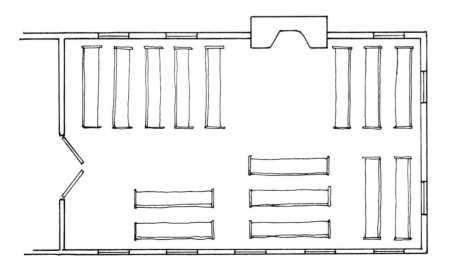

Fig. 5. A typical modern Quaker room for worship, characteristic of the meetinghouse in Lake Forest, Illinois, as well as those of Scarsdale and Chappaqua, New York. All were built within the last forty years. (author)

Fig. 6. Meetinghouse built in Pough-keepsie, New York, in 1928. The plan of this brick and limestone structure is more similar to the church buildings of other denominations than it is to traditional Friends' meetinghouses. (author)

nally built its own meetinghouse in 1928. The building's exterior is derived from the Colonial Revival style and is strikingly similar to eighteenth-century meetinghouses in urban Philadelphia and southern New Jersey (Fig. 6). However, unlike many of these antecedents, in this meetinghouse the double-entry door is placed in the gable end, giving the correct impression that the interior space is laid out like the nave of a church with an aisle extending from the doors to the pulpit (Fig. 7).

The development of this design is a story properly told in the recorded minutes of the meeting, but it is clearer and more dramatically embellished in the oral tradition of those few members who witnessed and recall it.[14] At the time the building plan was chosen, the meeting membership consisted of both Orthodox and Hicksite Quakers, the latter having been forced to abandon their rural meetinghouses, which no longer attracted sustaining numbers of members. Alfred Bussell, an architect from Chappaqua, New York, was designated to interpret the "sense of the meeting" and to design a place of worship that might satisfy all. Bussell heard talk from the Orthodox members about stained-glass windows, an organ, and a steeple, while the Hicksites wanted nearly to duplicate an old meetinghouse. The result was conservative. Built in brick and trimmed in white, the meetinghouse embodies many elements reminiscent of traditional buildings, including large, double-hung sash windows and a symmetrical facade. In this product, Bussell's kinship with one of the meeting's Hicksite members may be less important than the tenacity, clarity of mind, and sheer numbers of that group.[15]

All but a few of the meeting's members who lived through that period are deceased or have moved elsewhere. Most members are younger and are unaware of what conscious efforts to retain traditional elements actually entailed. However, those meeting elders

14. The author is grateful to Dorothy Carroll and Richard Lane, long-time members of the Poughkeepsie Meeting, for their help in obtaining the minutes and oral history of the development of the 1928 design of their meetinghouse.

15. Early meetinghouses generally were built with tall windows in the front wall, but the seated meeting faced the rear of the building, which typically was lighted with smaller windows set higher in the wall. Some meetinghouses still retain exterior wood shutters and interior sliding shutters.

made specific comments about architectural features that remind them of older, more comfortable forms and details. These include the partition on the south side of the main meeting room. While business meetings were no longer segregated, the partition lends a traditional feel to the worship room and functions as a practical divider from the adjacent wing. Clearly, the gable-end orientation reflects an important compromise with the Orthodox members. The benches also have been oriented toward the gable end of the building, but, in place of a pulpit, seated members face a contemporary facsimile of the old ministers' bench. This arrangement has, over the years, supported a tendency toward Orthodox programmed meetings for worship.

Some older members are aware that the wainscoting in this room is composed of hand-planed boards of uneven widths, a feature typical of eighteenth-century meetinghouses. An even more subtle feature is the single stairway leading from the foyer to the upper rooms. A large window crosses and lights the landing of the stair, as was often the case in older meetinghouses, where there was no electricity.

The exact intentions behind the decisions to build in this manner cannot be made clear without more extensive investigation. However, the origins of the design are part of the meeting's record and members' memories. Though the building's design was determined largely by Hicksites, the exterior appearance and the meeting's adoption of an Orthodox programmed service project the image of a community church rather than that of a Quaker meeting. This image contributed to the healthy growth of the Poughkeepsie Meeting between the 1930s and the 1950s. The traditional Quaker architectural elements, subtly incorporated into the church-like structure, were lost on a congregation that flocked to this place of worship because it was accessible and comfortably ambiguous. In no way did the architecture hinder those who put their radical, sectarian history behind them in order to seek assimilation into mid-twentieth-century America.

As Cleveland architect F. Charles Thum has written in his reviews of Quaker architecture, "The founders of Quakerism were experimenters, innovators, creative modern thinkers. While pledged to simplicity in all things, they used as their tools the most advanced ideas of their contemporaries."[16] This statement explains early Quaker adoption of sash windows, pent and hipped roofs, brick and stone fabric, and egalitarian spatial arrangements otherwise unheard of in their day. Thum's words are also applicable to the meetings' incorporation of important social spaces, such as kitchens and counseling centers. In earlier times, such areas were unnecessary, since those specific activities were part of the tightly knit Quaker communities. Today, the facilities allow Friends to continue functioning as a religious and social unit despite widely scattered residency.

Thum's remarks are significant, but to emphasize practicality

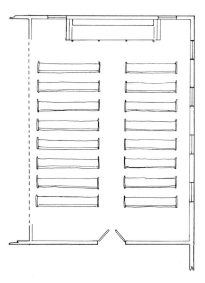

Fig. 7. Interior of the meetinghouse in Poughkeepsie, New York, showing fixed benches and a facing minister's bench set on a slightly raised platform. The left wall, indicated as a broken line, is actually a room-length sliding partition that may be raised to incorporate additional space into the worship area. (author)

16. F. Charles Thum, "Creative Quaker Architecture," *Friends Intelligencer* 107 (1950):587–88.

and simplicity is to ignore the deeper, semiotic meanings of cultural continuity in Quaker material culture. M. Estelle Smith has pointed out,

> Continuity . . . is a synthetic phenomenon with the property of appearing flexible and adaptive under some conditions and self-replicating under others. Since humans identify the conditions under which one or the other property is manifested, we are responsible for the apparent variation. In other words, continuity actually manifests both tradition and change at all times, but sociocultures may skew the cognitive orientation of their members to isolate certain conditions, thus factoring out one or the other manifestation.[17]

To this might be added another observation. In analyzing the competing values of groups in their material surroundings, Dell Upton observes, "The buildings that have survived in numbers are those that have been best adapted to the lives of subsequent generations. They do not necessarily represent the dominant or preferred modes of the past."[18]

Theoretical statements of this import are necessary, as is the ethnographic and sociological data presented in this essay. The placement of the fireplace in the new Lake Forest meetinghouse may be an innovation to that group, but it has historic precedent in eighteenth-century meetinghouses in the lake counties of England.[19] Moreover, the Clear Creek meetinghouse in Indiana does not represent a homogeneous or "consensus image of architecture as ideology."[20] Rather, it is an honorable but conscious attempt to skew or manipulate cognitive orientation. The Poughkeepsie Meeting now consists mainly of converted, or "convinced," Friends who wish to pursue a traditional, unprogrammed worship service much like those found over a hundred years ago in the rural Hicksite meetings of the surrounding county. Vaguely aware of Quaker architectural and spiritual traditions, they find themselves caught between the remembered image cherished by those few older members who prefer a church-like worship environment and their own needs to create anew the sectarian atmosphere of earlier times.

Quaker meetinghouse architecture, then, is not static. It is part of a shifting dynamic manifestation of cultural behavior. Proper study of the forms instructs scholars not to reify nostalgic stereotypes or to ignore the choices people make in taking control of their own cultural identity. By studying both the processes of choice and the material manifestations, it is possible to discern emergent qualities and specific architectonic meanings in the context of changing Quaker life.

17. Smith, "Sociocultural Continuity," p. 127.

18. Dell Upton, "The Power of Things: Recent Studies in American Vernacular Architecture," *American Quarterly* 35 (1983):279.

19. Butler, *Quaker Meeting Houses*, p. x.

20. Upton, "The Power of Things," p. 278.

IV. Elements and Forms of Vernacular Buildings

14

MICHAEL ANN WILLIAMS

The Little "Big House": The Use and Meaning of the Single-Pen Dwelling

To many, the term *big house* conjures images of plantation life in the lowland South. For some older rural people of mountainous western North Carolina, however, *big house* is used in reference to the smallest type in the regional repertoire of folk houses, the single-pen dwelling (Fig. 1). This consideration of the use and meaning of the big house grew out of a larger study of the spatial and symbolic use of folk dwellings in western North Carolina.[1] At first, it was easy to ignore the single-pen house. Compared to other folk houses of the region, it does not seem to be a very complex artifact—its system of spatial use seems rather self-evident. The extensive use of oral testimony, however, forced an examination of this assumption. In this case, simplicity of form belies a complexity of spatial organization.

Fig. 1. Log single-pen house still in use in Cherokee County, North Carolina. The house has been partitioned and the rear kitchen has been added. (author, courtesy of North Carolina Division of Archives and History)

1. Michael Ann Williams, "Home-place: The Social Use and Meaning of the Folk Dwelling in Southwestern North Carolina" (Ph.D. diss., University of Pennsylvania, 1985).

An understanding of the big house grew not from examining structures but from listening to people. In many cases, the individuals interviewed spoke of homes that have long since been destroyed. The choice not to limit interviews only to the consideration of extant structures had two unexpected benefits. With only the memory of a dwelling to prompt them, many individuals speak more freely of the experiential rather than the physical nature of architecture. Secondly, without a structure to examine, the interviewer is forced to concentrate solely on listening. Regretfully, students of folk architecture often fail to train their ears as acutely as their eyes. Careful listening, rather than careful looking, provides access to the meaning of the big house. It is important to point out that, although *big house* is used in reference to what appears to be a very small house indeed, the term is not used facetiously. No individual who knows and uses the term commented on the humor in it. Obviously, *big house* makes sense to them, and the logic of it must be understood.

Fig. 2. Kate Rogers of the Ellijay community in Macon County, North Carolina. (author)

By the time the majority of the individuals interviewed were born, most single-pen houses had separate kitchens. Whether the kitchen was attached or detached, this plan was referred to as the "big house and kitchen," a phrase as common as the term *big house* alone. Kate Rogers (Fig. 2) discussed this arrangement in her description of a childhood home: "The one on the hill was more straight up. They had the kitchen, just the kitchen and the big house . . . the beds went in the big house and then, you sat in there too. It was all the fireplace and back here was all kind of beds, and then there was the upstairs for beds."[2]

The perception of the rear kitchen as separate from the big house has led some individuals to conclude that the main part of the dwelling was called *big* in comparison to the kitchen. It is certainly possible to get that impression from examples in which the kitchen is a smaller, separate structure that served as an earlier family dwelling.[3] Assuming, however, that this relationship to a smaller kitchen explains the use of *big* ignores the fact that the single-pen house is still a *big house* even if it does not have a rear kitchen. Moreover, this assumption about the meaning of the term *big house* fails to take into account the probable origins of the term or its actual usage.[4]

Big house and kitchen is used in somewhat the same way vernacular architecture scholars might use the term *single-pen and kitchen*. The kitchen is not considered integral to the form, and, in many cases, it is indeed a later addition. Many people consider the kitchen an outbuilding rather than a part of the house. This attitude has its roots in the fact that, prior to the late nineteenth century, the majority of folk houses in this region had either combined kitchens and living rooms or completely detached kitchen buildings. This perception is also reflected in the many cases in which there is no interior access between the attached rear kitchen and the main block

2. Kate Rogers, tape-recorded interview, 3 October 1983.

3. A good example of this is the Walker Sisters' house in the Great Smoky Mountains National Park (Fig. 4). The term *big house* is used in reference to the main block of this dwelling (a partitioned single-pen house) in Robert R. Madden and T. Russell Jones, *Mountain Home: The Walker Family Homestead* (Washington, D.C.: National Park Service, 1977). The meaning of the term is not explained.

4. Also, only one individual interviewed who used the term *big house* gave this explanation for it.

of the house—it was necessary to step outside to pass between the two parts of the dwelling.

Another understanding of the term *big house* is that it refers solely to the living room. Kurath's *Word Geography of the Eastern United States* notes: "In the simple homes of the piedmont and the mountains of North Carolina (also on the Pee-dee in South Carolina, rarely in West Virginia) the living room is called the *big-house* or the *great-house*."[5] The term is used in this manner in western North Carolina, but generally only in a way that is consistent with its usage in reference to the single-pen house type. The frequent partitioning of or additions to the single-pen house during the early twentieth century probably did extend the use of *big house* to mean the living room.

To many individuals *big house* means both the main dwelling unit and an individual room. While asserting that their childhood home consisted of *just* a big house and kitchen, some people also speak of the big house as a room separate from the "upstairs."[6] In cases where the single-pen house is subdivided by a board partition, *big house* can again mean the whole unit and an individual room. In describing her grandmother's house, a single-pen dwelling that was partitioned but did not have a separate kitchen, Kate Rogers referred to the big house as the whole unit. Later, she described it as a room within the dwelling: "Now just grandma's, it was partitioned off, but the kitchen and the big room, the big house, was together; but there was plenty of room. They sat over on the side, most everybody did, and you cooked on the other."[7]

Linguistic antecedents may provide some clue to understanding the term *big house*. *House* was used to refer to the living room in early New England and in the northern parts of England as late as the 1700s, a fact that has been attributed to the continued persistence of one-room houses.[8] Though not common, this usage is still found in western North Carolina. In discussing terms for "the room with the hearth in it," one woman insisted that "it was the house."[9] Spatial patterns within the small folk house were consistent with this meaning of the term. Even in multi-room dwellings, family activity clustered heavily in one room. The "house" was a room for sitting, sleeping, entertaining, dancing, and, in the absence of a separate kitchen, cooking and eating. Some people also called it "the room we lived in." The word *big* also has older meanings, including, as a verb, "to dwell."[10] Thus, using *big house* to mean "dwelling" is not inconsistent with its use in reference to the plantation houses of the lowland South or to the single-pen dwellings of western North Carolina.

While individuals who use *big house* care little about its possible historical antecedents, they do think of the term as old. Asked about its meaning, ninety-two-year-old Zena Bennett said it was "old fashion talking," and seventy-five-year-old Monroe Ledford said, "I guess that's the way people thought of them then."[11] People under the age of seventy or those who grew up in communities where

5. Hans Kurath, *A Word Geography of the Eastern United States* (Ann Arbor: University of Michigan Press, 1949), p. 51.

6. See previously cited quote by Kate Rogers. If the second floor was used as a room rather than simply for storage, *upstairs* rather than *loft* was the preferred term.

7. Rogers interview.

8. M. W. Barley, *The English Farmhouse and Cottage* (London: Routledge and Kegan Paul, 1961), p. 46.

9. Vinnie McGaha, tape-recorded interview, 12 October 1983.

10. "Big," *Oxford English Dictionary*; "big," *A Dictionary of the Older Scottish Tongue from the Twelfth Century to the End of the Seventeenth*, ed. Sir William A. Craige (1973). The author is not attempting to revive the notion of antiquated Elizabethan speech in Appalachia, but the search for historical antecedents to house types and room use should involve the antecedents of the words and terms associated with them. Of course, antiquated word usages appear in regional speech across the United States.

11. Zena Bennett, tape-recorded interview, 18 October 1983; Monroe Ledford, tape-recorded interview, 21 October 1983.

single-pen houses were no longer common frequently had never heard of the term.

Whatever its origins, the fact is that *big house* makes sense to those who use it. *Big house* expresses the conception of a dwelling or room that has not had its functions split away. Rather, it is a functional unity: a big room where all—or most—of the living takes place. Understanding this term makes it possible to understand the idea of the single-pen house. The conception of the type of house as "big" in itself reflects a positive valuation of the single-pen plan. Though they may be seen as cabins, these houses are not necessarily a result of pioneer life-styles, extreme poverty, or low status within the rural community.

Many individuals did express a certain amount of ambivalence about these houses. In recalling childhood memories, they were quick to assert that the houses were really quite roomy and they "got along okay." On the other hand, they also expressed the growing preference for dwellings with separate rooms. Kate Rogers described the house where she boarded when she went to school: "They had a plank house . . . it was really built nice; it was roomy and everything was cut to itself."[12] Frequently, the single-pen houses that did continue in use were partitioned or "cut down" during the early twentieth century. Zena Bennett described the next generation's partitioning of a big house in this way: "They had it all cut down . . . they have a nice place now."[13]

Some simple conclusions may be derived from examination of the single-pen form. It seems to represent an extreme in generalized room use, a collective rather than an individualistic use of space, and a low valuation of personal privacy. Oral testimony, however, suggests that it is necessary to modify these assumptions. Though they may not be wrong, they do not account for the complexity of human attitudes and behavior.

Although the single-pen plan may enclose only one room, space was divided within the big house for practical, social, and symbolic purposes. The hearth was still the social and symbolic center of the house, though its practical role was eroded by the addition of a separate kitchen, and status was frequently expressed in the proximity of beds and chairs to the fireplace (Fig. 3). Parents often had designated chairs directly in front of the hearth, and, if there was a separate kitchen, the "chimney corner" was usually the preferred location for the head of household's bed.

Nonarchitectural means were sometimes used to divide space. Beds, one of the largest and most common pieces of furniture, frequently served this purpose. Kate Rogers described rectangular single-pen houses—"built long" as she said—and the "hallways" created within them: "Well it was built long and the middle here was just like a hall, but it wasn't a hall. They had a bed on one side and a bed on the other side, all the way back." Later she added: "There was different styles of houses, some of them long like I told you about. A hallway, not a hallway, just a walkway between the

12. Rogers interview
13. Bennett interview.

Fig. 3. A hearth in a single-pen log house—the social and symbolic center of the "big house." (Michael Southern, courtesy of the North Carolina Division of Archives and History)

beds and the living room on one end and the kitchen on the other."[14] Conceptually, there was, within this one room, a hallway, a living room, and a kitchen.

Without separate rooms, the use of space appears to be collective, rather than individualistic. However, family members did have their own places to sit and to sleep—even if it was in a bed shared with a sibling. Kate Rogers commented on the need for a youngster to assert his or her place in the household: "The big house and the kitchen, that was all you would hear them mention, never hear them mention the bedroom; they mentioned their bed though, 'my bed, now ain't nobody come in here and put me out of my bed and me have to sleep at the foot of mama's bed or on a pallet,' you would hear them say that."[15] Of course, children were frequently turned out of their beds when the family had overnight guests.

Collective use of space also suggests a low valuation of privacy. No designated bedrooms existed, and, even with the presence of added rooms, the heads of the household usually slept in the main room. The fact that no rooms were labeled as bedrooms, however, does not necessarily suggest a complete lack of regard for privacy. Again, nonarchitectural means were often employed. Blankets could be used to separate areas, and arrangements of beds could also serve this purpose. In describing a big house of her youth, Zena Bennett cited one instance of this:

Now Granny White's over there, talk about a big house, they did. Oh, they had a big farm, pretty farm there, and they raised everything. They had a kitchen built off too and the big, the living room, big house, they called it a big house. They had six beds in that one room, but they had

14. Rogers interview.
15. Ibid.

Fig. 4. Interior of the Walker Sisters' house on the Tennessee side of the Great Smoky Mountains National Park. (courtesy of Great Smoky Mountains National Park)

those big old high post beds, and the way you could turn every bed, you couldn't, nobody else couldn't see you behind the bed. Now that's the way they do it, now that's the truth.[16]

In the single-pen plan, as in some more complex house plans of western North Carolina, actual use may conflict with the physical limits of the house.[17] Individual space and personal privacy were achieved, even within a plan that seemed to ignore these concepts completely, just as individualism could be achieved within the confines of the cooperative values common to rural communities (Fig. 4).

The big house, then, is important because it helps to explain the complexities of meaning and use within even the simplest of folk houses. Among the range of cultural artifacts, dwellings are preeminent in the study of material culture because they are so complex, but, too often, this complexity is then ignored in the scholarship. If scholars are to study people through houses, then, at times, they also need to study houses through people—to come to terms with human as well as architectural complexity.

16. Bennett interview.
17. See Williams's abstract elsewhere in this volume.

In the absence of the possibility of ethnographic observation, oral testimony provides one of the richest sources for understanding the experiential aspects of houses. The use of oral history as a research tool in vernacular architecture scholarship has grown in recent years, and the value of this method is best expressed in the diversity of its application in recent studies.[18]

Usage has always been a concern in vernacular architecture scholarship, although too often this concern has been obscured by the variety of labels placed on this type of research. Scholars may shrink from being labeled *functionalist* or *behavioralist* and look instead to steal terms from other fields.[19] More important than labels is a widespread commitment to the study of architectural experience and meaning. Vernacular architecture scholars need to understand what a house is, what it does, and what it means in human terms and within specific cultural contexts.

Of course, oral testimony is not available for all folk houses. In these cases, oral history studies should not be used as mere fodder for ethnographic analogy, for the conclusions drawn from these studies may be culture-specific. Nevertheless, studies based on oral testimony demonstrate the need for caution in coming to conclusions. These studies may teach about human and artifactual complexity, about little houses that are big, about halls that are not halls, and about the capability of people to assert privacy and individual space within one room.

18. Recent studies incorporating oral history and vernacular architecture study include Charles E. Martin, *Hollybush: Folk Building and Social Change in an Appalachian Community* (Knoxville: University of Tennessee Press, 1984); George W. McDaniel, *Hearth and Home: Preserving a People's Culture* (Philadelphia: Temple University Press, 1983); Henry Glassie, *Passing the Time in Ballymenone: Culture and History of an Ulster Community* (Philadelphia: University of Pennsylvania Press, 1982).

19. The author suggests *pragmatics* as it is sometimes used in semiotics, relating to the use, rather than the formal structure, of language.

15

MARK R. WENGER

The Central Passage in Virginia: Evolution of an Eighteenth-Century Living Space

This paper deals with one aspect of early Virginia's gentry houses: the introduction of an entry space and its development from "passage" to "summer hall" to "saloon." This process was of crucial importance, for it ultimately involved the entire house and resulted in a realignment of the dwelling's traditional spatial hierarchy. To a considerable degree, the development of the gentry house throughout the eighteenth century revolved around what was happening to this important space.

The central passage made its appearance in Virginia during the first quarter of the eighteenth century (Fig. 1).[1] Prior to that time, many wealthy Virginians lived in houses having only two major ground-floor rooms. The larger of these—the hall—was a communal, multipurpose living space. Here, various members of the household might be found working, cooking, eating, sitting, or sleeping. It was the center of daily activity in the dwelling and was accessible to many sorts of people. Opening off this hall was a second, smaller room variously called the parlor, chamber, or inward room. As the last term implies, this space afforded a greater mea-

1. In 1717, John Custis of Williamsburg wrote to his factor in London, requesting a number of "good Comicall diverting prints to hang in the passage of my house"; John Custis to Perry, Lane and Perry, 1717, quoted in Mary Stephenson, "Custis Square," unpublished research report, Colonial Williamsburg Foundation, 1959, p. 5. The author is indebted to George Yetter of Colonial Williamsburg for this reference. In July of 1719, Thomas Nelson of York County contracted with Richard King of Williamsburg, carpenter, for construction of a story-and-a-half house having four major rooms and a passage on the lower floor. Loose papers, Clerk's Office, Circuit Court of Northampton County, Eastville, Virginia. This information was provided through the courtesy of Jean Mihalyka. The earliest known mention of a passage in Virginia probate records appears in the 1719 York County inventory of Matthew Ballard. See Dell Upton, "Vernacular Domestic Architecture in Eighteenth Century Virginia," *Winterthur Portfolio* 17 (1982):104. The author has relied heavily on this article in the discussion that follows.

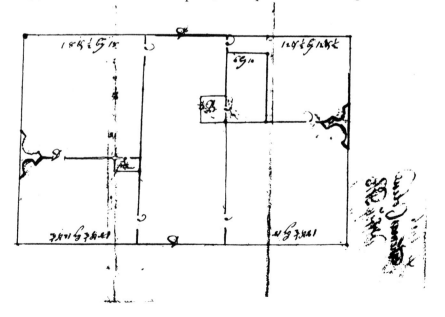

Fig. 1. Plan of a house to be built for Thomas Nelson of York County, Virginia, in 1719. Among loose papers in the Clerk's Office, Circuit Court, Northampton County.

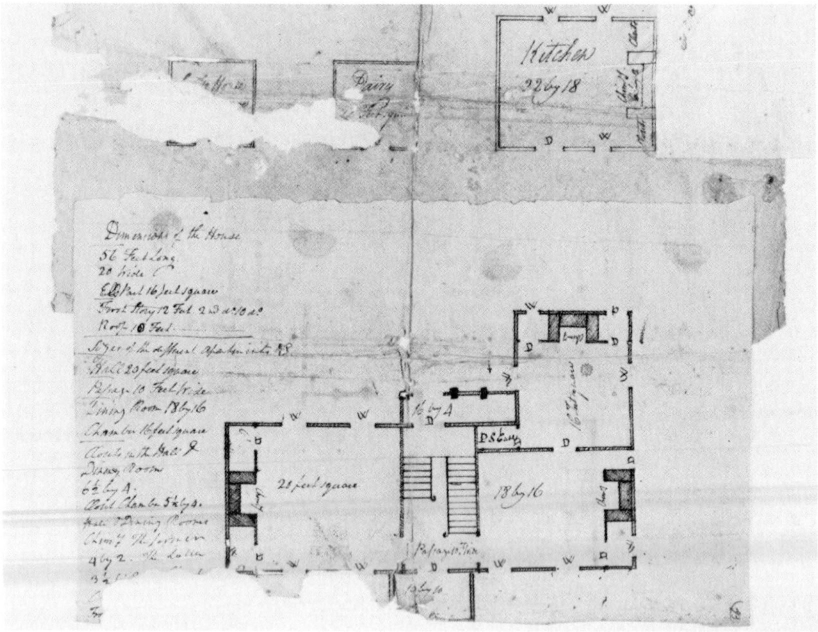

Fig. 2. Plan of a house to be built for William Cabell of Nelson County, Virginia, in 1784. From the Cabell Papers, Swem Library, College of William and Mary.

2. The most authoritative source on domestic planning in eighteenth-century Virginia is Dell Upton's "Early Vernacular Architecture of Southeast Virginia" (Ph.D. diss., Brown University, 1980). For a discussion on the introduction of the dining room and passage and the concurrent change in the social role of the hall, see pp. 240–71. See also Upton's "Vernacular Domestic Architecture," pp. 96, 102–4.

3. Henry Glassie observed, "In the new house the most public room was only as accessible as the most private room was in the earlier buildings." See *Folk Housing in Middle Virginia: A Structural Analysis of Historic Artifacts* (Knoxville: University of Tennessee Press, 1975), p. 121.

4. Ibid., pp. 121–22; Upton, "Early Vernacular Architecture," pp. 216–17, 265–71; Fraser Neiman, *The "Manner House" before Stratford* (Stratford, Va.: Stratford Hall, 1980), p. 35; Rhys Isaac, *The Transformation of Virginia, 1740–1790* (Chapel Hill: University of North Carolina Press, 1982), p. 75.

sure of privacy than the hall, often serving the family as a separate living and sleeping area. The typical gentry house thus incorporated these two living spaces on the ground floor.

As Dell Upton has shown, in the first quarter of the eighteenth century two new components were added to this plan: the central passage and the dining room. The latter was generally a front room and provided an intermediate space between the planter's threshold and the old chamber, which had been pushed deeper into the house. The promiscuous mix of persons and activities once accommodated in the hall was taken over by this new dining room. The old hall, in turn, became a formal "entertaining room" where those possessions expressive of one's station in society were assembled and placed on display. More than any other room, this richly appointed hall symbolized the social authority of the planter. Access to this setting was made increasingly selective by the new central passage through which visitors had to pass in order to reach the hall (Fig. 2).[2]

The effect of these new spaces, then, was to make the old hall and chamber far less accessible than they previously had been.[3] This change is thought to have represented a growing desire on the part of planters to distance themselves, in a ceremonial way, from persons outside their closely knit circle of family and social peers.[4] The role of the passage in this process is illustrated in the following description of an encounter between Robert Carter of Nomini Hall and one of his slaves:

About ten an old Negro Man came with a complaint to Mr Carter of the Overseer. . . . The humble posture in which the old Fellow placed himself before he began moved me. We were sitting in the passage, he sat himself down on the Floor clasp'd his Hands together, with his face directly to Mr Carter, & then began his Narration.[5]

Although Carter was willing to be confronted by an aggrieved slave in his own house, such an encounter could hardly have occurred in the inner sanctum of Carter's formal entertaining room. In this case, the passage was instrumental in restricting access not to Carter's person, but rather to his most important, most symbolic living space. This new passage was, then, an "instrument of control," a means by which to declare and maintain the social boundaries that separated the planter from his neighbors.

Very soon, however, Virginians came to appreciate the practical advantages of this new space as a refuge from the heat of summer. As early as 1724, Hugh Jones remarked that some Williamsburg houses were provided with "a passage generally through the middle of the house for an air-draft in summer."[6] In 1732, William Hugh Grove commented that, in Virginia, "The Manner of Building is much alike. They have a broad Stayrcase with a passage thro the house in the middle which is the Summer hall and Draws the air."[7] Grove's term, *summer hall*, is significant, for it points to the growing importance of the passage as a living space and emphasizes the seasonality of its use.

Perhaps architectural historians have overestimated the role of climate in determining how Virginians built their houses. Climate did, however, affect the way Virginians *used* their houses. This fact is convincingly portrayed in the diary kept by Sara Nourse of Berkeley County, Virginia. During the summer of 1781, Mrs. Nourse complained often of her discomfort from high temperatures and humidity. Occasionally, if breezes allowed, she remained "upstairs" in the passage, dressed only in a shift or undergarment, sometimes taking her meals there. When the breezes failed, she found it necessary to seek relief in the cellar, where she could be found working, dining, or even having tea.[8]

Landon Carter of Sabine Hall seems to have used his passage as a similar place of resort. In 1775, William Lee wrote to Carter, promising him "a line to repose on in a hot afternoon in ye cool passage."[9] Some time later, Carter commented in his diary on the "Gale's Pattent bedsteads on a new plan," adding, "I want one for my Passage in summer."[10] When, in July 1774, tutor Philip Fithian visited the house of George Turberville in Westmoreland County, he found the captain seated with his company "in a cool passage."[11] Clearly, Virginians made seasonal adjustments in their use of domestic space, and the passage played an important role in that process.

Clothing also figured prominently in this adaptive change of routine. According to William Hugh Grove, Virginians "affected

5. Philip Vickers Fithian, *Journal and Letters of Philip Vickers Fithian, a Plantation Tutor of the Old Dominion, 1773–1774*, ed. Hunter Dickinson Farish (Williamsburg: Colonial Williamsburg, 1965), p. 129. The passage seems to have served as a sort of waiting area for those wishing to see a member of the owner's family. When Alexander Macauley visited Williamsburg in 1783, he was obliged to wait among black servants in the passage to see Mrs. Campbell. Peevishly, he wrote, "As I did not approve of waiting for her in the passage, I . . . led Bettsy into the cold parlour." See Jane Carson, *We Were There, Descriptions of Williamsburg, 1699–1859* (Williamsburg: Colonial Williamsburg Foundation, 1965), pp. 68–69. In some instances the passage appears to have served as a waiting area for servants not immediately engaged in some household task. Eliza Custis recalled singing songs as a child to entertain her father's friends while "the servants in the passage would join in the mirth." See Daniel Blake Smith, *Inside the Great House* (Ithaca: Cornell University Press, 1980), p. 43. See also Fithian's account of an episode in the passage at Nomini Hall involving a slave boy quoted in Isaac, *Transformation*, p. 75.

6. Hugh Jones, *The Present State of Virginia*, ed. Richard L. Morton (Chapel Hill: University of North Carolina Press, 1956), p. 71.

7. William Hugh Grove, "Virginia in 1732: The Travel Journal of William Hugh Grove," ed. Gregory Stiverson and Patrick H. Butler III, *Virginia Magazine of History and Biography* 85 (1977):28.

8. Sara Fouace Nourse, Diary 1781–83, Nourse and Morris Family Papers, Alderman Library, University of Virginia, entries for July 1781. This source was brought to the writer's attention by Linda Baumgarten of Colonial Williamsburg Foundation.

9. William Lee to Landon Carter, 19 May 1775, Letterbook of William Lee, Virginia Historical Society, quoted in William Rasmussen's "Sabine Hall, a Classical Villa in Virginia" (Ph.D. diss., University of Delaware, 1979), p. 132.

10. Landon Carter, *The Diary of Colonel Landon Carter of Sabine Hall, 1752–*

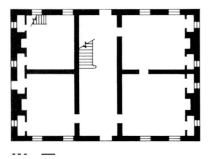

Fig. 3. First-floor plan of Wilton, formerly Henrico County, now Richmond, Virginia. After a drawing by Thomas Tileson Waterman. (author)

London Dress and wayes" during the winter months but, with the coming of summer, attired themselves in waistcoats and breeches of white linen.[12] Shortly before departing for Virginia in 1765, Edward Hawtrey received the following admonition from his brother concerning a summer wardrobe: "Your cloathing in summer must be as thin & light as possible for the heat is beyond your conception . . . you must carry a stock of linnen waistcoats made very large and loose that they may not stick to your hide when you perspire."[13]

Staying cool was a prime concern that Virginians often indulged at the expense of formal routine. Englishman Edward Kimber was shocked to find local gentlemen dispensing with the customary wig, that "distinguishing badge of gentlefolk," and wearing white caps of cotton or linen to cover their shaved heads.[14] Having set aside the trappings of social rank, Virginians moved into their passages, intent on spending the summer in as little discomfort as possible.

Life in the passage came to be associated closely with these seasonal periods of informality. As a result, this space was considerably less formal than either the hall or the dining room. Whereas the hall was superior and socially symbolic, the passage was subordinate and socially neutral, a setting in which the gentleman planter could, with propriety, let down his hair—or even take it off.

Initially, this subordinate relationship of the passage to the hall and dining room was reflected in the dwelling's interior embellishment. At Wilton, a mid-century house in Henrico County, the passage is adorned with a simple cornice, and its woodwork exhibits relatively plain molding details (Fig. 3). In contrast, the dining room boasts rather more complex panel moldings and a full-height entablature with Doric pilasters flanking the chimney breast. In the hall these pilasters are more elaborate still; they are carried completely around the perimeter of the room. The paneling of this hall, moreover, is assembled in such a way as to eliminate visible fastenings, a technique analogous to the blind-nailing of floors in finer rooms.[15] The ornamentation of these spaces reflects, then, the ascending degrees of importance initially attached to the passage, dining room, and hall.[16]

1778, ed. Jack P. Greene (Charlottesville: University Press of Virginia, 1965), p. 786. This reference was kindly provided by Liza Gusler of Colonial Williamsburg. While visiting Westover in 1814, James Kirk Paulding "lay on the sopha in the stately hall during the sultry part of the day," reading "with wonderful gusto" the manuscript of William Byrd's dividing-line histories. James Kirk Paulding, *Letters from the South* (New York: James Eastburn and Company, 1817), p. 28.

11. Fithian, *Journal and Letters*, p. 130.

12. Grove, *Virginia in 1732*, p. 29.

13. Stephen Hawtrey to Edward Hawtrey, 26 March 1765, Faculty/Alumni file, Archives, Swem Library, College of William and Mary. The writer wishes to thank John Hemphill of Colonial Williamsburg Foundation for information on this source.

14. Edward Kimber, "Observations on Several Voyages and Travels in America," and Devereaux Jarratt, *The Life of the Reverend Devereux Jarratt*, both quoted in Isaac, *Transformation*, pp. 43–44.

15. At Gunston Hall in Fairfax County, the floors of the elaborate parlor or "Palladian Room" are doweled together on their edges and blind-nailed. In the lesser rooms, all floors are butted at the edges and face-nailed. These floors are original throughout the house. Similar hierarchical treatment of floors is evident in builders' accounts and insurance property assessments from Philadelphia. See Nicholas Wainwright, *Colonial Grandeur in Philadelphia* (Philadelphia: Historical Society of Pennsylvania, 1964), pp. 142, 145, 150; *Mutual Assurance Company for Insuring Houses from Loss by Fire: The Architectural Surveys, 1784–1794* (Philadelphia: Mutual Assurance Company, 1976).

16. The writer is indebted to Edward A. Chappell, Director of Architectural Research at Colonial Williamsburg Foundation, for his observations on the hierarchical structure of Virginia house interiors. See Chappell, "Looking at Buildings," *Fresh Advices: A Research Supplement to the Colonial Williamsburg Interpreter* 5, no. 6 (1984):i-vi. Appraisals from eighteenth-century room-by-room inventories indicate that this hierarchical finish of surviving interiors correlates with a similar "pecking order" among their contents.

The third quarter of the eighteenth century witnessed a transformation of the passage that resulted in a realignment of this spatial "pecking order." This change was due, in part, to the growing importance of the passage as a living space. More and more, Virginians were coming to regard this space as a year-round living area. Such was certainly the case at Gunston Hall in Fairfax County, where owner George Mason is believed to have installed an iron stove in his passage, knocking a hole in the wall to carry its metal flue into the chimney breast of an adjacent room.[17]

The growing popularity of the double-pile house in Virginia around mid-century may have resulted from—and encouraged—this trend.[18] This house form, with its two-room-deep plan, effectively doubled the size of the passage, which was increasingly likely to contain greater quantities of furniture. When Robert Tucker of Norfolk County died in 1758, his passage contained, among other things, ten chairs, four tables, a couch, a candlestand, and a corner cupboard.[19] In 1760, Gawen Corbin of Richmond County had several chairs, a gaming table, two other small tables, a couch and a harpsichord in his passage.[20] Clearly, people were living in these spaces.

This fact may explain the occasional application of the term *hall* to this space. When Fithian visited the Tayloes at Mount Airy, he found the ladies "in the Hall playing the Harpsichord."[21] Later in the century, a French traveler was more explicit in his reference to "a sort of corridor called a hall . . . [where] the residents live when the cold season is over."[22]

Concurrent with this change in nomenclature was a tendency to give the passage—or hall—an identity of its own, separate and distinct from that of the stair.[23] George Mason's stair at Gunston Hall stands beyond an archway, expressing, if only equivocally, its separateness from the rest of the passage (Fig. 4A). In some instances, the stair was removed from the passage altogether, as at Sabine Hall or Mount Airy, creating an unobstructed, flue-like space (Figs. 5 and 6).

Socially and architecturally, this new living space was approaching the old hall in importance. Recent investigations have revealed that the passage at Gunston Hall was once adorned with

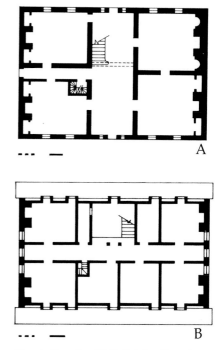

Fig. 4. Gunston Hall, Fairfax County, Virginia. A. First-floor plan. B. Second-floor plan. After drawings by Thomas Tileson Waterman. (author)

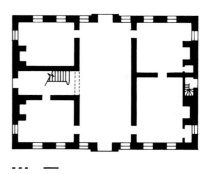

Fig. 5. First-floor plan of Sabine Hall, Richmond County, Virginia. The arrangement of the service stair is conjectural. After a drawing by Thomas Tileson Waterman. (author)

17. Personal communication with Paul Buchanan, former Director of Architectural Research, Colonial Williamsburg Foundation, and with Bennie Brown, Jr., former librarian/archivist Gunston Hall.

18. For a discussion of the detached house form in Virginia, see Camille Wells, "Kingsmill Plantation: A Cultural Analysis" (M.A. thesis, University of Virginia, 1976), pp. 125–27.

19. Norfolk County Records, Appraisements 1755–1783, fols. 117–20.

20. Inventory typescripts, Department of Architectural Research, Colonial Williamsburg Foundation.

21. Fithian, *Journal and Letters*, p. 152.

22. Kenneth Roberts and Anna M. Roberts, trans. and ed., *Moreau De St. Mery's American Journey, 1793–1798* (New York: Doubleday and Company, 1947), p. 52.

23. Upton notes this tendency in smaller houses. See his "Early Vernacular Architecture," p. 274.

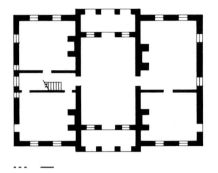

Fig. 6. First-floor plan of Mount Airy, Richmond County, Virginia. The stair location is conjectural. After a drawing by Thomas Tileson Waterman. (author)

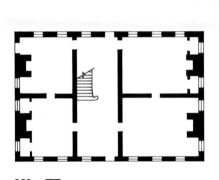

Fig. 7. First-floor plan of Westover, Charles City County, Virginia. After a drawing by Thomas Tileson Waterman. (author)

24. Buchanan and Brown, personal communication.

25. Mark R. Wenger, "Westover: William Byrd's Mansion Reconsidered" (M.A. thesis, University of Virginia, 1980), pp. 23–27.

26. Washington's correspondence mentions "Papier Machee for the Ceiling of two Rooms, one of them 18 Feet Square, the other 18 x 16 with Cr. Chimneys." George Washington, *The*

Doric orders and a full-height entablature.[24] The passage was still subordinate to the old hall—but the gap was closing.

At Carter's Grove, the passage—or hall—at last overtook all the other rooms in importance. Ionic orders, standing nearly six inches out from the surface of the wall, carry a full-height entablature completely around the room. In the two flanking rooms, full-height entablatures occur only over the chimney breasts, carried on simple Doric orders that appear relatively flat and two-dimensional when compared with those in the hall. The embellishment of Carter Burwell's mansion left no doubt as to which room was the most important.

William Byrd's remodeling of Westover, early in the 1760s, provides a revealing example of this realignment in the old spatial hierarchy of planters' dwellings. Byrd's passage, like that at Wilton, was initially less elaborate than the hall and dining room (Fig. 7). About 1763, Byrd added elaborate rococo plaster ornaments to the ceilings of two rooms.[25] Had the old scheme of order been respected, these ornaments would have been applied to the ceilings of the hall and dining room, as they were at Mount Vernon in 1757.[26] At Westover, however, the ceilings of the hall and of the passage received these embellishments. In Byrd's mind, the passage had overtaken the dining room in importance, and the mansion's decorative scheme was adjusted accordingly.

The new preeminence of this living space also found expression on the dwelling's exterior. At Mount Airy, the "hall," as Fithian called it, is a broad, well-lit space, emphasized on the outside by a three-bay pavilion of light-colored, finely detailed stonework that contrasted rather dramatically with the less refined materials to either side (Fig. 8). This articulation of the new hall or passage found its culminating statement at Tazewell Hall, the Williamsburg residence of John Randolph. Before its alteration early in the nineteenth century, Randolph's passage was a full two stories in height, occupying the entire extent of the dwelling's upward-thrusting, central mass (Figs. 9 and 10).[27]

Referred to as the "saloon" in a 1775 inventory,[28] this magnificent space points up a second factor that contributed to the transformation of the passage: a desire on the part of wealthy Virginians to affect the manners and customs of their peers in England. By 1760, this affectation of English ways was readily apparent in the names local gentry were applying to the rooms of their houses. During this period, such terms as *saloon*, *drawing room*, and even *dressing room* began to appear in the documents.[29] These were all English denominations with little or no prior use in Virginia.

Even more revealing, however, was Virginians' use of an old term, *parlor*, in a totally new sense. Originally, this word referred to the smaller room of the old hall-and-parlor house. About 1760, however, *parlor* began to replace *hall* as the name for the best room of larger gentry houses.[30] This new meaning derived from English

Fig. 8. River front of Mount Airy, Richmond County, Virginia. (Edward A. Chappell, courtsy of Colonial Williamsburg Foundation)

Writings of George Washington from the Original Manuscript Sources 1745–1799, ed. John C. Fitzpatrick, 39 vols. (Washington, D.C.: U.S. Government Printing Office, 1931), 2:23. Obviously, the eighteen-foot-square room was the hall. Washington's request earlier in the invoice for wallpaper for "a Dining Room 18 x 16" indicates that the second set of ceiling ornaments was to be used in that location.

27. Singleton P. Moorehead, "Tazewell Hall: A Report on Its Eighteenth-Century Appearance," *Journal of the Society of Architectural Historians* 14 (1955):16.

28. Inventory typescripts, Department of Architectural Research, Colonial Williamsburg Foundation.

29. Traveling through Virginia in 1779, Thomas Anburey described the saloon at Tuckahoe, noting, "These saloons answer the two purposes of a cool retreat from the scorching and sultry heat of the climate, and of an occasional ball-room." Thomas Anburey, *Travels Through the Interior Parts of America*, 2 vols. (1789; rpt. New

York: Arno Press, 1969), 2:359. Shortly after 1790, Isaac Weld commented on the prevalence of such rooms, noting, "An apartment like this, extending from front to back, is very common in a Virginia House; it is called the saloon, and during summer is the one generally preferred by the family, on account of its being more airy and spacious than any other." Isaac Weld, *Travels Through the States of North America* (1800; rpt. New York: Johnson Reprint Corporation, 1968), 1:207. Drawing rooms appear in the inventories of William Hunter (1761), John Randolph (1775), Fielding Lewis (1781), and Thomas Nelson (1789). Inventory typescripts, Department of Architectural Research, Colonial Williamsburg Foundation. Among the Armistead-Cocke Papers, Box 1, Folder 61, Swem Library, College of William and Mary, are first- and second-floor plans for an unidentified house, dating from "c. 1760." The primary first-floor room is designated "Drawing Room." Shippen likewise mentioned a drawing room at Westover during his visit there in 1783. Thomas Lee Shippen to his par-

ents, 30–31 December 1783, Shippen Papers, Library of Congress. Col. Thomas Lee's house at Stratford had a dressing room in 1758. Inventory typescripts, Department of Architectural Research, Colonial Williamsburg Foundation. George Fairfax had a dressing room at Belvoir when he was preparing to sell his house in 1774. Inventory, Fairfax Family Papers, Virginia Historical Society. The architectural plans, cited above, show a dressing room on the upper floor.

30. In 1760, Gawen Corbin's house had a parlor, but no hall, as did those of Edward Ambler in 1769, George Fairfax in 1774, Landon Carter in 1779, Rawleigh Downman in 1781, Robert Gilmour in 1783, George Washington in 1799, and John Belfield in 1802. Inventory typescripts, Department of Architectural Research, Colonial Williamsburg Foundation. In 1770, Joseph Kidd advertised lodgings for gentlemen at the former residence of John Custis, where there was "a very elegant parlour, intended to be appropriated to the use of lodgers." See Stephenson, "Custis Square," p. 26.

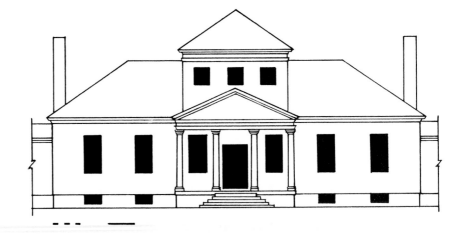

Fig. 9. South elevation of Tazewell Hall, formerly Williamsburg, now Newport News, Virginia. (author, courtesy of Colonial Williamsburg Foundation)

usage, wherein the term connoted "a fair lower Room design'd principally for the Entertainment of Company."[31] That definition corresponded very closely with Virginians' concept of the old hall as *the* entertaining room, although in England, *parlor* could refer in a general way to *any* such room in the house. This broader sense of English usage was occasionally adopted in Virginia, as in Robert Carter's 1762 order for wallpaper "to hang three Parlours" of his house in Williamsburg.[32]

Like saloons and drawing rooms, these new parlors reveal a desire on the part of local gentry to appropriate certain outward signs of English culture. John Randolph's residence epitomized this attitude. Built on one of the choicest sites in Williamsburg, Tazewell Hall was an uncommonly elegant house, modishly appointed with furnishings of the highest quality.[33] Among the rooms mentioned in Randolph's 1775 inventory were a saloon, drawing room, dining parlor, and gallery. This elaborate residence exemplified the growing fashionability of English room nomenclature during the third quarter of the eighteenth century. In no other Virginia house of this period was the new terminology so completely embraced.

The growing Englishness of gentry houses after mid-century was also evident in the increasingly frequent use of English architectural publications as sources of inspiration and detail. This is not to say that such material was copied indiscriminately. Rather, as Dell Upton has asserted, the selection and adaptation of academic models were directed by local intention and circumstance.[34] Not until the passage had surpassed the old hall in size and importance did houses with articulated central masses like Brandon become popular in Virginia (Figs. 11 and 12). The adoption of English prototypes in this and other instances represented a momentary correspondence of academic form with local priorities.

31. *The Builders' Dictionary* (1734; rpt. Washington, D.C.: Association for Preservation Technology, 1981), entry for "parlour."

32. Robert Carter to Thomas Bladon, 16 February 1762, Robert Carter Letterbook 1761–64, quoted in Mary Stephenson, "Carter-Saunders House" (unpublished research report, Colonial Williamsburg Foundation, 1956), p. 20. The generic sense of English usage is exemplified in a letter written by Sir William Chambers to a client "with regard to the painting of your Parlours." See John Fowler and John Cornforth, *English Decoration in the Eighteenth Century* (London: Barrie and Jenkins, 1974), p. 205.

33. Inventory typescripts, Department of Architectural Research, Colonial Williamsburg Foundation.

34. Upton, "Early Vernacular Architecture," p. 96.

Fig. 10. Saloon of Tazewell Hall, formerly Williamsburg, now Newport
News, Virginia. (author, courtesy of Colonial Williamsburg Foundation)

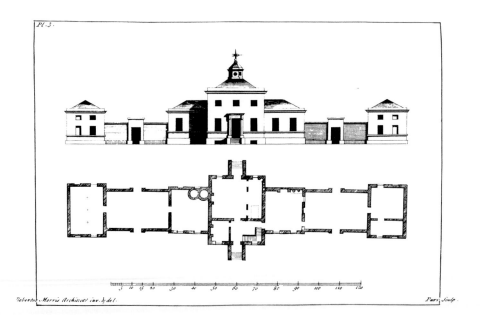

Fig. 11. Plate 3 from Robert Morris's *Select Architecture*, published in London, 1755.

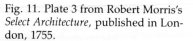

Fig. 12. West elevation of Brandon, Prince George County, Virginia. After a drawing by Clay Lancaster. (author)

35. The furnishings of second-floor passages generally suggest a room of relatively minor social importance. "Old" furniture and trunks filled with linen are the items that appear most frequently among the inventoried contents of these spaces. As a rule, their architectural finish is unremarkable as well. Exceptions to this are to be found at Carter's Grove in James City County, and at Sabine Hall in Richmond County, where the ornament of the upper rooms is relatively elaborate. See Rasmussen, "Sabine Hall," pp. 163–67.

In Virginia, the changing role of the passage had created a need for new ways of packaging the planter's domestic environment. Typically, both first and second floors had been laid out on the same plan. As long as the upper and lower passages continued to function as circulation spaces, this arrangement was satisfactory. By the middle of the eighteenth century, however, the social importance of the lower passage had increased rather dramatically, while that of the upper passage remained largely unchanged. The resulting difficulty is evident at Carter's Grove, where the great room over Carter Burwell's entry was disproportionately large in relation to its traditional function as a secondary circulation and storage area (Figs. 13A and B).[35]

This problem resulted in a tendency to dissociate the plans of the first and second floors. At Gunston Hall, George Mason's narrow second-floor corridor—primarily a circulation space—is independent of the larger first-floor passage, which was primarily a liv-

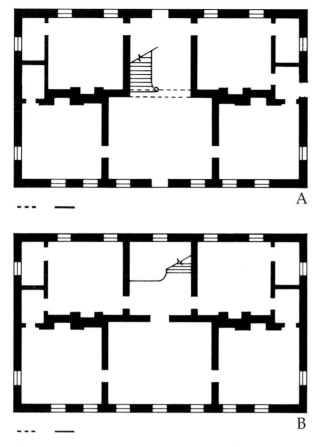

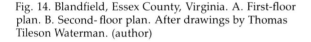

Fig. 13. Carter's Grove, James City County, Virginia.
A. First-floor plan. B. Second-floor plan. After drawings
by Thomas Tileson Waterman. (author)

Fig. 14. Blandfield, Essex County, Virginia. A. First-floor
plan. B. Second- floor plan. After drawings by Thomas
Tileson Waterman. (author)

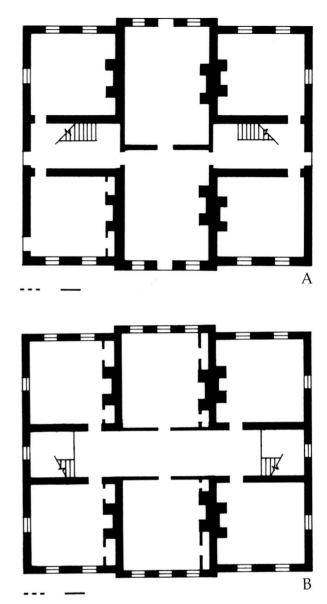

ing space (Figs. 4A and 4B). In light of this example, it should be
clear that the bookish plan of Blandfield, in Essex County, was selected precisely because it offered a solution to the increasingly
problematic relationship between the first and second floors (Figs.
14A and 14B). The assimilation of academic influences was pro-
foundly affected, then, by the changes that were reshaping the old
central passage.

Increasingly, wealthy Virginians came to associate their lower
passages with the halls or entries of contemporary English houses.
This connection is particularly clear at Carter's Grove, where the

36. For a discussion of the English formal plan see Mark Girouard, *Life in the English Country House* (New York: Penguin Books, 1980), p. 119.

37. Mecklenburg County Records, Wills 1802–1807, fols. 326–34. The writer was led to this information by Vanessa Patrick of Colonial Williamsburg Foundation.

38. Norfolk County Records, Appraisements 1755–1783, fol. 180.

39. *Virginia Gazette* (Dixon), 7 August 1777, p. 2, col. 2.

40. Charles Santore, *The Windsor Style in America* (Philadelphia: Running Press, 1981), pp. 33, 48; Nancy Goyne Evans, "A History and Background of English Windsor Furniture," *Furniture History* 14 (1977):33; Jane B. Kolter et al., *The Branded Windsor Furniture of Independence National Park* (Philadelphia: Independence National Park, 1981), pp. 5–6. The author wishes to thank Martha Theobald, formerly of Colonial Williamsburg Foundation, for calling his attention to the latter two sources.

41. Inventory typescripts, Department of Architectural Research, Colonial Williamsburg Foundation.

42. Frances Norton Mason, ed., *John Norton and Sons, Merchants of London and Virginia* (Richmond: Dietz Press, 1937), p. 125. This reference was provided through the courtesy of Betty Leviner of Colonial Williamsburg Foundation.

43. Santore, *Windsor Style*, pp. 29, 35. Santore admits, however, that, "Because Windsors used as outdoor furniture were almost a fad in London in the mid–1700's and because no Philadelphian could have a proper garden without the proper furniture, imported Windsors of the green-painted variety were almost certainly first used in America in the gardens of the wealthy." In Virginia, these chairs continued to be artifacts of the wealthy through the end of the eighteenth century.

44. Personal communications with Ron Hurst and Carl Lounsbury, both of Colonial Williamsburg Foundation. In Norfolk County, Virginia, Windsor chairs appeared in the inventories of six decedents between 1755 and 1783. The appraised values of these estates ranged from a high of £6797 to a low

monumental quality of the entry echoes the general effect of many such rooms in England. At Blandfield, the parallel was carried even further by dividing the great central space into a hall and saloon in the manner of the English formal house (Fig. 14A).[36] Although no eighteenth-century record naming these rooms has survived, a similar pair of rooms at Prestwould in Mecklenburg County were called the *hall* and *saloon* in an 1804 inventory.[37]

This identification of the passage with the English hall is further revealed in the occasional mention of "passage chairs" in various records after 1760.[38] What was this specialized seating form, so closely linked with the passage as to have taken on its name? Reference to "green Passage Chairs" in a 1777 newspaper advertisement[39] suggests that these were Windsor chairs, a form that was often painted green.[40] In 1758, Norfolk County appraisers listed ten Windsor chairs among the furnishings of Robert Tucker's passage.[41] Writing to his factor in 1770, Mann Page of Spotsylvania County ordered "1 dozn. Windsor Chairs for a Passage," probably for use at Mannsfield, his estate near Fredericksburg.[42]

Some historians have emphasized the utility and democratic availability of this seating form in America, pointing to its maintenance in a wide variety of social contexts throughout New England and the middle colonies.[43] In Virginia, however, the use of Windsor seating seems to have followed a different course. Probate inventories suggest that, during the second half of the eighteenth century, Windsor chairs were to be found primarily in wealthier Virginia households. They do not appear in the appraisals of lesser estates, nor do they seem to have been used much in taverns and public buildings as they were in the North.[44] The attitude of Virginians toward the Windsor chair more closely resembled that in England, where such seating was used primarily in parks and gardens.[45] Frequently, these chairs appear as props in outdoor portraits, contributing to the fashionable informality of the setting.[46]

The green-painted chairs acquired by Virginians seem to have been used outdoors as well. In 1775, the contents of John Randolph's basement at Tazewell Hall included, among other things, "five green Windsor Chairs and one green Settee belonging to the Summer House."[47] This sort of outdoor use may account for the frequent appearance of Windsor chairs in passages, from which they could be carried easily out of the house. Such chairs were actually kept outdoors at Mount Vernon, where, in 1799, the inventory of George Washington's estate mentioned thirty Windsors "in the Piazza" facing the river.[48]

Although it was a relatively inexpensive form of seating, the Windsor chair was, in Virginia at least, a genteel object. Through its association with the pleasure garden, an amenity enjoyed by a wealthy minority, the Windsor connoted ease, fashionability, and status. The presence of a dozen or so of these chairs in the passage of a house identified its owner as a person of considerable means and high social rank.

Furniture historian Wallace Gusler has suggested that these Windsor chairs functioned much like another English seating form—the hall chair. As the name implies, these chairs were typically kept in halls of English country houses. Frequently the backs of these hall chairs were emblazoned with the owner's coat of arms, a clear statement about inherited social position. Like Windsors, they had unupholstered wooden seats and were intended for occasional outdoor use.[49] There was a marked similarity, then, in the physical character, architectural context, and social use of these two forms. Elements of both are to be seen in a Windsor chair—now in the Victoria and Albert Museum—decorated on its back with the arms of Sir John Perceval, second Earl of Egmont (Fig. 15). Like Windsor seating in Virginia, this chair was as suitable for the garden as it was for the entry.[50] In the light of this chair, the link between hall seating in England and passage seating in Virginia—between English halls and Virginia passages—becomes especially clear.

With its escalating level of decoration, genteel furniture, and fashionable new names, the old passage had evolved from its beginnings as an agent of social control to become a viable living space and, ultimately, an icon of status—a symbol of the social distinctions it had once enforced. In the process, the entire house had been transformed—its outward form, its interior arrangement, its response to extralocal influences, its social meaning. In this space, then, lies an important key to understanding the houses of Virginia planter oligarchs, and the way of living that endowed those houses with meaning.

Fig. 15. Windsor chair bearing the arms of Sir John Perceval, Earl of Egmont. (Victoria and Albert Museum)

of £385. Norfolk County Records, Appraisements 1755–1783. Windsors seem to have become rather more common by the early years of the nineteenth century. In 1800, a dozen Windsor chairs were ordered for the Public Hospital in Williamsburg. According to Travis MacDonald of Colonial Williamsburg Foundation, these were possibly intended for use in the directors' meeting room. Eastern State Hospital Court of Directors' Minutes, 1770–1801, p. 203, Virginia State Library. See also Michael Anne Lynn, "Curator's Report to the Furnishing Committee, May, 1981," Research Report, Point of Honor, Lynchburg, Virginia.

45. Santore, *Windsor Style*, pp. 31–34; Evans, "History and Background," p. 33.

46. Arthur Devis and Johann Zoffany were particularly fond of using Windsor chairs in such portraits. See Evans, "History and Background," pp. 82b, 86.

47. Inventory typescripts, Department of Architectural Research, Colonial Williamsburg Foundation.

48. *Inventory of the Contents of Mount Vernon, 1810* (Cambridge: The [Harvard] University Press, 1909), p. 6. Washington owned six *green* Windsor chairs, possibly for his passage, by 1764, p. xvii.

49. Thomas Sheraton, *Thomas Sheraton's Cabinet Dictionary*, 2 vols. (1803;

rpt. New York: Praeger Publishers, 1970), 2:250; Thomas Chippendale, *The Gentleman and Cabinet-maker's Director* (1762; rpt. New York: Dover Publications, 1966), p. 3, pls. XVII, XVIII. Chippendale offered "Six Designs for Halls, Passages, or Summer-Houses," which could be "either of Mahogany, or any other Wood, and painted," usually with "wooden Seats." The above references were supplied by Liza Gusler. In outlining the relationship between hall chairs and Windsor chairs, the author has relied heavily on the ideas of Ms. Gusler and those of Wallace Gusler, both of Colonial Williamsburg Foundation.

50. Evans, "History and Background," pl. 81, p. 38.2.

16

A R L E N E   H O R V A T H

Vernacular Expression in Quaker Chester County, Pennsylvania: The Taylor-Parke House and Its Maker

For more than two centuries, members of the Abiah Taylor family have responded to the promise of Penn's new province with both spiritual affirmation and practical endeavor. Early generations of the family repaid Chester County's welcome with a small cluster of domestic and commercial buildings, eight of which still stand, along the east branch of the Brandywine Creek and a tributary called Taylor's Run.

In 1702, the founding Taylor arrived in Pennsylvania from Berkshire, England. A member of the Society of Friends, Abiah Taylor settled in predominantly Quaker Chester County. By 1724, he had built a saw and grist mill on his property, established a succesful farm, and replaced his first dwelling with one reflecting his improved material circumstances.[1] More importantly, he had rooted the family in their modes of work and worship and in their building traditions.

By 1768, his namesake grandson, also a Chester County farmer, miller, prominent citizen, and Friend, had constructed a substantial farmhouse within view of the elder Abiah Taylor's 1724 brick dwelling. The "mansion house," as the younger Taylor's fieldstone farmhouse was termed in early deeds, was a complex response to the culture in which it was constructed. As an artifact, this stone structure—now known as the Taylor-Parke house—is a rich source for interpreting the values, attitudes, and assumptions of its maker and, inferentially, of the larger community to which he belonged.[2]

The importance of asking analytical questions of historic artifacts is now rarely questioned by historians. Furthermore, the potential for understanding inaccessible ways of life through surviving objects and structures is central to all vernacular architecture studies. Still at issue, however, is precisely what cultural meanings are embodied in the forms and structures of artifacts. The Taylor-Parke house serves as a case study: does it reflect the personal commitment of Abiah Taylor to Quaker tenets? How might its form have been influenced by this and by more general local interpretations of Quaker values?[3] Does this dwelling represent a "Quaker style"

1. J. Smith Futhy and Gilbert Cope, *The History of Chester County, Pennsylvania* (Philadelphia: J. B. Lippincott and Company, 1881), p. 164; Taylor genealogy, Chester County Historical Society, West Chester, Pennsylvania.

2. The name *Taylor-Parke* reflects a hundred and eighty years of family ownership, concluding with Samuel Parke's sale of the property in 1949.

3. The belief system of the Society of Friends in the eighteenth century was subject to a variety of individual and regional interpretations. Failure to consider this lack of homogeneity could lead to a misreading of the cultural signals expressed in Quaker artifacts.

150

of architecture, or does it, instead, reflect the incorporation of widely accepted Anglo-American house forms?

To find the meaning in the house and to understand its maker, it is necessary to consider Taylor's social status, economic circumstances, and cultural orientation in conjunction with his religious affiliation. Also important is the role of family tradition in shaping his beliefs and assumptions about what his house should be. It is the artifact itself, however, that leads to an understanding of its maker. The substantial and carefully detailed farmhouse provides evidence of the compromise between Taylor's Quaker ideals and the approved uses of his prosperity, between a provincial interpretation of house form and his urban associations, between his basic conservatism and a subtle but stubborn independence.

The documentary evidence related to the house and to Taylor himself reveals similar compromises in the man and in the mansion house. He was one of the most successful businessmen in the county—a farmer, miller, land speculator, and estate builder—and he served as a state legislator until his death in 1801.[4] His worldly affairs took him into Philadelphia, as did his representation of Bradford Meeting at Philadelphia Yearly Meeting.[5] He thus had an opportunity to become familiar with urban architecture, cosmopolitan tastes, and a somewhat more liberal interpretation of Quaker testimonies.

Taylor was, however, a provincial in most aspects of building and furnishing his house. His seating furniture was limited to the more modest products of the rural craftsman,[6] and receipts indicate his expenditures to have generally conformed to a Quakerly rejection of excess or extravagant display,[7] although his house suggests a taste for items "of the best sort, but plain."[8] His library of religious works, contemporary histories, law books, and business readings was well within the strictest purview of approved Quaker reading material.[9] Even his drinking habits adhered closely to Friends' principles as they were locally perceived.[10] Like his father and grandfather, he did not neglect the "inward plantation" in his pursuit of prosperity and stature within the community.[11]

These practices continued to be typical of Taylor's life even after he was "read out" of Bradford Meeting in 1791 for recurring indebtedness.[12] By that time, his estate in Chester County had grown significantly, and he owned at least two large tracts of land elsewhere in the state.[13] As a result, Taylor was at times land rich and cash poor, contrary to Friends' "Advices," which were taken quite strictly during that late eighteenth-century period of spiritual reform.[14] This represented his only known point of departure from the local interpretation of a distinctly Quaker way of life.

The local architectural context in which the Taylor-Parke house was built had undergone a transformation since the first Abiah Taylor had constructed his brick hall-parlor house with a steeply gabled roof and asymmetrical fenestration. This and other early dwellings in the area represent a building tradition brought to Penn's province

4. "Assessment Lists of Chester County, 1785," *Pennsylvania Archives*, ser. 3, 12 (1897):663–823, indicates that Abiah Taylor II paid the highest taxes in Bradford Township and was one of the highest taxpayers in Chester County. "Proprietary Tax Lists of Chester County, 1765–1771," *Pennsylvania Archives*, ser. 3, 11 (1896):20, lists Taylor as a miller with saw and grist mills and also numbers him among the large landowners and livestock owners of the county. "County of Bedford, 1771–1893, Warranties of Land," *Pennsylvania Archives*, ser. 3, 25 (1898):447–673, and "Returns of Taxables for County of Huntingdon," *Pennsylvania Archives*, ser. 3, 22 (1898): 327–66, document Taylor's large land holdings outside Chester County. Journal of Samuel Taylor, 1798–1799, Cope Collection, Chester County Historical Society, mentions Abiah Taylor's assembly seat.

5. "Philadelphia Yearly Meeting Minutes, 1681–1827," Quaker Collection, Haverford College Library, Haverford, Pennsylvania.

6. Estate of Abiah Taylor II, Inventory No. 4898 (1801), Chester County Historical Society. Household contents include:

7 feather beds and bedding	kitchen dresser furniture
2 chaff beds and bedding	books
2 pair sheets	clock
1 counter pain	bookcase and desk
4 pair pillowcases	dining table
5 cases of drawers	oval table
candlestand	dressing table
large oblong table	tea table
1 looking glass	tenplate stove
2 fine tablecloths	1 cupboard
1 D[itto] D	lot of pewter
2 small D D	chest
2 large coarse D	4 small spinning
5 fine napkins	wheels
8 coarse D	real
6 blue rush bottomed chairs	spooling wheel swifts
	kitchen furniture
5 red D D	4 iron pots
pr andirons	1 iron skillet
bake iron, gridiron, spit	brass kettle
toaster	cedar ware
	watering pot
	shovel and tongs
	hand irons

7. Miscellaneous papers, Abiah Taylor Estate, Chester County Historical Society.

8. Frederick Tolles, *Meeting House and Counting House* (New York: W. W. Norton and Company, 1948), p. 128. The passage is from a 1738 letter from John Reynell in Philadelphia to Daniel Flexney in London.

9. Estate of Abiah Taylor II. His library included: *Proud's History of Pennsylvania, Read's Digest of Laws of Pennsylvania, Sewel's History, Penn's Selected Works, Barclay's Appollogy, Declaration of Friends' Principles, Laws of the United States, Laws of Pennsylvania, Trader's Guide, Baily's Dictionary, Thomas Taylor's Works, Woolman's Journal, Griffith's Journal,* and *Churchman's Journal.* The last four titles are diaries of Quaker "saints."

10. Miscellaneous papers, Abiah Taylor Estate. These records contain Taylor's personal and business receipts and bills, including his running tab with West Chester innkeeper Samson Babbe for 1795. This itemized bill indicates a temperate use of alcohol, an occasional brandy sling or rum grog, which conforms to the Quaker prohibition against grain alcohol but not to the extremist abstention rum, product of slave labor.

11. *Two Hundred Fifty Years of Quakerism at Birmingham, 1690–1940* (West Chester, Pa.: Birmingham Monthly Meeting, 1940); Estate of Abiah Taylor I, Inventory No. 1066 (1747), and Will of Samuel Taylor, Will Book 4, p. 159, both at the Chester County Historical Society. See also Tolles, *Meeting House,* pp. 3–11.

12. "Bradford Monthly Meeting Minutes and Index, 1737–1800," Chester County Historical Society.

13. "Proprietary Tax Lists of Chester County," p. 20; "County of Bedford Warrants of Land," pp. 447–673; "Returns of Taxables for the County of Huntingdon," pp. 327–66.

14. Tolles, *Meeting Houses,* p. 58.

15. Hugh Braun, *Elements of English Architecture* (Devon: David and Charles, 1973), pp. 20, 24; R. J. Brown, *The English Country Cottage* (London: Robert Hale, 1979), p. 240.

16. Henry Glassie, "Eighteenth Century Cultural Process in Delaware Valley Folk Building," *Winterthur Portfolio* 7 (1972):43–45; R. W. Brunskill, *Vernacular Architecture* (London: Faber and Faber, 1974).

17. Glassie, "Cultural Process," pp. 43–45.

18. Patricia Irvin Cooper, "A Quaker-Plan House in Georgia," *Pioneer America* 10, no. 1 (1978):15–34. See also Robert C. Smith, "Two Centuries of Philadelphia Architecture," in *Historic Philadelphia from the Founding until the Early Nineteenth Century* (Philadelphia: American Philosophical Society, 1953), p. 292. Smith attributes the plan to English architectural tradition and cites examples of the corner fireplace in vernacular buildings in London and Dublin. Henry Glassie, *Passing the Time in Ballymenone: Culture and History in of an Ulster Community* (Philadelphia: University of Pennsylvania Press, 1982). Glassie also mentions an example of the angled fireplace in Ireland.

19. Cooper, "Quaker-Plan House," pp. 25–29. Cooper discusses occurrence of the Quaker plan with angled fireplace "wherever there has been Quaker settlement from Pennsylvania . . . to South Carolina" and attributes its dissemination primarily to Quaker migration. Although not aware of any corner fireplaces in British or western European vernacular architecture, Cooper did attribute their use in some parts of Virginia to the 1670 introduction of such fireplaces into English academic building.

20. Hugh Morrison, *Early American Architecture from the First Colonial Settlements to the National Period* (New York: Oxford University Press, 1952), p. 503.

from England. Using that English architectural vocabulary, each first-generation builder created his own vernacular expression, usually with only small modifications in deference to climate, materials, or topography. The resulting houses followed essentially the patterns of design common to late seventeenth-century England. This tradition included a steeply pitched gable roof, a minimal number of small windows placed in response to interior spatial needs, and interior end chimneys with brick shafts that were square in section, similar to those that were concurrently replacing the central chimney in the smaller English dwellings.[15] In plan as well, most early eighteenth-century houses of Chester County were constructed according to the vocabulary of the seventeenth-century English vernacular tradition.[16] The hall-parlor plan was the most common, with variations involving the relative sizes of the two principal rooms and the positions of fireplaces, stairs, and entrances.[17]

Some dwellings incorporated or were influenced by the "Quaker plan," consisting of two or three rooms and corner fireplace. That configuration has been attributed to an early Swedish influence in the province, but the angled fireplace so integral to the ethnic identity of the type is not peculiar to any single northern European country and has appeared, in fact, in Britain.[18] The Quaker plan is also found in the American South, where English influence was largely unchallenged, although its appearance there may be due to Quaker migration.[19] The "Penn plan," as it is also termed, is actually three similar eighteen-by-thirty-foot plans recommended by William Penn in a tract for prospective immigrants from the Palatinate.[20] The "Quaker" appellation probably derives from this Penn connection and from the fact that, although used by many different religious and ethnic groups, the plan was first introduced into a predominantly Quaker province.

In Chester County, the transplanted English vernacular tradition was expressed in local terms and most commonly executed in native fieldstone.[21] Where brick clay was found, builders from areas of Britain—such as Berkshire—that had a strong tradition of brickwork could build as they would have in their native shires.[22] Whatever the generating factors, only a relatively small number of these tall single-pile brick structures have survived in the part of Chester County that is located west of the Wertenbaker line.[23]

In degree of elaboration, the county's early eighteenth-century buildings evidence a prevailing mode of simplicity and practicality that is not unsympathetic with English vernacular traditions. Materials were used frankly and honestly without complex detailing. Although the simplicity of these early house exteriors may be misread as a distinctly Quaker characteristic, these structures speak more to ethnic origins, economic status, and the practical concerns of early settlers than to religious beliefs. Nevertheless, all these influences, including Friends' tenets of simplicity, separately and together mitigate toward the plainness of style found in dwellings dating from this period of early Quaker settlement. With some exceptions, these underlying assumptions about design remained consistent into the middle of the eighteenth century.[24]

By 1768, the steeply gabled roof had given way to a lower profile, windows were larger and regularly placed, and new features, such as paneled shutters, had increased in popularity. There were also new variations in house plans. The two unequal-sized rooms of the traditional hall-parlor house had become symmetrical and were often separated by a central passage. Other Chester County houses are examples of both the one-third and the two-thirds Georgian house types. Still others represent fusions of the basic Georgian form with pre-Georgian elements.[25] These synthetic types often display exteriors that mask the asymmetry within. A closer look at the 1768 Taylor-Parke house will place that structure and its builder in the midst of these transformations.

The Taylor-Parke house looks south across Strasburg Road toward an early nineteenth-century Taylor dwelling and toward the site of the original Taylor mills. Beyond the mill race, following the southeast course of Taylor's Run across a broad field, the first Abiah Taylor house is visible on a small rise. Strasburg Road leads eastward through rolling countryside to West Chester, located about a mile away. The house (Fig. 1) is set against the foot of a small hill and hidden from the road by an overgrowth of trees and shrubs. It has a two-and-a-half-story main block that is abutted on its east side by a one-and-a-half-story kitchen to which a summer kitchen was later added. It has a gable roof, interior end chimneys with decorative brick caps, symmetrical fenestration on all four walls, and proportions similar to those of other Chester County and Taylor family dwellings.

21. Glassie, "Cultural Process," p. 45; Barte Anderson and Ned Goode, "Historic American Buildings Survey, Chester County, 1958–1962" (manuscript, Chester County Historical Society).

22. Braun, *English Architecture*, p. 20; John Penoyre and Jane Penoyre, *Houses in the Landscape* (London: Faber and Faber, 1978), p. 92.

23. Thomas Jefferson Wertenbaker, *The Founding of the American Civilization: The Middle Colonies* (New York: Charles Scribner's Sons, 1938), p. 236. Wertenbaker notes: "If we draw a line on the map from Princeton to Wilmington, we find that in the region east of it, including Philadelphia, both banks of the Delaware and southern New Jersey, the [eighteenth-century] houses are generally of brick, whereas to the west they are almost invariably of stone." According to Anderson and Goode material, only 3 percent of surviving pre–1780 dwellings are brick, and these tend to be concentrated in the lower townships closer to the Wertenbaker line.

24. Anderson and Goode, "Historic American Buildings Survey."

25. Glassie, "Cultural Process," p. 44.

Fig. 1. Facade of the Taylor-Parke house, built in 1768 in Chester County, Pennsylvania. (author)

Fig. 2. West end of the Taylor-Parke house. The room that is accessible from the northwest corner door probably served as Taylor's office. (author)

The four-bay, south-facing facade is constructed of dressed and coursed hornblende that was quarried on the property. The other three faces are built of uncut rubble stone also from the premises (Fig. 2). Twelve-over-twelve double-hung sash windows are costly features that were used only in the finest county houses. The original shutters, like those on other eighteenth-century houses in Chester County, are double-paneled on the first story and louvered on the second story. The symmetrical fenestration of the Taylor-Parke house is somewhat offset by the west-of-center placement of the main entrance. Five wide stone steps lead up to the entrance, where a sturdy, double-paneled batten door is surmounted by a four-light transom. Four of the five eighteenth-century Taylor dwellings exhibit this feature.[26]

Centered in the entrance facade just below the cornice is a circular datestone, surrounded by radiating dressed compass stones. Its design is identical to one in the gable of the house built by the first Abiah Taylor. Datestones, also known in a number of English shires, are scattered throughout the county and appear in three of six surviving Taylor dwellings.[27]

The pent eave that separates the first and second stories and carries the cornice on the gable ends was an accepted feature of Chester County architectural design, and it appeared frequently in Philadelphia, where an English heritage also predominated.[28] Of the eight surviving Taylor structures, seven were built with this feature. Five of these buildings date from the period before 1780 and two others were built by 1824. This represents a higher rate of occurrence than was common among early houses in Chester County.[29]

Despite the incorporation of many local elements and materials, the use of coursed cut stone on the facade, coupled with the decorative chimney details, the refined window treatment, and the grand entrance steps, suggests that Abiah Taylor II had a taste for something more imposing. In this, he may have been influenced by the stately mansions of Philadelphia's wealthy Quaker aristocracy, whom he would have known. That his farmhouse suggests a rural version of Benjamin Chew's newly constructed Cliveden may not be accidental.

Structural evidence indicates that the kitchen predates the main block of the house, thus reinforcing family oral history.[30] The kitchen wing, with its ovens and large cooking fireplace and its loft, could have provided an adequate dwelling by itself, whereas the main block, with only small corner fireplaces, would not have been sensible without nearby food preparation facilities. The widely mismatched levels between kitchen and main block create interior problems but suggest a pragmatic set of priorities. The solid, workmanlike construction and careful detailing of the house indicate that Abiah Taylor II was not slipshod, and his relatively broad experience suggests that he knew how fine houses were supposed to fit together neatly. Nonetheless, he was satisfied to accept a practical

26. Anderson and Goode, "Historic American Buildings Survey." Transom-lighted doorways are reported in 20 percent of pre–1780 houses both in East Bradford and in Chester County as a whole.

27. Ibid.

28. Glassie, "Cultural Process," pp. 35–43.

29. Anderson and Goode, "Historic American Buildings Survey." The pent eave is seen in Chester County at least by 1704. By 1780, it had been incorporated into 45 percent of the recorded structures in East Bradford Township.

30. Walter Parke Thompson, personal interview, 24 May 1980.

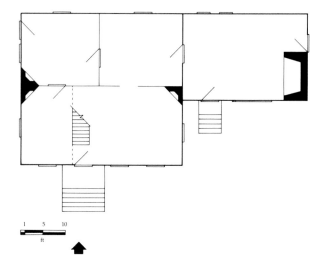

Fig. 3. Plan of the Taylor-Parke house. The parlor and dining room are on the east end of the house. One or both of the two west rooms served functions relating to Taylor's business. (author)

Fig. 4. Entrance and stair of the Taylor-Parke house. (Historic American Buildings Survey)

if somewhat jerry-rigged solution to a structural problem that presented itself in the service sphere of the house.

In plan, the house represents an intersection of the Quaker plan and the central-passage double-pile Georgian configuration (Fig. 3). A combination of the Georgian aesthetic with local forms such as the corner fireplace was common in Chester County during this transition period. In Taylor's synthesis, the internal asymmetry probably grew out of a desire to place the stair directly opposite the main entrance. This arrangement reduces the size of the west front room and creates a larger room to the east of the entrance. The unusual steepness of the staircase was required to reduce its depth and to accommodate an equally unusual arched passage behind it. The passage originally connected the two front rooms and led to a basement stair. In these and other instances, Taylor devised original but practical means to approximate elements that were not part of the local vernacular traditions. Like his peers, he borrowed what appealed to him from houses with which he was familiar, but he had a broader exposure than many of his fellows. The Philadelphia country houses he observed combined formal Georgian attitudes and Palladian features with many vernacular elements. Similarly, Abiah Taylor II drew from many sources to create a well-considered design that suited his own needs.

The two large east rooms are the parlor and dining room; the latter communicates directly with the kitchen wing. The two west rooms appear to have been segregated as the business end of the house. Separate access to the northwest room is provided by the west side entrance, and the likelihood that this room served as Taylor's office is reinforced by a cash drawer beneath the interior sill of the west-facing window. Iron straps on the shutters of the southwest windows and hooks in the ceiling of that small room also suggest a business function. The straps provided extra security, and the hooks are believed to have been used for the business manager's bed—supposedly of a hammock type that could be pulled up during the day.

The interior scheme includes three corner fireplaces, fairly common in the local vernacular expression and found in four of the six extant Taylor dwellings. The popularization of that particular construction was most likely stimulated by the traditional Quaker plan, although the economy of the form appealed to many besides the Friends.

The interior of the Taylor-Parke house indicates a taste for plainness and quality. The spare staircase bears a chamfered newel post that supports a simple handrail without balusters. The chair rail is deeply molded and strong in profile, and the fielded paneling under the closed string staircase is an example of local joinery at its best (Fig. 4).

The style and detail of the two surviving original mantels appear sufficiently often in Chester County dwellings to suggest that these were accepted forms among those at the upper end of the social and economic scale. The small southwest room is dominated by a boldly proportioned corner fireplace with a ceiling-high overmantel. The deep mantel shelf and cornice combine ogee and ovolo moldings to create complex forms with strong projecting contours (Fig. 5). This fireplace shares a wall with the corner fireplace in the northwest room. In this case, the fireplace treatment is distinguished by a glass-paned cupboard in the overmantel (Fig. 6). Plain overmantel cupboards were not uncommon in Chester County, but the glass panes and the keystoned arch of Taylor's example were unusual enrichments. This room, which also contains the cash-drawer window and a ceiling-high, four-door cupboard with fielded panels, would have been an impressive office in which to transact business. It is most likely the room where Taylor placed his expensive secretary desk, one of the few possessions—besides his fine house—in which he must have felt a twinge of un-Quakerly pride.[31]

To construct a house with decorative restraint was clearly within the contemporary aesthetic of Chester County domestic architecture. This plain style reflects a fortuitous dovetailing of practical concerns, economic and technical capability, a common English

31. Estate of Abiah Taylor II.

Fig. 5. Mantel in the southwest room of the Taylor-Parke house. Also visible is the ceiling hook that is said to have accommodated a hammock-type bed. (Historic American Buildings Survey)

architectural heritage, provincial priorities, and a shared orientation toward plainness as a virtue, rather than any conscious choice or establishment of a "Quaker style."

Although Friends did not create the plain style to accommodate their beliefs, it would be a mistake completely to dismiss the role of their religion in reinforcing the use of the plain style and its entrenchment in areas of Quaker hegemony. Friends did not refrain from establishing unique patterns of dress, speech, and education, as well as distinct legal, social, and political practices that were based on Quaker tenets. However, when prevailing attitudes, behaviors, and artifacts coincided with their beliefs, Friends comfortably retained them over long periods of time.[32] In such a homogeneous community that was largely dominated by members of the Society of Friends, the Anglo-American plain style would have been strengthened and sustained by its support in the Quaker community. The plain style was further perpetuated as it became the prevailing local tradition and was adopted by Quakers and non-Quakers alike in an increasingly diverse Chester County.

32. See Moore's essay elsewhere in this volume.

Fig. 6. Detail of the northwest room of the Taylor-Parke house, showing the glass-paned cabinet in the overmantel and the cash drawer in the sill of the window. (Historic American Buildings Survey)

Only a step outside the norm—some obvious departure— would allow the issue of Quaker influence on any specific dwelling to be isolated for more accurate evaluation. If Abiah Taylor II had constructed his house with a pedimented entrance like the one at Cliveden, or if he had added fluted pilasters to his plain arched passage behind the stair, it would be obvious that he had violated certain codes. He would have gone beyond not only local architectural traditions but also his Quaker community's interpretation of what was acceptable for even a wealthy man. That same degree of elaboration and fashionability would have had a different reading among Philadelphia Quakers, who had a more liberal view.

But Taylor's house did not flaunt Friends' testimonies, family tradition, or assumptions of his cultural group. Since those values and attitudes were so interwoven with local building patterns, it cannot be said from the evidence of the house itself whether Taylor conformed because of religious conviction, aesthetics, social and economic conservatism, available expertise, or a combination of these factors. Only the stark stair rail, plain even by local standards and almost public in the statement it makes just inside the entrance, can inform modern speculation.

Extrinsic information is necessary to fill out the picture. Taylor's life, as revealed in his legal and financial papers, public records, and local diaries, conforms, with the jarring exception of his indebtedness, to the mores of his Quaker community and the basic conservatism of the area. His relative sophistication and taste for quality can be explained by his urban exposure. Any conflict Taylor experienced between Quaker ideals and the luxuries permitted by prosperity was shared with most well-to-do Quakers of his day.[33] The Society of Friends did not question the prerogatives of wealth or social status retained from its English background, and this attitude complicated the requirements of the plain style of life.[34] To live moderately according to one's station did not necessarily mean asceticism, but the line was a fine one to draw. The rural interpretation of such matters was more strict than that in urban areas, and the "mansion house" speaks of Taylor's worldly success with appropriate restraint. He was, however, no ascetic.

He is best understood as an estate builder with membership in a religious group that encouraged economic success but condemned financial imprudence. His independence from that group and his broader perspective are evident, not so much in his extensive land holdings around the state as in his continuing indebtedness and in the resulting religious disenfranchisement he was willing to tolerate. The record indicates he also maintained, until his death, a standard of living befitting his station, the respect of his community, and his ability to borrow.[35]

The attitudes and values associated with the rural conservative combined with cosmopolitan taste are the most obvious forces embodied in Abiah Taylor's substantial and carefully detailed farmhouse. Beyond that, the structure itself and its relationship to the common vernacular expression appear to have more to do with social and economic status and prevailing Anglo-American architectural practices than with any singular Quaker tenet. Abiah Taylor's assumptions about house form did not differ significantly from those of his peers of equal wealth and station, and only in a few individualized details does his house reveal that the amalgam of his social, political, aesthetic, and religious conservatism was tempered by a surprising independence and élan.

33. William J. Frost, *The Quaker Family in Colonial America* (New York: St. Martin's Press, 1973), p. 190.

34. Ibid., pp. 196–97; Tolles, *Meeting Houses*, pp. 109–13. Quaker egalitarianism did not infer a communist disavowal of class distinctions, and a hierarchical view of society was explicitly accepted by Quaker apologists William Penn and Robert Barclay. However, decent respect was due to all men, and each was required to live modestly within his means and his station.

35. Miscellaneous papers, Abiah Taylor Estate.

17

THOMAS C. HUBKA

The New England Farmhouse Ell:
Fact and Symbol of Nineteenth-Century
Farm Improvement

Between 1800 and 1850, the common New England farm was spatially and functionally reorganized. Perhaps the most pronounced aspect of this development was the widespread adoption of the farmhouse ell, which extended outward from the major domestic building to form an L-shaped plan (Fig. 1). This ell contained the farm kitchen, an important room that previously had been incorporated within the central-chimney farmhouse on most eighteenth-century farms. By 1850, the new ell linked a series of work rooms in an increasingly standardized arrangement that usually included a kitchen, a kitchen workroom, a wagon house, a wood house, and a workshop. This organization became so popular with New England farmers that, by 1867, an agricultural writer even cautioned against the excesses of ell building. He recommended a more compact plan, "rather than buildings stretching off in a continuous line, as we too often see where ell upon ell is added to the main structure."[1] New England farmers, however, found great advantage in their "ell upon ell" system, and they continued to build versions of it well into the twentieth century.

The New England farmhouse ell has antecedents in the building traditions that English settlers brought with them to America. Attached buildings were often found among high-style and vernacular building complexes of the colonial period. In spite of these precedents, however, the vast majority of New England houses constructed before 1800 included all major domestic rooms within the principal dwelling. Irregularly placed adjoining buildings were generally used for minor support activities, such as wood or vehicle storage. During the next fifty years, the placement of kitchens within connecting ells gradually became popular for all segments of society, signaling fundamental change in the pattern of living for rural New Englanders.

Perhaps the most important reason that farmers began to reorganize their buildings was a gradual shift in farm production from a self-sufficient economy to one increasingly structured by multiple commercial enterprises.[2] Although farming for self-sufficiency continued to be significant, New England farmers, like those in all parts

1. *Maine Board of Agriculture, Twelfth Annual Report of the Secretary* (Augusta, Maine: Stevens and Sayward, 1867), p. 30.

2. Several leading agricultural historians of New England emphasize this point. See, for example, Clarence H. Danhof's *Change in Agriculture: The Northern United States, 1820–1870* (Cambridge: Harvard University Press, 1969).

Fig. 1. A typical New England farmhouse ell at the Marston-Lawrence farm, North Yarmouth, Maine. The ell was built in 1864. From *Big House, Little House, Back House, Barn: The Connected Farm Buildings of New England.* (author; all illustrations for this essay appear courtesy of University Press of New England)

of America, adopted more commercial practices so that they might acquire the goods and services of an expanding industrial economy. These market changes had a fundamental effect on the pattern of building and living on many New England farms.

In the seventeenth- and eighteenth-century building system, a kitchen located within the major domestic building effectively served the needs of a small-scale colonial farm operation (Fig. 2). In the nineteenth century, the commercialization of kitchen-related activities, such as the production of butter, influenced many farmers to construct their kitchens in readily expandable ell additions. The specialization of work activities in the separate rooms of the ell had distinct advantages over the all-purpose, one-room colonial kitchen. It was also consistent with a continuing trend toward the abandonment of medieval communal customs in favor of more spatially differentiated room arrangements.

The placement of the kitchen in an attached structure or ell was an English practice known to the colonists, but, for various reasons, it was not commonly selected by rural inhabitants.[3] The practice of kitchen-ell construction seems to have developed slowly in eighteenth-century towns. By 1800, houses with kitchens located within attached ells were beginning to appear among the structures built by New England's gentlemen farmers and town dwellers. The kitchen-ell arrangement was used in some early Federal mansions such as the Deering estate of Portland, Maine, and vernacular builders also developed a popular version of the kitchen ell attached to their one-room-deep, hall-parlor houses. While some farmers adopted the kitchen-ell arrangement, many others continued to build houses with integral kitchens until technical innovations made ell construction more desirable.

One of the most significant changes in the colonial pattern of New England housing was effected by the introduction of the stove.

3. The practice of locating a kitchen in the ell seems to have become popular for all levels of society after 1800. A survey of three hundred and fifty houses in southwest Maine found no original kitchens built in ells, although many were moved to this arrangement after 1800. Thomas C. Hubka, *Big House, Little House, Back House, Barn: The Connected Farm Buildings of New England* (Hanover, N.H.: University Press of New England, 1984), p. 38.

This transformation occurred between 1820 and 1860 during a period of intensive rural remodeling and expansion.[4] No factor was more influential to the rapid popularization of the kitchen ell than was the availability of the cast-iron stove. It enabled common farmers to install practical and efficient heat sources away from a single core, causing the gradual elimination of the central-chimney fireplace system and facilitating the expansion of work spaces on the nineteenth-century New England farm. The introduction of multiple stoves also allowed for a greater differentiation of room uses throughout the house, fostering the post–1840 diversity of domestic rooms such as the living room, dining room, and individual bedrooms (Fig. 3).

The size and shape of the connecting kitchen ell took many forms, but the linear pattern of room organization became standardized in New England by the middle of the nineteenth century (Fig. 4). The kitchen, which continued to be the major work and gathering place for the farm family, was almost always the first room in the extended ell. It was followed by a kitchen-related workroom that was often given a name derived from the principal activity conducted in this space. "Wash room," "milk room," "buttery," and "pantry" were all common. The practice of moving the stove to this back room for working comfort during the summer is apparently the reason that many modern owners of these buildings refer to this room as the "summer kitchen." The term does not seem to have been used during the nineteenth century.

The next room was usually a firewood storage area or "wood

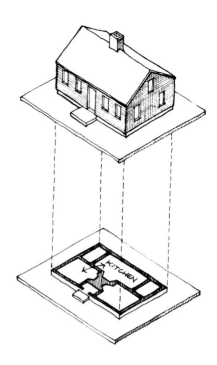

Fig. 2. Plan and form of a Cape Cod house, showing the integral kitchen location. From *Big House, Little House, Back House, Barn: The Connected Farm Buildings of New England*. (author)

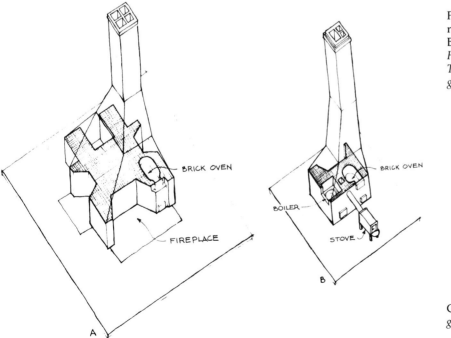

Fig. 3. New England kitchen chimneys. A. Pre–1830 fireplace chimney. B. Post–1850 stove chimney. From *Big House, Little House, Back House, Barn: The Connected Farm Buildings of New England*. (author)

4. William J. Keep, "Early American Cooking Stoves," *Old-Time New England* 22 (1931):70–87.

Elements and Forms of Vernacular Buildings / 163

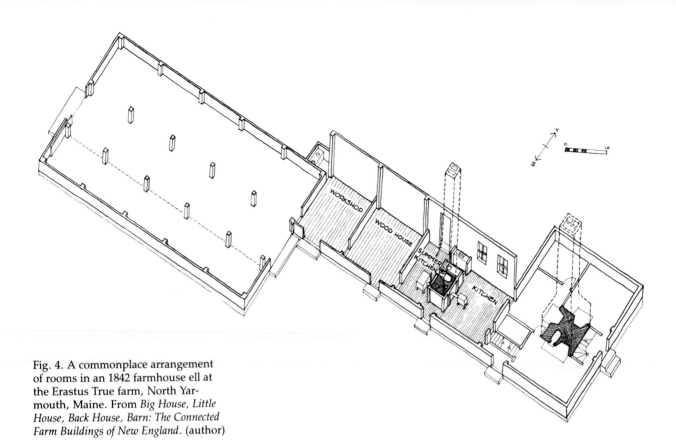

Fig. 4. A commonplace arrangement of rooms in an 1842 farmhouse ell at the Erastus True farm, North Yarmouth, Maine. From *Big House, Little House, Back House, Barn: The Connected Farm Buildings of New England.* (author)

5. Benjamin, *The American Builder's Companion* (1830; rpt. New York: Da-Capo Press, 1972).

house." Although the order of the following rooms varied, most farm ells also included a storage area for wagons and carriages, a farm workshop, and a general storage room. In the New England tradition, an "outhouse" or "privy" was usually built into or alongside the last room of the ell. Farmers could obtain this linear form by building a continuous structure stretching out from the house, but, more often, several existing buildings were moved into place and joined together.

The New England farmhouse ell employed the latest nineteenth-century planning concepts and technological devices that were available to most farmers. One of the more common "improvements" to the New England farm was the "set-kettle" or "boiler," an iron pot built into a masonry shell alongside a chimney. It was used for cooking, washing, and animal food preparation. The boiler was an eighteenth-century European development introduced in the Federal period to estates like the Rundlet-May house of Portsmouth, New Hampshire. Early nineteenth-century pattern books, such as Asher Benjamin's *American Builder's Companion*, pictured boilers and thus contributed to their rapid popularization throughout New England.[5] By 1850, the boiler was a familiar feature of the kitchen ell and was usually built into a compact chimney system that included stove flues and a brick bake oven.

The entire ell was considered to be a place of applied technology and labor-saving devices, including a brick cistern that was usu-

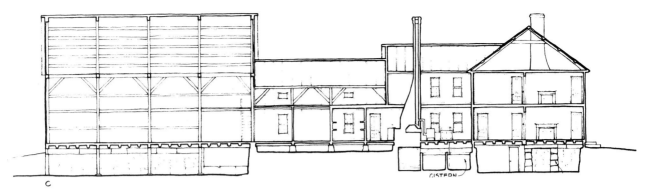

C

Fig. 5. An elaborate assemblage of
work spaces within an ell at the
Marston-Lawrence farm, North Yar-
mouth, Maine. From *Big House, Little
House, Back House, Barn: The Connected
Farm Buildings of New England.* (author)

ally located underneath the kitchen, as well as metal pumps, sinks,
ice containers, and an increasing variety of hand-powered tools and
food-processing machines, such as the crank-and-barrel churn. Together, these rooms and their technological improvements supported a combination of farming and home-industry activities that
usually included the production of butter and cheese, clothes and
leather products, handicraft and woodworking items, all for home
use and commercial sale. Most of these activities took place in the
kitchen and its adjoining workroom, performed by women in daily
and seasonal cycles of production.

The spatial relationship of work tasks within the farmhouse ell
is demonstrated at the Marston farm of North Yarmouth, Maine
(Fig. 5). Its large ell was built in 1864 and contains an arrangement
of rooms considered advanced for the period. The rooms of the ell
formed the center of a farm production system that also included
grain and corn storage on the second floor of the ell, a cistern underneath the kitchen, a cellar milk room for buttermaking, a cellar
arch beneath the fireplace of the main house for perishable food
storage, and a barn cellar for manure and root-crop storage.

The development of the kitchen ell is also associated with a
significant reorganization of the yard system that surrounded the
New England farm (Fig. 6). The ell standardized a three-part division among frontyard, dooryard, and barnyard that corresponded
to the functional division of the farm buildings themselves into formal house, kitchen ell, and barn. In the colonial period, most rural
houses and barns faced south with only minor regard for the orientation of the adjacent road. The development of the ell allowed
the kitchen and its workrooms to maintain a south-facing orientation, while the major dwelling and its formal frontyard usually
faced the road.

Growth of the farmhouse ell represented a distinct break from
traditional vernacular construction practices and signaled the establishment of a flexible modular structural system. New England
builders perfected a framework of uniform bays that could be expanded indefinitely and subdivided at any point to produce rooms

Elements and Forms of Vernacular Buildings / 165

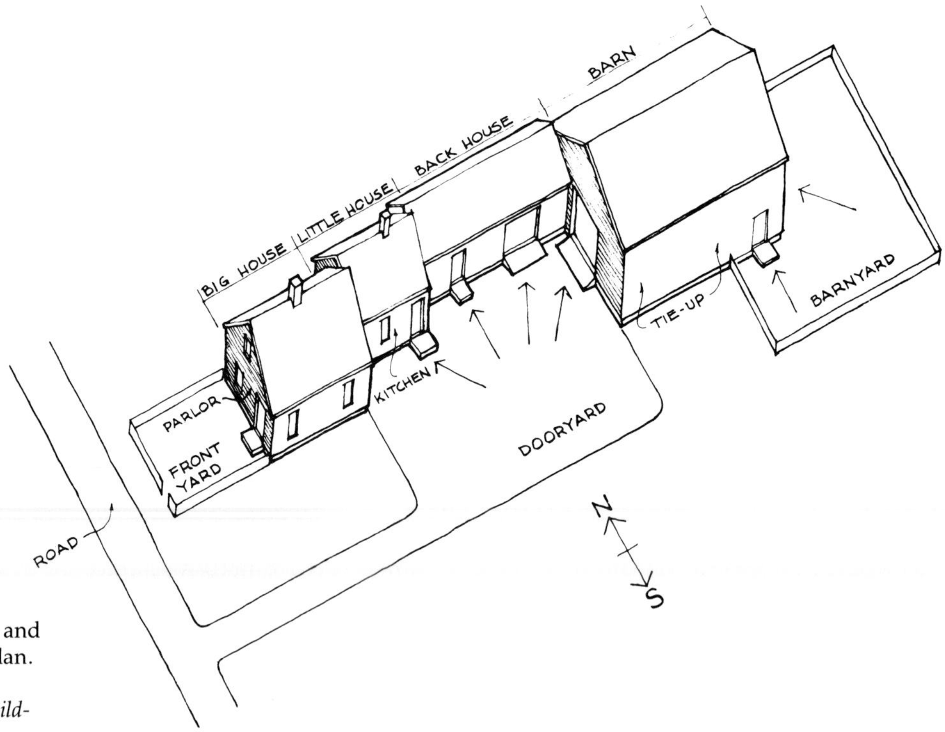

Fig. 6. A New England farmhouse and ell, showing a typical three-yard plan. From *Big House, Little House, Back House, Barn: The Connected Farm Buildings of New England*. (author)

in various sizes. This was the same type of module expansion system that New England builders also used to extend their barns. By 1840, the typical structural system for the ell combined both balloon framing and older mortise-and-tenon techniques. The result was a framework of great flexibility that allowed farmers to accommodate the changes of nineteenth-century agricultural production.

The standardization and popularization of the multipurpose, technologically advanced New England ell was a progressive response to changing economic circumstances in the nineteenth century. In the face of agricultural competition from other areas of the country, New England farmers had little choice but to abandon traditional practices in favor of a more commercialized, mixed-farming and home-industry system. They adopted the ell because it was well suited to this diversification. Despite such aggressive modernization, however, New England farmers could not change the essential nature of their agricultural system. They ultimately could not adapt their operations to the mechanized single-crop agricultural capitalism that came to be so profitable in other regions. Thus, the New England farmhouse ell is both a fact and a symbol of a new system of agriculture that was itself rapidly becoming obsolete. Today, the farmhouse ell has an old-fashioned, antiquated appearance. During the nineteenth century, however, it was built by people who considered it to represent the most progressive form for their New England farms.

V. Buildings in Their Social Contexts

18

JANET HUTCHISON

The Cure for Domestic Neglect:
Better Homes in America, 1922–1935

At the end of World War I, a group of nationally prominent individuals began to express a concern about the role of women and domestic architecture in America. These people perceived that the era of the twenties was different from previous periods. As a result of war mobilization, more women were in the work force. Divorce rates were also rising, and new inventions—notably the automobile—were giving women greater potential freedom from the home. Moreover, data from the census of 1920 revealed that less than half of the American people owned their own homes, an issue of crucial importance to those who believed that American freedom and safety rested with a home-owning democratic population. Both the American family and national security seemed to be threatened.

In 1922, concerned individuals formulated a unique housing campaign, Better Homes in America. The purpose of this campaign was to cure home neglect through an educational program that combined the nineteenth-century republican values of thrift and self-reliance with twentieth-century household technology. While the prescribed woman's place remained in the home, promoters believed that the modern twentieth-century housewife should be a trained expert, discriminating consumer, and moral arbitrator within a defined architectural setting. The Better Homes campaign promoted these goals through visual instruction.

Marie Meloney, editor of *The Delineator*, a Butterick publication with a circulation of over 1 million female readers, was a principal founder of the Better Homes Movement. Using *The Delineator* as an instrument, Meloney obtained the endorsement of federal and state officials, including President Harding and twenty-eight state governors. She established a National Advisory Council with Vice-President Coolidge as honorary head and Secretary of Commerce Herbert Hoover as chairman. Other members of the council included Secretary of Agriculture Henry Wallace and Julius Barnes, president of the United States Chamber of Commerce. The editorial offices of *The Delineator* became the bureau of information and general headquarters of the Better Homes Movement. This combination of government approval and magazine circulation contributed to the success of the campaign. In addition, the campaign benefited

Fig. 1. The National Better Home, built on the Capitol Mall of Washington, D.C., in 1922. From *Books of a Thousand Homes*, published in 1923, p. 25. (Home Owners' Service Institute)

both politicians and *The Delineator*, offering the former a means to address voting women about their concern for the American home, while providing the latter with justification as a service-oriented magazine.[1]

By 1924, government officials took greater control, readjusting the organizational structure of the movement. Better Homes in America was incorporated as a national educational organization with an executive board and advisory council that were expanded to include both government officials and prominent representatives from women's clubs, welfare and health organizations, and farm and home bureaus. James Ford, Harvard professor of social ethics, was appointed executive director. Although *The Delineator* relinquished official sponsorship, the magazine continued to support the campaign enthusiastically. Moreover, Meloney and George Wilder, owner of *The Delineator*, retained influential positions on the executive committee.[2]

To launch the Better Homes campaign and gain nationwide attention, the National Better Home was erected in Washington, D.C., in 1922 (Fig. 1). It was built by the General Federation of Women's Clubs with the support of the national Better Homes organization, *The Delineator*, and the contributions of industries and businesses. The home embodied deliberate messages designed to educate the American viewers. The first message lay in the location of the National Better Home on public ground behind the Treasury Building near the Shaw Monument and the White House. Moreover, President Harding officiated at the 1922 opening ceremony of

1. "Better Homes in America," *The Delineator*, October 1922, p. 17.
2. "Better Homes in America," *The Delineator*, April 1924, p. 2.

Fig. 2. President Harding at the 1922 opening ceremony of the National Better Home. From *Books of a Thousand Homes*, p. 41. (Home Owners' Service Institute)

the National Better Home (Fig. 2). In these ways a national concern with the American home and with the role of women was demonstrated.[3]

The design and furnishings of the house also contained symbolic value, emphasizing both the romance of history and the benefits of modern technology. These messages were not left to individual interpretation. *The Delineator* provided readers with deliberate direction through description. The National Better Home was planned as a modern replica of the "Home Sweet Home" house, a seventeenth-century building in Easthampton, Long Island. *The Delineator* informed its readers that the "Home Sweet Home" house was the birthplace of John Howard Payne, author of the famous song. In his youth, Payne immigrated to Europe where he wrote his song in 1822. He died in Tunis in 1852. Thirty years later, his body was brought to the United States and reinterred near Washington at Oak Hill. The ceremony was attended by President Hayes, his cabinet, and a military escort.[4]

The John Payne house was an appropriate choice for reproduction, for it appealed to a national consciousness on several historical levels. First, the seventeenth-century colonial house embodied community and familial values to the twentieth-century reader. In addition, the image of the nineteenth-century exile yearning for his homeland was particularly poignant after World War I. Payne himself had received government and presidential recognition through ceremonial burial. His popular song romanticizing the American home represented both music and culture. Furthermore, the centennial of the song was celebrated in 1922.

Although the modern "Home Sweet Home" house attempted to evoke the image of the seventeenth-century dwelling, the build-

3. Donn Barber, "Our First National Better Home: The Modern Version of Home Sweet Home," *The Delineator*, September 1923, pp. 2, 20.

4. Ibid., p. 2.

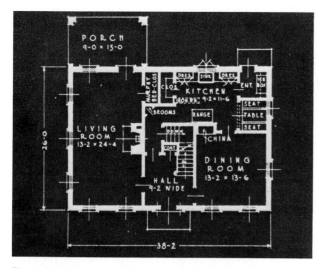

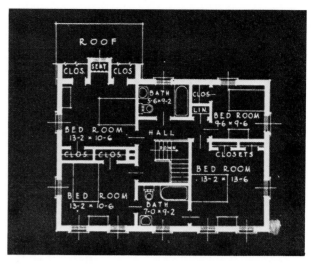

Fig. 3. First-floor plan of the National Better Home. From *Books of a Thousand Homes*, p. 24. (Home Owners' Service Institute)

Fig. 4. Second-floor plan of the National Better Home. From *Books of a Thousand Homes*, p. 24. (Home Owners' Service Institute)

ers' intentions, plans, and materials differed. The original Payne house had a hall-parlor plan with a central chimney, a small entry, and two upstairs chambers. It was constructed of timber frame with clapboard siding and a shingled roof. During the nineteenth century, the cladding was replaced with shingles. The builders of the original Payne house had expressed their traditional values to the surrounding community.

In contrast, the designers of the twentieth-century building made deliberate cultural mandates to a national audience. The 1922 National Better Home had a central passage (Fig. 3). To the right of the passage, the living room extended the entire width of the house. The dining room and breakfast nook were located to the left of the passage, and the kitchen connected the living room and breakfast nook. A central stairway led to a second-story passage surrounded by four bedrooms and a bathroom (Fig. 4). To modernize, the builders of the National Better Home substituted concrete blocks, Portland cement, and other twentieth-century commercial products for seventeenth-century materials.

In keeping with the architecture of the house, the furniture contained historic symbolism within a twentieth-century context of modernity. According to *The Delineator*, the living room was fitted with a colonial small-paned glass door, colonial gray paper, a colonial chair, a colonial tilt-top table, an old-style fireplace of rough red brick with colonial andirons, and a narrow colonial mantel beneath a colonial painted mahogany mirror. None of the objects was actually old. Rather, the magazine gave them validation through historic imagery. The living room also stressed the importance of instruction

Fig. 5. Living room of the National Better Home, showing "colonial" furnishings. From *Books of a Thousand Homes*, p. 140. (Home Owners' Service Institute)

Fig. 6. Kitchen of the National Better Home, where the emphasis was on efficiency and cleanliness. From *Books of a Thousand Homes*, p. 140. (Home Owners' Service Institute)

5. Lida Hafford, "Furnishing the 'Home Sweet Home' House," *The Delineator*, April 1924, pp. 2, 74, 76.

and culture in the home: books, a piano, a phonograph, and copies of masterpieces all confronted the viewer (Fig. 5). Unmistakable allusions to American history and authority were made by a reproduction portrait of Abraham Lincoln and a mahogany sofa similar to one owned by the Washington family.[5]

While the living room was designed and described to evoke sentimental images of family unity, the kitchen conveyed efficiency and cleanliness (Fig. 6). Conforming to rules established by home economists in the Department of Agriculture, the kitchen concentrated on modernity, convenience, order, and sanitation. An enameled sink was set at a specific height to avoid backaches. A double drainboard was designed to save dish-washing time. A worktable mounted on rollers, a clock, and a tin wastebasket all contributed to the scene. Also featured in the kitchen were washable wall coverings, cushioned cork linoleum, and a curved baseboard to eliminate the "dust gathering crack, unsanitary and annoying to the less than modern housewife."[6] The kitchen as the woman's workplace needed standardization and modernization.

Better Homes in America promoted its educational messages by public exhibition of the "Home Sweet Home" house and through coverage in *The Delineator* and newspapers. The national house fulfilled other goals of the movement as well. After the home was displayed on the Capitol Mall, it was moved to a site across from the Corcoran Gallery, where it was used as a training center for Girl Scouts of America. There, scouts learned the skills of hostessing and housekeeping in a proper environment.[7]

The Better Homes campaign also sponsored an annual contest of model demonstration houses planned by local committees around the country. Committee members decorated these homes in order to instruct viewers in aesthetics, thrift, and proper housekeeping. Houses were opened to the public during an annual Better Homes Week, and the National Advisory Council judged the demonstration homes, choosing a national winner. According to *The Delineator*, participation in Better Homes in America ranked as "the most important public work to which women in this country could give their time."[8] Apparently, many women agreed. In 1922, the first year of the movement, over five hundred committees exhibited homes. Over one thousand communities competed in 1923, and, by 1930, the national Better Homes administration claimed a total of 7,279 Better Homes committees.[9] The national Better Homes administration circulated guidelines formulated by experts, but local communities added their individual interpretations of the needs of the average American family.

The 1924 model home in Kalamazoo, Michigan, winner of first prize in the national contest, embodied one local response to the national campaign (Fig. 7). Like the National Better Home, the prize-winning dwelling displayed popular middle-class nineteenth-century notions of the home as the woman's sphere, and it applied these values within a modern context of comfort, convenience, and efficiency. However, the Kalamazoo house created a "new style of architecture, a home built around mother."[10] In effect, the 1924 Kalamazoo home represented an extension of the Better Homes concern to ameliorate domestic neglect. In addition to exhibiting the model home, the head of the Kalamazoo committee, Caroline Crane, published *Everyman's Home*, a book that described in detail the prize-winning house and its ideal inhabitants.

6. Ibid., p. 74.

7. Girl Scouts of America, Washington House Folder, Box 11, Better Homes in America Papers, Hoover Institute, Stanford, California.

8. Blanche Brace, "Good Homes: The Right of All Citizens," *The Delineator*, January 1925, p. 13.

9. The quantity of local committees showed an increased awareness of the Better Homes Movement, but Better Homes committees did not always manage to display houses. While the actual number of demonstration homes is difficult to determine, research suggests approximately a thousand houses were displayed throughout the country in 1930.

10. Brace, "Good Homes," p. 13; James Ford, "Chapter XXII Governmental and Other Educational Organizations: Better Homes in America," in *The Better Homes Manual*, ed. Blanche Halbert (Chicago: University of Chicago Press, 1931), p. 743.

Fig. 7. The Kalamazoo, Michigan, model home of 1924, winner of first prize in the national Better Homes contest. From *The Delineator*, February 1925, p. 2. (Butterick Publishing Company)

According to Crane, visitors to the Kalamazoo house entered a hall (Fig. 8). To their right, the living/dining room extended across the entire width of the dwelling. The "mother's room" was located on their left. Behind the mother's room was a bathroom. At the rear of the house was the kitchen, with doors leading to both the mother's room and the dining area. The girls' room, the boys' room, and another bathroom were located on the second floor (Fig. 9).

The living/dining room contained a couch and chairs in front of a central fireplace with a dining table and chairs set to one side (Fig. 10). The mother's room was furnished with a double bed, a crib, and a number of innovations for nursing and rocking the infant to sleep (Fig. 11). In accord with the Better Homes emphasis on efficiency, the kitchen was fitted with storage cupboards and modern utensils recommended by home economists (Fig. 12).

The Kalamazoo committee named the mother's room, bathroom, and kitchen *the mother's suite*. Ideally, the proximity of the mother's room to the kitchen allowed her to care for her baby while performing household tasks. The downstairs bathroom saved the woman steps. In addition, the bedroom and bathroom could be converted into a sickroom.[11]

Although Crane and *The Delineator* discussed the importance of the father's presence in the house, they failed to give him proper space—they defined the house as the woman's domain. While advocating men's participation in the home, Crane, *The Delineator*, and

11. Blanch Brace, "A Home Built around Mother," *The Delineator*, February 1925, pp. 2, 66, 68, and 71; Caroline Crane, *Everyman's Home* (New York: Doubleday, Page, and Company, 1925).

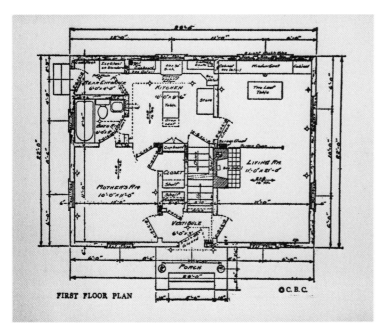

Fig. 8. First-floor plan of the Kalamazoo model home. From Caroline Crane's *Everyman's Home*, p. 12. (Doubleday and Company)

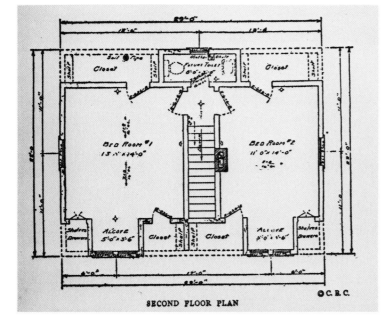

Fig. 9. Second-floor plan of the Kalamazoo model home. From *Everyman's Home*, p. 13. (Doubleday and Company)

Buildings in Their Social Contexts / 175

Fig. 10. Living/dining room of the Kalamazoo model home. From *Everyman's
Home*, p. 18. (Doubleday and Company)

Fig. 11. The "mother's room" of the
Kalamazoo model home. From *Every-
man's Home*, p. 138. (Doubleday and
Company)

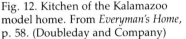

Fig. 12. Kitchen of the Kalamazoo model home. From *Everyman's Home*, p. 58. (Doubleday and Company)

the Better Homes Movement reinforced the nineteenth-century separation of spheres. The home built around a mother and a baby allowed the father only limited participation. He could read his newspaper in the living room after work or eat dinner with the family. Crane also gave the father a small workshop in the basement, a twentieth-century use of house space. Even though the imaginary father must have slept in the mother's room, his presence there was not mentioned. Thus, the Kalamazoo house displayed the Better Homes concentration on the mother as the trained supervisor of the domestic reformed environment; the man's place remained outside the home. Although the actual plan of the Kalamazoo dwelling was not unusual in 1924, the description of room usage and home furnishings marked an increased specialization and gender-identification of living and work space.[12]

According to *The Delineator*, adherence to and success of the Better Homes Movement could be seen in model homes such as the Kalamazoo prize winner, as well as through the existence of demonstration homes in such diverse places as Cleburne, Texas; New Haven, Connecticut; Montclair, New Jersey; Coxton, Kentucky; Santa Barbara, California; and Blue Grass, Minnesota. Additional proof could be derived from one visitor's experience.

In 1925, *The Delineator* recounted a story about an unidentified Italian mother that exemplified the reception of the goals of the movement as they were conveyed through a demonstration home. Although this example addressed the conversion of immigrants to the Better Homes Movement, campaign promoters felt that all

12. Brace, "Built around Mother," pp. 2, 66, 68.

Americans, especially rural people, miners, and blacks, would benefit from proper instruction. The immigrant woman, whose husband had made a "considerable" amount of money in the United States, entered a model dwelling with her children.

> She pointed to the fireplace exclaiming, "That's the fire to sit around and talk all together, not stand around on the sidewalks . . ." She noted the piano. In the kitchen she cried, "No grease! No smells! We must learn to live like that!" And, in the bedroom she observed, "In rooms like this clean minds. And this for clean bodies," she added as the quartet moved on to the bedroom. As she turned to go from the Better Home, she said, with tears in her eyes to her children, "Here is the place where they learn you how to live! This is what America means!"[13]

The Italian woman expressed the goals of the Better Homes campaign: health, learning, and culture within an American setting.

The Delineator and the Better Homes movement declared that the problems of the United States could be solved through specific instruction in the construction, organization, and supervision of proper homes. The rooms of the house that the Italian woman visited revealed the ideology of the campaign. The story also exemplified negative middle-class American beliefs about immigrants' houses and lives. In effect, the Better Homes campaign attempted to design ethnicity out of the appropriate landscape. Assuming that immigrants interacted outside on the sidewalks, the movement sought to bring them indoors to the proper controlled domestic sphere. Within the dwelling, immigrants needed dictates on cleanliness of kitchens, minds, and bodies, for they, assumed *The Delineator* fearfully, lived in filthy ignorance. Visual instruction could convert viewers, thereby insuring stability within the home, the community, and the nation.

For campaign supporters, the goals of encouraging cohesiveness in the home and training the housewife to her role justified the Better Homes Movement. Through model homes, proponents instructed Americans in the importance of the woman to the domestic environment. From all sectors of the movement came verbal and visual mandates defining correct American living. These dictates combined a popular sentimentalized version of the American past with standards of modern regulation and efficiency in a program designed to cure twentieth-century neglect of the American home.

13. Brace, "Good Homes," p. 52.

19

PAUL GROTH

"Marketplace" Vernacular Design:
The Case of Downtown Rooming Houses

In every American city, thousands of people live in "invisible" homes, all within a short walking distance of the central business district. Stores, restaurants, nightclubs, and bars occupy the ground floors on these blocks, and their visually insistent awnings and neon signs conceal the small, often unmarked doors that lead to second- and third-floor commercial housing. It is all too easy to miss structures built as rooming houses. Quite appropriately, two recent studies call the people who live in such homes "The Unseen Elderly" and "Invisible."[1]

This visual vacuum challenges students of vernacular architecture with new twists to four old methodological issues: focusing, sampling, classifying, and characterizing. First, the social needs of people currently living in unusual and invisible housing cry out for the focus of scholars who are interested in building types. Second, because so many examples of the buildings still exist in complicated urban situations, it is necessary to experiment with effective and defensible sampling methods. Third, in order to classify residential hotel buildings, it is necessary to understand them not so much by their form but as they relate to the social position and purchasing power of their occupants. Finally, such buildings cannot be easily understood in terms common to vernacular or popular design. The compromises of form gradually developed between building owners and their tenants are better characterized by the term *marketplace design*.

In many American cities, a large share of the downtown housing stock is made up of single-room units, usually without kitchens or private baths. Most often, these homes are for rent in rooming houses and hotels. In San Francisco, a full tenth of the city's housing units are single rooms. In America as a whole, between 1 and 2 million people live permanently in such homes—more than in all of the country's public housing. Hotel residents are generally single, and their existence is a reminder that a household is not always a family. In 1930, a third of New York City's population over fifteen years old was single; today in New York the number of single elderly women living alone is equal to the population of Des Moines. For

1. J. Kevin Eckert, *The Unseen Elderly: A Study of Marginally Subsistent Hotel Dwellers* (San Diego: Campanile Press, 1980); St. Louis Institute of Applied Gerontology, *The Invisible Elderly* (Washington, D.C.: National Council on the Aging, 1976).

2. James Ford, *Slums and Housing: History, Conditions, Policy with Special Reference to New York City* (Cambridge: Harvard University Press, 1936), pp. 337, 752; Michael Mostoller, "The Single State: Shelters, Lodging Houses, Boarding Houses, and Residential Hotels" (manuscript, Columbia University School of Architecture and Planning, 1981). On the lack of interest in nonfamily and single people's housing, see an excellent study by Arnold Rose, "Interest in the Living Arrangements of the Urban Unattached," *American Journal of Sociology* 53 (1947):483–93.

3. On San Francisco's losses in single-room residences, see Scott Dowdee, "The Incidence of Change in the Residential Hotel Stock of San Francisco, 1975–1980: A Report to the San Francisco Department of City Planning" (Berkeley: University of California Department of City and Regional Planning, 1980), p. 38. On New York, see Susan Baldwin, "Salvaging S.R.O. Housing," *City Limits: The News Magazine of New York City Housing and Neighborhoods*, April 1981, p. 15. For national surveys on the situations of fragile elderly, see the California Governor's Office of Planning and Research and the California Department of Housing and Community Development, "Residential Hotels: A Vanishing Housing Resource," proceedings from a conference held in San Francisco, 11–12 June 1981. A terse and authoritative review is included in Frances E. Werner and David B. Bryson, "A Guide to the Preservation and Maintenance of Single Room Occupancy (SRO) Housing, Part 1," *The Clearinghouse Review*, April 1982, pp. 999–1002. See also United States Senate, Special Committee on Aging, *Single Room Occupancy: A Need for National Concern*, information paper, 1978.

4. The most notable exception is a study of present-day conditions: John K. C. Liu, *San Francisco Chinatown Hotels* (San Francisco: Chinatown Neighborhood Improvement Resource Center, 1980). This work provides detailed drawings and complete resident pro-

many of these people, renting rooms in hotels has been their choice of making a home.[2]

There is now a crisis in the downtown world of single-room occupancy. Tenants are losing their supply of inexpensive housing units at staggering rates. Between 1979 and 1985, San Francisco lost six thousand single-room units—the equivalent of twenty-five large housing projects. In the same period, New York lost almost two-thirds of its units. The majority of today's tenants in rooming houses and hotels are elderly. Their independence is fragile and highly intertwined with the unique setting and convenience of their hotel buildings. In a real sense, the residents' lives are as endangered as their one-room homes.[3]

Examining the available literature about the single-room occupancy crisis reveals a large void. Sociologists and social workers fully describe the human situation. Urban planners count units lost and measure rental categories based on computer printouts of property tax roles. Policy planners have written about the changes needed in housing codes and federal programs. Yet, very little literature describes the building types or the social history woven into the available range of single-room housing.[4]

The buildings themselves are an important aspect of current problems. As one single-room housing activist put it, "We're Johnny-come-latelys compared to the buildings we're working with."[5] The physical shells and original intentions of the hotels set clear limits on what activists can do. In this case, social need calls for academic research that can explain the physical form and history of single-room housing. Students of vernacular architecture are uniquely prepared to perform such a task.

A bewildering range and number of structures greet anyone who sets out to study urban buildings. In order to ascertain what typical single-room housing looked like historically, random samples were drawn from listings of hotels, boardinghouses, lodging houses, and furnished rooms in the 1880, 1910, and 1930 city directories of San Francisco. From twenty-six hundred possible listings, this process yielded a manageable study group of three hundred buildings. Insurance maps, water company records, and the street surveyor's forms from the Works Projects Administration's Real Property Survey supplied information for demolished buildings. Tax assessors' records described extant ones. Thus, for each of the sampled buildings, it was possible to determine the location, basic building outline, functions of various floors and adjacent plots, configuration of light wells, and number of baths. In some cases, basic floor plans were also available.

Classifying the buildings at first presented a formidable problem. Categories in the city directories and names of the establishments often correlated poorly with building types and neighborhood status. Before 1920, names were particularly fluid: the Isabelle Grant Lodging House could be renamed the Central Hotel for a year and then become the Evergreen Club—all with no corresponding remodeling or neighborhood change.

The most useful classifying scheme proved to be socioeconomic status of the housing tenants. As might be expected, the rent each class could afford to pay for single-room housing clearly influenced building form. From the 1860s through the 1950s, four distinct classes of people lived in four ranks of single-room hotel homes. The wealthy lived in palace hotels; middle-class professionals and business people lived in middle-priced hotels; skilled laborers lived in inexpensive rooming houses; and migrant or casual laborers lived in cheap lodging houses.[6]

Neither facades nor total size of buildings distinguished the four social classes of hotels, but provision of plumbing did. At least among structures built after 1890, hotel housing can be sorted effectively by using a plumbing ratio: the number of bathrooms divided by the number of guest rooms.[7] By the 1890s, the best single-room homes—those in palace hotels—each had a private bath. Not until the 1920s did most middle-priced hotels have a one-to-one bath ratio. By 1910, rooming houses had reached one-to-four or one-to-six ratios. At the bottom of the scale were the cheap lodging houses built for migrant and casual laborers whose commercial homes had a plumbing ratio of no better than one to twelve in 1910.[8]

From 1880 to 1930, the third rank of hotel housing—the rooming houses for skilled laborers—made up about one-third of San Francisco's single-room housing. The evolution of those buildings provides a good example of the architectural issues raised by hotel housing in general.

Up to the 1880s, many people in urban centers lived in boardinghouses, so named because the tenants could take meals there at a large family-style dining table. By the turn of the century in most cities, boarding had been largely replaced by merely rooming—that is, tenants rented single rooms and took meals elsewhere. In Boston between 1885 and 1895, the proportion of roomers among all people in single-room housing shifted from 60 to 86 percent.[9]

In the older cities on the East Coast, the shift from boarding to rooming caused few changes in building types. Both boarding and rooming establishments were originally single-family houses built close to downtown in previous generations. Most typically, the owners had moved to new residential districts and had leased their old houses to women who hoped to make a living by renting rooms. When landladies gave up providing meals, they had much less work and servant expense. They could also rent out the dining room, just as they had already rented out the parlors.

The room sizes and arrangements in these improvised rooming houses did not adapt ideally to the new functions (Fig. 1). The parlors and major bedrooms were often too large and expensive for one person to rent, yet they offered no privacy when two people rented them jointly. Tiny, cheap side rooms were always in demand

files of several hotels, along with discussions of the hotels' plans and entrances.

5. Richard Livingston in California Governor's Office of Planning and Research, "Residential Hotels."

6. For a full discussion of the sampling and categorization plus detailed descriptions of all four social and building ranks, see Paul Groth, "Forbidden Housing: The Evolution and Exclusion of Hotels, Boarding Houses, Rooming Houses, and Lodging Houses in American Cities, 1880–1930" (Ph.D. diss., University of California at Berkeley, 1983), pp. 28–36, 47–287.

7. Two separate toilet rooms (without bathtubs) equal one full bath. Room sinks are not included in the plumbing ratio, but any later refinements of this ratio should set a reasonable factor for them.

8. The rise of plumbing as a feature of modern vernacular buildings and the influences of electricity and other utilities on urban life and architectural forms deserve more attention. For steps in the right direction, see May N. Stone, "The Plumbing Paradox: American Attitudes towards Late Nineteenth Century Domestic Sanitary Arrangements," *Winterthur Portfolio* 14 (1979):283–309; Albert Eide Parr, "Heating, Lighting, Plumbing, and Human Relations," *Landscape* 19 (1970):9–13; David Glassberg, "The Design of Reform: The Public Bath Movement in America," *American Studies* 20 (1979):5–21; Mark H. Rose and John G. Clark, "Light, Heat, and Power: Energy Choices in Kansas City, Wichita, and Denver, 1900–1935," *Journal of Urban History* 5 (1979):340–64.

9. Albert Benedict Wolfe, *The Lodging House Problem in Boston* (Boston: Houghton, Mifflin and Company, 1906), pp. 6, 38, 42–44. Listings in San Francisco's city directories show parallel changes in the proportions of rooming houses compared to boardinghouses during the 1880s and 1890s.

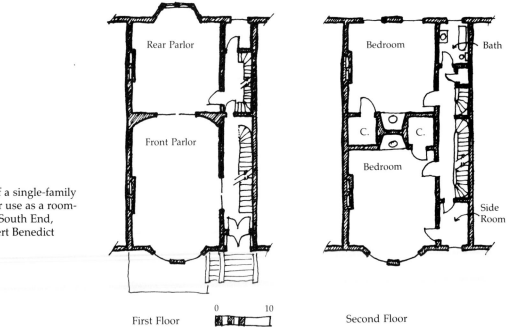

Fig. 1. Typical plans of a single-family row house adapted for use as a rooming house in Boston's South End, about 1900. After Albert Benedict Wolfe. (author)

Rear Parlor

Front Parlor

Bedroom

Bath

Bedroom

Side Room

C.   C.

0   10

First Floor   Second Floor

but rarely available. Building codes made it either illegal or difficult to partition the larger rooms into smaller units. Significantly, whether a rooming house had nine or eighteen rooms to let, it had only the one original bathroom.[10]

The housing stock was different in newer cities like San Francisco that, in 1880, had a relative shortage of single-family houses. Over half the rooming businesses were established not in discarded houses, but on the upper floors of new generic loft buildings (Fig. 2). These structures usually filled their entire plot. The walls of neighboring buildings obviated side windows, and light wells were either minimal or absent altogether. "Dark" rooms—those with no direct exterior light—had windows opening into daylit corridors or into interior stairwells with skylights and balconies. In such rooming houses, tenants were lucky if the building was new or well maintained so that the skylights were clean and their movable sash still offered ventilation.[11] Space inside these loft buildings was intended for easy conversion to a variety of uses including warehousing, restaurants, shoemaking, office work, or housing. Three or four of these functions could take place simultaneously on different floors of the same building. Developers thus kept plumbing minimal and near the edges of the floor space to facilitate changes.

From 1880 to World War I, as growth of commercial districts created demands for more business space, the owners of downtown properties gradually rebuilt on hundreds of lots, using a new, specialized building type: the downtown rooming house (Fig. 3). In the cities of western America, downtown rooming houses still are very

10. Ibid., pp. 1–2, 36–37, 52–71. Ford, *Slums and Housing*, p. 341. Community Services Society, Committee on Housing, "Life in One Room: A Study of the Rooming House Problem in the Borough of Manhattan" (mimeographed report, New York City, 1940).

11. Because of the fire of 1906, no extant building or plan of the improvised loft-building type remains in San Francisco. This description is based on Sanborn Insurance Maps and extrapolations from middle-class Victorian hotels in Oakland, California.

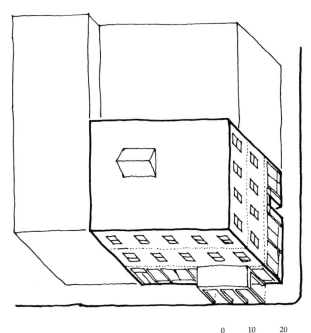

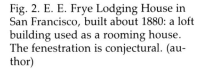

Fig. 2. E. E. Frye Lodging House in San Francisco, built about 1880: a loft building used as a rooming house. The fenestration is conjectural. (author)

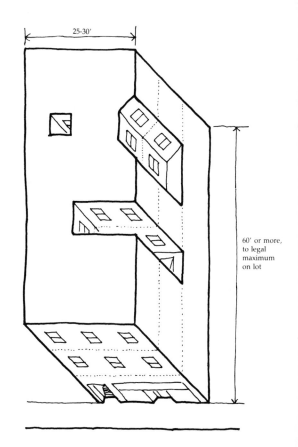

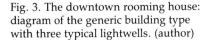

Fig. 3. The downtown rooming house: diagram of the generic building type with three typical lightwells. (author)

common. The plans of these buildings include and also improve on the living characteristics of the converted house and the generic loft building. On the ground floor are commercial spaces with forms, uses, and lease incomes that clearly say "downtown" to observers on the street. On the one, two, or three floors above are between fifteen and forty single-room living units. The front windows of these upper floors reveal the function of the rooms only if tenants have left residential items such as milk bottles, clothing, or domestic curtains in view.

Throughout the period of downtown rooming-house construction, the vast majority of people who lived in these rooming houses were single and young skilled workers, half of them men and half of them women. They had recently arrived in the city and were struggling along on low salaries. In 1906, the sociologist Albert Wolfe characterized this group as the "great army of clerks, sales-men, barbers, restaurant-keepers, policemen, nurses . . . journey-men carpenters, painters, and machinists," upon whom the expansion and management of the city depended.[12]

The renters sometimes called their homes "upstairs hotels," and the phrase aptly describes most downtown rooming houses.

12. Wolfe, *Slums and Housing*, pp. 1, 5–6. Also compare Wolfe's study with a very similar work, Franklin K. Fretz, "The Furnished Room Problem in Philadelphia" (Ph.D. diss., University of Pennsylvania, 1912). Fretz privately printed his dissertation, and it is generally available.

Fig. 4. View of the Delta Hotel, built in San Francisco about 1910. The ground floor is currently occupied by a pawn shop. (author)

Fig. 5. Entrance to the Delta Hotel. (author)

Many had the word *hotel* in their title. As with more elaborate hotels, their rooms could be rented by the day, week, or month. However, downtown rooming houses had no lobby or other hotel space on the ground floor. Usually, the only public area was a wide section of the second-floor hall near the office. The light wells that lit the upstairs rooms indicated more physical and financial commitment to rental housing than had been the case in either the old converted houses or the loft buildings. Downtown rooming-house forms no longer needed to be experimental or temporary; the market was sure and speculators had tested close-to-downtown locations for over a generation.

The form of the upper floors connoted not only permanence but also permanent residence. The light wells of these new rooming houses were comparable to those of the flats and apartments that developers were building for family groups in this same economic class. The plumbing was better than that in converted houses. Downtown rooming houses usually had about one bath and toilet for every six rooms instead of one bath and toilet for every twelve to eighteen rooms. Another important step upward in plumbing quality was a small sink in every room, typically next to a case closet. Sinks, along with smuggled-in hot plates, made light housekeeping possible for tenants.

San Francisco's Delta Hotel exemplifies the small downtown rooming house of 1906 (Fig. 4).[13] The Delta is three stories tall and twenty-five by eighty feet in plan. The facade on the upper floors is simple but vaguely classical. The ground floor, like so many urban storefronts, has seen at least three remodelings, so its original details are unknown. On either side of the Delta Hotel are other small downtown rooming houses. A pawn shop currently occupies the ground floor. Narrow flights of stairs extend from a single door on the street to eighteen rooms on the upper floors (Fig. 5). In tenants' letters home and in the novels about rooming-house life, the long and dark stairways have often become symbols for loneliness and for the difficult climb to economic comfort.

The second and third stories of the Delta have light wells that are seven feet by fourteen feet. The rooms receive maximum attention in the floor plan (Fig. 6). Each is roughly the same size—there are no oversized and difficult-to-rent rooms comparable to the parlors of old converted houses. Although they are only about eleven by ten feet, the individual living units are as large as the plot and light wells allow. A bathroom and a separate toilet room accommodate the nine dwellings on each floor. The hallways, created from the spaces left over, are less-than-elegant forms that snake around pilasters, stairs, and cleaning closets (Fig. 7).

Just as rooming-house bathrooms were usually down the hall, food was usually available down the street or around the corner. Individual freedom in eating was a primary advantage of restaurant-and-rooming-house life over boarding life. On the boarding plan, tenants had to eat at predetermined times and pay for meals they often missed. On the rooming plan, tenants could vary the times, places, and expenses of dining—perhaps adding a glass of beer and a free lunch in a saloon to the routine of cafés and small dining rooms.[14]

This scattering of daily life is a distinguishing element of most single-room life downtown, and particularly of rooming houses. The surrounding sidewalks and the commercial establishments function as parts of a rooming-house patron's home. The "house" is distributed up and down the street: the dining room is at the end of the block, the laundry is three doors down, and the living room and den are at bars, coffee shops, or favorite corners.

Small buildings like the Delta and its neighbors may also function as the basic units of larger rooming houses (Fig. 8). The plan can be doubled, tripled, or twisted to fit odd-shaped lots. As it does for other types of downtown buildings, the shape of the plot plays a very active role in determining the shape of the building. The Sierra House, for instance, is a longer variation of the Delta Hotel form (Fig. 9). Owners of the Sierra opened its sixty-two rooms for business in 1908. In isometric view, the light wells indicate the build-

13. The Delta was so named in 1910. In 1985, the hotel still stood at 41 Sixth Street. It was known as the Whitaker Hotel and was under the management of a family from Bombay.

14. Wolfe, *Slums and Housing*, pp. 38, 46–48. For a sharply negative opinion of the commercial nature of dining, and of rooming-house life in general, see Harvey Warren Zorbaugh, *The Gold Coast and the Slum: A Sociological Study of Chicago's Near North Side* (Chicago: University of Chicago Press, 1929), esp. chaps. 3 and 4.

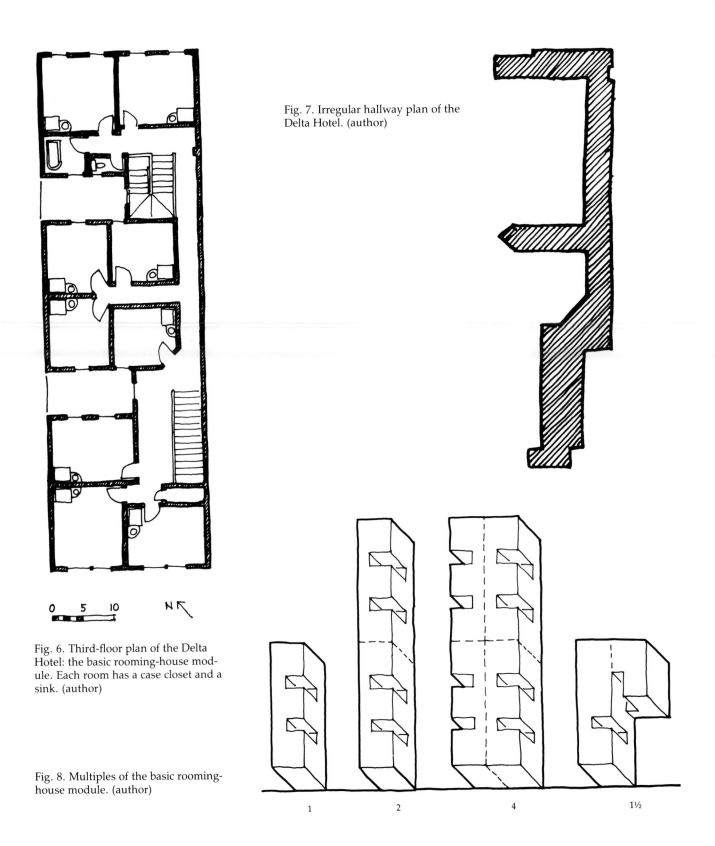

Fig. 7. Irregular hallway plan of the Delta Hotel. (author)

Fig. 6. Third-floor plan of the Delta Hotel: the basic rooming-house module. Each room has a case closet and a sink. (author)

Fig. 8. Multiples of the basic rooming-house module. (author)

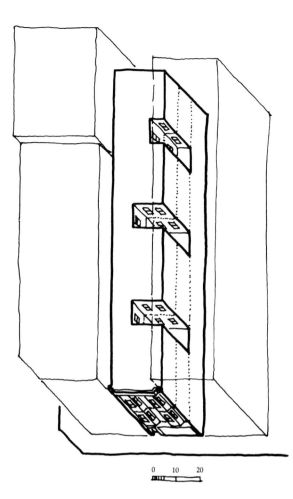

Fig. 9. Isometric of the Sierra House in San Francisco. (author)

Fig. 10. View of the Sierra House from Broadway. The hotel is above Big Al's nightclub. (author)

ing's function as housing. The modern street view, however, suggests why single-room housing is often called "invisible" (Fig. 10). The Sierra House is directly above Big Al's nightclub at Broadway and Columbus Avenue—the middle of San Francisco's most notorious adult entertainment district. Few people notice housing when they walk or drive on such streets. Yet within three hundred feet of Sierra House are over three hundred vernacular housing units, most of them single-room dwellings.

As was true in all four of the hotel ranks from palace hotels to hobo flophouses, investors could build rooming houses within a set price structure. Rooming-house rents were high, low, or medium, depending on the building or site amenities. The Delta Hotel represents the center price in the rooming-house range. The Sierra House represents a lower price because of its location near the historic center of the Barbary Coast. For a relatively high rooming-house rent, it is possible to live in a building like the Eastman House, a forty-room establishment built in 1913 (Fig. 11).[15] Several

15. The Eastman House is presently operated as The Pension, at 1668 Market Street, and caters more to tourist trade than to permanent residents.

Fig. 11. View of the Eastman House—now The Pension—built in San Francisco as a high-rent rooming house. (author)

16. The history of the small apartment, in particular, has yet to be written. In the meantime, see Elizabeth Cromley, "The Development of the New York Apartment, 1860–1905" (Ph.D. diss., City University of New York, 1982); Miriam Beard, "New York Squeezes into the 'Domestic Unit,'" *New York Times Magazine,* 7 November 1926, p. 4; William Benslyn, "Recent Developments in Apartment Housing in America," *Journal of the Royal Institute of British Architects,* ser. 3, 32 (1925), pt. 1, pp. 504–19, pt. 2, pp. 540–51; John Hancock, "The Apartment House in Urban America," in *Buildings and Society: Essays on the Social Development of the Built Environment,* ed. Anthony D. King (London: Routledge and Kegan Paul, 1980), pp. 151–89.

of the rooms in the Eastman House have private baths; the other rooms have a bath-to-room ratio of one to four. The building's location near San Francisco's Civic Center, as well as the expense and care invested in the design of its entry, confirm its position at the top of the rooming-house price range (Fig. 12). The ample windows at the wide doorway make the Eastman's first flights of stairs less dark than those of other rooming houses. However, the stairs are no less long, and on the upper floors they are typically narrow and dark.

San Francisco property owners built downtown rooming houses of all prices largely from the 1890s up until World War I. No extant rooming house in the city was built after 1915. Visual surveys in other cities suggest that there, too, developers built few new rooming houses in the 1920s, as factory-prepared foods and a diversity of electric appliances made small apartments with kitchenettes more feasible. Simultaneously, capital investment and new jobs were shifting to the suburbs.[16]

Whether they were built in 1890 or in 1915, downtown rooming houses represent an urban variation of vernacular design processes, a type that might be called "marketplace design." Unlike the builders of most rural buildings, the owners of rooming houses were not intimately connected with the design and construction of their properties. As rooming-house facades and available records show, San Francisco's individual landowners hired architects to design their investment projects. Moreover, as was the case with converted single-family dwellings, the owners rarely managed rooming houses directly. Typically, they or their designated real estate firm leased the residential sections of the buildings to entrepreneurs

Fig. 12. Door detail of the Eastman House. (author)

who lived in one or two rooms behind the office and struggled to attract enough steadily employed and reliable tenants whose rents could meet lease and operating expenses. Owners and lessees alike carefully examined the rooms or the arrangements shown on the floor plans. Their goal was to avoid rooms that would be hard to rent. This concern accounts for the regular, nearly square rooms characteristic of most rooming-house designs, even when hallways were perforce haphazard.

Although the clerks and secretaries living in rooming houses did not directly influence the form of individual buildings, owners and managers paid careful attention to what the most reliable tenants wanted. Thus, the tenants exerted distinct market pressure on building forms. Although they could not demand changes or additions in structures, they could do "design by moving." During a few hours in a new city, a young worker could inspect a dozen housing options in a single neighborhood. Furthermore, since rooming-house residents had few possessions, they could move very easily. If their initial choice of residence failed to meet their expectations, they could pack their suitcases and move on within a week.

Diaries and letters indicate that rooming-house clients noticed and cared about a building's image and the appointments of their rooms. Such concerns are expressed in the letters of Will Kortum, an eighteen-year-old lumberyard clerk from a small California town. Kortum moved into a very large, new rooming house on his arrival in San Francisco a few months before the great earthquake and fire of 1906. He excitedly wrote his parents to say that he had found a fine urban home on his first day: "The hotel is a new one.

Everything is neat and clean, although not large. My room is very light, has hot and cold water, double bed, bureau, wash stand, chair, and small table. It also has a closet for clothes."[17] Kortum *had* gotten a good room at a good price, although his new home was only a hundred yards from the very center of the city's hobo labor market. When his father expressed concern over Kortum's housing choice, the young man wrote: "Rest assured that my present place of lodging is no low class hotel [not a cheap lodging house], but a clean, plastered room, and that the bed is also clean and comfortable."[18]

Kortum's letters show sharply tuned material concerns. He gave a precise list of furnishings, noticed that there was a built-in closet instead of a case closet, and knew that hot water was not on tap at all rooming houses. These skills of discernment quickly expanded beyond the boundaries of his room to include the surrounding neighborhood. Within weeks he moved far from the migrant workers' district. He rented a room in a converted single-family house, and he wrote that he missed the amenities and the privacy he had enjoyed downtown.

While Kortum and other skilled workers often came to the city with middle-class aspirations of respectability, their low wages forced calculated and conscious compromises. For several years, Kortum could not afford what he really desired: a room in a middle-class residential hotel with a ground-floor lobby and restaurant. Nevertheless, even on his first day in town, he had been careful to avoid the "low-class" lodging houses of the wintering migrant workers and casual laborers.

To please good renters like Will Kortum, building owners were also compromising. In an effort to emulate the better hotels, they spent money on embellishments for the facade—especially the doorway—and on interior details. They fitted and furnished individual rooms in ways that distinguished their upstairs hotels from cheap lodging houses, which had only the minimum facilities required by building and health codes. Most of all, it was in the extra expenses for daylighting and plumbing that the building owners made compromises with their tenants. Yet owners were *not* asking architects to design truly distinctive buildings with unique identities. Such places were for middle-class tastes, demands, and budgets.

This give-and-take of desires and prices resulting in an identifiable class of structures is at the core of marketplace vernacular design. Architects might be involved in the design process, but they merely packaged a product already tightly circumscribed by rent prices and the owners' knowledge of their clients' preferences or complaints. Like tailors, they adjusted the market patterns so that they would fit on a given site. The most important aspects of the buildings—the size and number of their rooms, bathrooms, sinks, as well as access to daylight and fresh air—were the result of social

17. Quoted in Roger R. Olmstead, Nancy Olmstead, et al., *The Yerba Buena Center: Report on Historical Cultural Resources* (San Francisco: San Francisco Redevelopment Agency, 1979), p. 227.

18. Ibid., p. 232.

and cultural pressures hammered out by cash transactions and rent agreements.

Studies of vernacular architecture often reject the significance of blatantly commercial housing: buildings constructed for an anonymous market are "mere commodities," in the views of leaders in the field. Traditionalists hold that rented dwellings deserve consideration as human places only when they are altered or embellished by an inhabitant.[19] Yet even before tenants arrange bedspreads or hang pictures, rooming houses are distinctly human places shaped by social-group processes. They have meaning both for owners and for potential residents.

Downtown rooming houses speak bluntly about a class of people who are not necessarily place-identified. Unlike members of the middle class who attach great significance to homeownership and domestic virtues, long-term rooming-house tenants derive little of their personal identity from their living quarters. Although many single-room homes are elaborately personalized, it is not uncommon for individuals to live in a space for many years and never make any sort of individualizing statement.[20] Whether or not they decorate their rooms, the residents of upstairs hotels derive a social identity—literally a place in society—from the location and basic conditions of their homes.

This focusing, sampling, classifying, and characterizing of downtown rooming houses differs from most vernacular architecture studies. For that reason this study should be approached as an experiment, a case study of an unexamined building type developed and used by renters and owners. More important than the subject itself, however, is its attempt to bridge a gap in the field of American vernacular architecture: that concerning the generic buildings of marketplace design. To dismiss these buildings as unworthy of study because they are "impersonal" is not only short-sighted, it is irresponsible. Marketplace design has shaped and continues to shape much of the built environment—suburban housing tracts represent the same vernacular give-and-take as downtown rooming houses. Furthermore, as this consideration of single-room living units indicates, architectural historians who study all types of common buildings have important contributions to make toward the fuller understanding of social issues that affect large sectors of the American population.

19. See R. W. Brunskill, *Traditional Buildings of Britain: An Introduction to Vernacular Architecture* (London: Gollancz and P. Crawley, 1983); Henry Glassie made the "mere commodities" comments at the paper session on house types at the Vernacular Architecture Forum meeting in Newark, Delaware, 4 May 1984. A striking exception to this point of view is Mary Ellen Hayward, "Urban Vernacular Architecture in Nineteenth-Century Baltimore," *Winterthur Portfolio* 16 (1981):33–63.

20. See the range of living situations described in Liu, *Chinatown Hotels*. For a photographic comparison, see Ira Nowinski, *No Vacancy: Urban Renewal and the Elderly* (San Francisco: Carolyn Bean Associates, 1979).

Completion of this article was made possible by a National Endowment for the Humanities research fellowship at the Office of Advanced Studies, Winterthur Museum and Gardens, Winterthur, Delaware.

20

ALICE GRAY READ

Making a House a Home in a Philadelphia Neighborhood

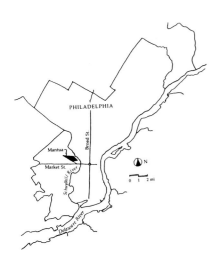

Fig. 1. Map of Philadelphia showing the Mantua neighborhood. (author)

In most parts of the United States, a new house built to order is an uncommon luxury. The vast majority of the population, particularly in the urban Northeast, lives in second-hand houses or "off the shelf" models designed and built by profiteering developers for an anonymous public. In large industrialized cities, domestic architecture has been taken out of the hands of residents so completely that developers and architects rarely know the people for whom they design and rarely concern themselves with residents' opinions when a project is complete. The gulf between designer and occupant is compounded in cities such as Philadelphia and Boston, for a large percentage of the current housing stock is old. Most urban residential neighborhoods were built in the nineteenth and early twentieth centuries according to the tastes of the period. These houses stand twice removed from their present owners: they were built by strangers and they were built nearly a century ago.

In these cities, this great displacement of architectural authorship to designers outside the community has modified the meaning of *house* and *home*. The significance of a house has been reduced to the brick and wood of which it is made. There is no longer a singular identification of building and resident as in communities where houses have the same name as their owners. As physical shells, the existing houses that fill large urban neighborhoods are relics of turn-of-the-century design principles that have now been discarded. An unoccupied house exists in the same strange void of meaning as an empty theater. The actors that defined the space with drama are gone and a new company has not yet possessed the stage. The house is anonymous and mute. Only when it is touched by an owner, lived in, and made over inside and out does it begin to bear the identity of its occupants. It is they who see "character" in its empty rooms and transform an existing house into their home. In a sense, the city is an enormous and complex ruin of anachronistic forms occupied by residents who constantly must modify and reinterpret their found spaces to accommodate new needs and changing priorities. Renovation is the decorating, furnishing, painting, and planting that homeowners do to claim a house as their own and to make it a part of their community.

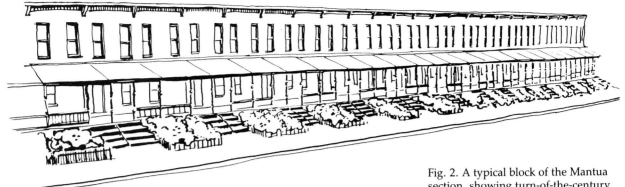

Fig. 2. A typical block of the Mantua section, showing turn-of-the-century urban residential architecture. (author)

Remodeling is usually done by a homeowner for his or her own use in response to some specific need or perceived inadequacy in the existing design. A homeowner may find suggestions for renovation from popular magazines or retail stores' advertisements, but, within a coherent community, design ideas are often passed through local networks of neighbors and friends. The actual work of renovation may be done by the homeowners themselves or by builders and handymen from the immediate area. This local economy is so consistent that remodeling styles often characterize neighborhoods within the city and distinguish one area from the next.

Materials available to a homeowner or handyman are plentiful, flexible, and inexpensive, allowing a broad range of choice for even the simplest details. With a repertoire enriched by whole catalogs of decorative options, renovation must be addressed as a self-conscious and articulate form of architectural expression. By considering renovations this way, it becomes possible to approach the spatial aesthetic of a community that has never had the opportunity to build new. This essay explores the architectural aesthetic of one urban community—the Mantua section of west Philadelphia (Fig. 1).[1]

Bounded by railroad yards on the north and east and by a deteriorated commercial strip on the south, Mantua is a dense urban neighborhood of two-story brick row houses set on long, uniform blocks (Fig. 2). Developed in the mid-nineteenth century as high-density housing for workers, Mantua has been a stopping place for a succession of railroad and factory workers of differing ethnic backgrounds who remained only until they could become established more comfortably elsewhere. The area was notorious for unrest during late nineteenth-century labor struggles against the railroads and was the scene of periodic street violence that did not encourage the munificence of Philadelphia City Hall. The area has thus suffered from poverty, abuse, and governmental neglect. Since World War II, it has become a relatively stable black community consisting largely of families from rural areas of the South. Homeownership

1. This study began while the author was working on the design of a church building for a congregation in Mantua. It was initially an attempt to understand local spatial preferences so that the new building might respond more effectively to its users. The church was never built, but this study may suggest one way in which architects might begin to learn from their clients.

in Mantua, rare in the past, has risen recently in some neighborhoods, for the housing, while deteriorated, is sound, inexpensive, and pleasant.

In Mantua today, the almost ancient masonry establishes a background rhythm against which current householders must set their new variations, adding their own strains to the work that has gone before. Brightly painted porches, awnings, flower gardens, and outdoor carpeting are the more recent flourishes played out in elaborate variation down each neighborhood block. Layer upon layer, new construction is added to old. Little is removed. Over the years, a neighborhood street becomes dense with detail. Awnings, railings, furniture, and gardens each take their place as families grow and become part of the life of the community (Fig. 3).

The buildings of Mantua acquire a visual density, and social ties among neighbors fill the space between them. In a sense, "remodeling" is almost a metaphor for the whole of neighborhood life. The expressed intent of homeowners and elected block captains is to "beautify" their area and to distinguish it as a community—in their words, to make their houses their homes. An additive, outward-looking approach to building is a consistent style of architecture in Mantua that exists independently of ideas on house renovation that prevail in the rapidly expanding areas of white "urban renaissance" (Fig. 4).

In Mantua, improving a house or beautifying a neighborhood invariably means adding to it either in actual construction or in dec-

Fig. 3. A typical Mantua house, before and after renovation. (author)

oration. Brick is painted, cornices are sheathed and redecorated, siding is added. Astroturf covers porch decks and steps; stone facing conceals facades; and bright paint sets off railings and trim. Porches and gardens receive special attention as outside living spaces with a view of the street. Dependencies such as awnings and cornices extend the surface of the wall out toward the sidewalk so that the facade itself acquires depth. The facade literally becomes three-dimensional, enclosing space of its own. In effect, the house is a structural frame from which layer upon layer of construction extends out into space. In the language of aesthetician Robert Plant Armstrong, it is an architecture that may be described as "extensive" as it reaches out from a central core, extending to engage a larger space than it actually encloses.[2]

The elaboration of porch and garden strengthens the area between street and house and blurs the border between inside and outside. The ubiquitous porch is an extension of interior living space, profusely decorated, furnished, and commonly used as a summer living room. Railings and posts are often articulated with two or three different colors of paint. The porch deck is covered with outdoor carpeting, and another textured surface such as formstone, stucco, or paint is added to the first-floor facade, thus distinguishing the entire porch area as a finished room (Fig. 5). To complement this extension of living area toward the street, a walkway from the sidewalk to the door is generally kept visually open and physically direct. The property line dividing public space from private front walk is rarely marked by a gate or fence. The walk itself is identified by a railing, strip of carpeting, or painted concrete that offers a broad passage up the porch steps to the front door.

A suburban curving stepping-stone path across a sea of green lawn would be foreign in this part of Philadelphia, as would the pedimented and paneled entrance doors common in other parts of the city. In Mantua, the entrance door does not receive the same attention that is lavished on the porch and garden. Doors are plain, painted the same color as window trim, and are rarely adorned with doorknockers or wreaths. The absence of specific marking at the doorway—the inside/outside boundary—or at the property line—public/private boundary—further softens any spatial division between the individual house and the neighborhood as a whole. The porch and the garden negotiate these transitions as "in-between" spaces where public and private, inside and outside may coexist.[3]

This in-between space is essential to the social life of Mantua. Neighborhood life is street life, and it requires participation. The covered porch offers a place to sit outside during the summer in a shaded spot open to the breeze. Here, residents are separated from the public way yet close enough to be both audience and actors, maintaining both the possibility of distance and the possibility of involvement. Neighborhood life is built around talk from sidewalk to porch, words passed without interruption or excuse.

This place for sitting out in front of the house is so essential to

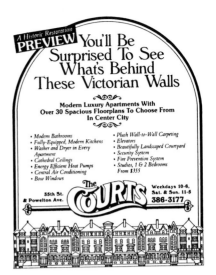

Fig. 4. A recent real estate advertisement for Victorian houses that have been stripped and transformed into "urban renaissance" apartments. (*Philadelphia Inquirer*)

2. The notion of "extensive" as opposed to "intensive" design is taken from Armstrong's *The Affecting Presence: An Essay in Humanistic Anthropology* (Chicago: University of Chicago Press, 1971).

3. The idea of an architectural space partaking of two worlds—an "in-between"—was suggested by Dutch architect Aldo van Eyck, in his lectures at the University of Pennsylvania in 1979. See also his observations published in *Via I* (Philadelphia: University of Pennsylvania Graduate School of Fine Arts, 1966).

Fig. 5. A Mantua porch decorated and furnished as an outside living room. (author)

Fig. 6. A decorated and furnished sidewalk serves as outside living space for a porchless Mantua house. (author)

neighborhood life that there can be no compromise. The backyard will not serve as a substitute. It is a service area, used only as a storage space, a laundry yard, or a pen for dogs. Residents of houses that were built with no frontyard or porch will not furnish a back lot. Rather, a sitting area in front of the house is made out of a piece of the sidewalk, always within the lot lines of the house and always adjacent to the front door (Fig. 6). Acting with the consent of the community, individuals literally stake out a part of the street to serve as a part of the house. A covering on the ground is enough to identify an area of the sidewalk as a spot claimed by a particular homeowner or to distinguish a part of the public way that is set aside and maintained by a shopkeeper.

Whether this front space is given or made, homeowners plant it and furnish it with grass-green carpets, hanging baskets, and other details, creating a pastoral setting for summer afternoons. Decorative elements for the front garden are frequently drawn from the vocabulary of the country—roses, picket fences, and box hedges—and a lush Astroturf lawn may be set down across the sidewalk to the curb of the street. Vegetables are not considered appropriate for front gardens. Those who plant them draw local criticism. Ambitious flower gardens, by contrast, are the subject of pride and encouragement. Enthusiastic gardeners may extend their

Fig. 7. Section showing a front garden extended out onto the sidewalk. (author)

attention to planting boxes placed across the sidewalk on the concrete curb or hanging baskets suspended from street-side trees (Fig. 7). Into these city gardens passersby become fleeting visitors or trespassers on a sidewalk that is no longer neutral ground.

The sidewalk is common ground held by a neighborhood that has the same stolid existence as the houses themselves. The street is the arena for community interaction and cooperative physical design, just as the individual house is the arena for a householder's interior design. Within such a cohesive neighborhood, the design of a single house is meaningless if divorced from the whole block. The exteriors of houses have become the interior of a neighborhood.

The block of houses presents a visual pattern of three-dimensional form and color stretching out horizontally and parallel to the street. Most of the emphasis is on the ground story—even on the ground plane. A line of awnings cuts low across the visual horizon, and railings and fences, flower gardens and furniture reinforce the horizontality of the picture. Often the first story is distinguished from the others by a change in color or facade sheathing. A wall surface underneath a porch roof often is more strongly identified with its neighbor than with the facade above, reinforcing the horizontal theme. A section cutting through the street makes this low and horizontal emphasis even more apparent (Fig. 8). It directly addresses pedestrians on the sidewalk, for decorative elements seem within reach. In linear perspective, the vanishing points of all horizontal lines are at eye level. This is a very human horizon to which the space between ground and sky is concentrated in distance. The low architecture of Mantua gathers detail and color within a narrow band close to this horizon.

As horizontality is emphasized, the vertical plane of the facade wall is weakened. In graphic design, an artist may use color tonality

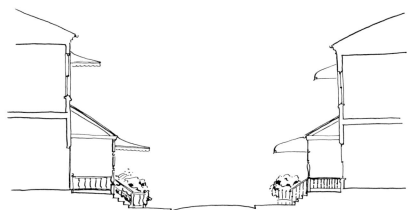

Fig. 8. Section cut through a street and flanking houses, showing the emphasis on low spaces and horizontal lines. (author)

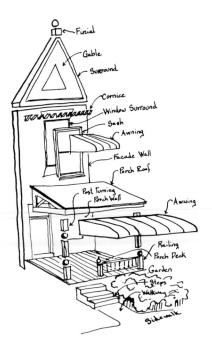

Fig. 9. Facade of a renovated Mantua house, showing the contrasting shapes that have been used to enhance and extend the two-dimensional surface. (author)

4. Sally Price and Richard Price, *Afro-American Arts of the Suriname Rain Forest* (Los Angeles: University of California, 1980). A marked similarity between the Mantua house in Fig. 10 and an Afro-American quilt was pointed out to the author by Henry Glassie and John Vlach at the Vernacular Architecture Forum meeting in Newark, Delaware, 4 May 1984.

5. Many of the characteristics of Mantua houses are parallel to qualities of African art and dance emphasized by Robert Farris Thompson in *African Art in Motion* (Los Angeles: University of California Press, 1980). Thompson describes dance of the Niger River area as characterized by low horizontal movements with specific attention to the ground plane. He also sees in African art the accomplished arrangement of discrete elements into a decorative composition.

to create depth in a composition. Darker colors and cooler colors—blues and greens—will appear to be farther away than light warm colors—reds and yellows. In juxtaposition, these contrastive colors create a visual modulation that contradicts the planar surface of the actual work. Painted facades along a block of houses in Mantua often work on the same principle. A pattern of color exists independently of the masonry structure, apparently lifting off the surface of the front wall and unfolding in its own rhythm, dissolving the vertical plane in favor of a variable pattern not unlike those of Afro-American quilts.[4] As with quilt designs, the colors are chosen from within a close range of hue density so that they complement each other in much the same way as pastel colors. Along this "quilted" block, each house is picked out individually in bright colors. Unlike the cacophony of individualism on the American strip, however, these singular houses converge in a pattern that contains all while allowing each to stand alone.

Within the design of a single facade, a similar compositional logic applies. The house front is a congeries of separate pieces clearly delineated by changes in color or by a contrasting band that traces the extent of that color and separates the shape from other areas. Parts of the facade are picked out with color: the triangle of the gable end, the rectangles of windows and doors, the triangular form of projecting awnings, the terminal stripe of a cornice (Fig. 9).

Fig. 10. A Mantua house facade with patterns of brick emphasized by different colors of paint. (author)

Each part is crisply isolated from every other part as if called out by name.[5] White-painted mortar joints on stone walls emphasize the irregular stones as abstract shapes that exist independently of the wall itself. Visually dissolving any sense of solidity, the patterning of brick relies on principles of formal isolation and emphasis in order to create an animate surface from static building materials. It becomes a wall that will not stand still (Fig. 10).

Making a house a home in the Mantua section of Philadelphia means more than a new coat of paint. It implies an affective transformation of an anonymous masonry shell into a personal architecture that not only accommodates domestic life but also participates in a broader visual aesthetic shared by the neighborhood. These houses are singular statements not of an isolate individualism but of an individualism strengthened by its communal base. Houses do not retreat from one another behind their facades but reach out to contribute to a larger sense of place and, in doing so, establish an arena for personal expression. Together these houses create an identity that allows neighbors to belong to their neighborhood as villagers belong to their country towns. In Mantua, renovation is a part of the necessary making of a home, at once individual and communal, arbitrary and ordered.

The author wishes to thank the homeowners of Mantua for discussing their houses and for allowing them to be photographed. Robert St. George contributed sound advice and encouragement.

21

ROBERT L. ALEXANDER

A Shopkeeper's Renaissance: Academic Design and Popular Architecture in Late Nineteenth-Century Iowa City

The Renaissance Revival style traveled from the East Coast to the Midwest in 1893, making its mark at the World's Columbian Exposition in Chicago. Although it took another five years to migrate to Iowa City, it required much less time to spread from an academic monument to pragmatic commercial blocks. This last transformation, involving a new building material and a special group of patrons, offers a case history in the relationships between high art and vernacular art.[1]

The revival first appeared in Iowa City in Schaeffer Hall, a classroom building begun by the University of Iowa in 1898, after the designs of Proudfoot and Bird, an architectural firm of Des Moines (Fig. 1). Dated three years later and located three blocks away.was the Woodburn block, a vernacular or popular version of the same revival (Fig. 2). Many differences distinguish the two: the university building is a large freestanding monument of stone, while the commercial block proffers a small brick facade hemmed in by its neighbors on either side. But there are instructive similarities, too: both are divided into three major sections, both have a precise, rectilinear articulation, and both are distinguished by decorative forms that cling to the wall plane. The large disk, or *patera*, in the frieze above the pilaster is a common device of the academic Neo-Renaissance and a hallmark of Proudfoot and Bird compositions. Its repetition indicates that the design of the commercial building was derived from Schaeffer Hall.

Closer examination of the Woodburn block shows more clearly the popular nineteenth-century conception of the Renaissance. The Ionic capital and cornice were enriched with unorthodox moldings, but in general there was abbreviation of the Beaux-Arts manner. For example, the base was reduced to a single molding and a shallow plinth, and the architrave was omitted from the entablature. The smaller pilasters were of an indeterminate order, for the bases and capitals were identical.

This change was not simplification alone. The decorative parts of this building were of stamped metal; in order to shape the top

1. The basic information on the vernacular buildings discussed here comes from the manuscript Transfer Books in the Johnson County Courthouse. The several editions of the city directory offer some corroboration of dates, and Charles Ray Aurner, *Leading Events in Johnson County, Iowa*, 2 vols. (Cedar Rapids, Iowa: Western Historical Press, 1912–1913), provides much historical and biographical information.

Fig. 1. Schaeffer Hall, designed by Des Moines architects Proudfoot and Bird for the University of Iowa, Iowa City, 1898. (author)

Fig. 2. The Woodburn block, built in Iowa City in 1901. The building has been demolished. (author)

and bottom elements of the small pilasters, the local tinsmith employed simple molding dies that he already owned. For the capitals of the tall pilasters, he clearly acquired a new set of dies that followed the new revival fashion. The builder of the block purchased the stamped-metal parts from the tinsmith and had them set in place by bricklayers. No architect was necessary. While the metal dies enforced a limited standardization, details were "customized" for the individual client. For example, a variety of separate cast-metal elements was available to compose the garlands bolted to the sheet-metal friezes.

By the turn of the century, Iowa City had experienced sixty years of growth and change. It was founded in 1838. Two years later, the Greek Revival Old Capitol, designed by architect John Rague, was built to serve as the territorial government building. In 1846, this became the state capitol, and, after 1857, it functioned as the main building of the University of Iowa.[2] For many decades, the university had no rival as the state's center of learning in the sciences, humanities, and professions. Its medical complex was created to serve the entire state, as it still does. In Iowa City, the university has always represented a force for change and modernity.

Iowa City was not only an important governmental and academic center; it was also a city of commercial importance. For several years after 1850, the city was the western terminus of the railroad. Even when the tracks pressed farther on, Iowa City remained an important stop for passengers and freight. The city also served as a market and shipping center for a widely dispersed population. From an effectively one-street community at mid-century, the city had developed an L-shaped business district some three blocks deep and long by 1910. A few Neo-Renaissance buildings replaced old structures, and more of them expanded the business district after the turn of the century.

Iowa City was built of brick. From several huge clay pits came the millions of bricks, fired in local kilns, that make up the richly textured facades of pink common brick. To this basic masonry structure, local designers and builders adapted the products and processes of the Industrial Revolution. While there was little need for the steel skeleton structure developed for the skyscraper, cast-iron columns replaced bulky masonry and brick piles on the street-level fronts, and I beams permitted broad shop windows. Most popular of the newly available options was pressed tin.

From the mid-nineteenth century on, pressed-tin elements became widely used in architecture, often for interiors—especially ceilings—but exterior forms also became very popular. Many small cities acquired at least one manufactory, and Iowa City was no exception. The major tinsmith of the city, Vaclav W. Maresh, constructed his workshop and sales building in 1883, using the front of the building to as a catalog of then fashionable motifs (Fig. 3). The columns on the ground floor were of cast iron, while the rest of the brick structure was covered by the thin sheet of metal—cut, pressed, and soldered into a rich decorative vocabulary.[3]

In the 1870s, the firm of Maresh and Holubar was established in Iowa City, and its products were used on houses as well as public and commercial structures. As a tinsmith, Maresh certainly used that material, but galvanized iron was employed more frequently on buildings. Unpainted sections show corrosion, and occasionally

2. Henry-Russell Hitchcock and William Seale, *Temples of Democracy* (New York and London: Harcourt Brace Jovanovich, 1976), p. 111.

3. Maresh and his partner, Joseph Holubar, first appear in the city directory for 1875–1876, advertising stoves and tinware. In the 1878 directory, their entry shows expanded activities: "Iowa City Galvanized Iron Works, mnfrs of cornices, window caps, jobbers in roofing and spouting." The 1890–1891 directory shows them at the address of the Maresh building. Although this building still stands, its front has been covered with aluminum and plastic, perhaps the modern equivalent of pressed tin.

Fig. 3. Maresh building, constructed in Iowa City in 1883. The facade has now been drastically altered. From Edwin Charles Ellis's 1946 thesis, "Certain Stylistic Trends in Architecture in Iowa City." (Courtesy of University of Iowa)

it is possible to see where a galvanized iron tab has rusted out so that the metal has sprung away from the wall.

As is customary when any new material appears, metal was substituted for elements that had been developed in traditional materials. The rather simple pieces introduced in the 1850s and 1860s adhered closely to traditional structural forms, such as the triangular and arched window pediments produced in stone and wood. By the middle of the 1870s, stamped metal window caps clearly imitated high Victorian forms of brick and stone. For sheer imitation, nothing can surpass a group of three shop fronts of the early

1880s in which the upper windows were flanked by permanently open shutters, all in stamped tin.[4]

Builders could use the material for a quick and easy means of enriching surfaces, just as they used millwork, but the material also was susceptible to the control of the architect. One of the Iowa City's few identified architects of the nineteenth century, Chauncy Lovelace, designed the College block of 1883. With a more sophisticated design than Maresh's building, it has thin metal shells that build up a rich plasticity reaching out over the brick wall plane. Such a form as the arch becomes abstract sculptural ornament exemplifying the bulky elaboration that characterizes the high Victorian style.

The large formal and aesthetic changes of the later nineteenth century affected the architecture of Iowa City. One commercial building, the Whiteway block, illustrates a major change in formal preferences in the space of eight years. The north half of this structure was built in 1873, and the south half was added between 1881 and 1882, when the whole building received a tin cornice and a mansard roof faced with pressed tin. The original front of stucco scored to imitate ashlar was succeeded by the even texture of brick, and instead of three-dimensional tin hoods, windows acquired flat, cast-stone arches. Even popular taste, then, responded to formal change. Thus, it might be reasonable to expect a ready acceptance of the Neo-Renaissance that dominated the Columbian Exposition of 1893. The change came, but it was a traumatic experience. The decision made in 1898 by the university's board of regents to adopt the Neo-Renaissance style for its new building nearly precipitated riots.

In 1898, the regents called Henry Van Brunt from Kansas City for advice on using architecture to achieve the image of a modern university. Van Brunt devised the scheme known today as the Pentacrest: four buildings in light gray limestone placed at the corners of the Old Capitol, designed in the style fostered by the Columbian Exposition. Although the plan echoed the classicism of the Greek Revival monument, large numbers of students, faculty, and townspeople opposed the regents. In every way, the new scheme denied the existing perception of the campus, which has been preserved in a late nineteenth-century print. In this print, the university campus is a rural Downingesque retreat, fenced in, filled with trees, bosky nooks, and a grotto with a fountain. Red brick buildings were aligned with the Old Capitol, and, in the print, even this white Greek Revival structure was colored brick red. The regents persisted in the face of opposition and in 1898 began construction of the Neo-Renaissance Schaeffer Hall, their symbol of the modern university. The county selectmen, at almost the same time, reaffirmed their commitment to picturesque tradition. In the spring of 1899, they commissioned a new Johnson County courthouse in the Richardsonian Romanesque style that had become standard for such buildings.

Thus, when the merchants in town chose not to continue the

4. These windows are illustrated in Constance M. Greiff, *Lost America, from the Mississippi to the Pacific* (New York: Weathervane Books, 1972), fig. 150.

Fig. 4. Patterson block, built in Iowa City in 1899. The facade of this building has been partially destroyed. (author)

Richardsonsian model and developed a popular version of the Neo-Renaissance style, they made a conscious decision to show their modern spirit. Built only months later than Schaeffer Hall and just a block away is the Patterson block (Fig. 4).[5] Here is the Renaissance interpreted by the tinsmith and brickmason for the small businessman. Old photographs show that it originally bore a tin parapet with the name of the block and the 1899 construction date, and only in recent years were the white metal parts painted in darker tones. Nevertheless, there is an attempt to achieve a Palladian design through the slight projection of the center bays and the use of pilasters for subdivision. The order of the pilasters is again indeterminate. The tin capitals and bases applied to the brick shafts are identical forms, shaped by the same dies that Maresh used for the Woodburn block. To embellish the arched windows, he simply cut and soldered the sheet-metal parts, and their broad surfaces show bulges and dents from damage received over the years. For the large window frieze he provided elegantly simple and fine garlands in accord with the new taste, while other forms, especially the oversized keystones, suggest a nostalgia for the plasticity popular a decade or two earlier.

In 1900, a more considered version of the Renaissance Revival appeared. Exactly across the street from Schaeffer Hall, three old buildings were refronted as the Seifert block (Fig. 5). The street level of the Seifert block, where cast-iron columns once stood, was set into a white, glazed brick surround during the 1960s. A light, buff-colored brick and stone structure framed by a tin Ionic order, the original front showed the turn-of-the-century aesthetic. Gone are

5. Attorney Lemuel B. Patterson appears in the directory for 1875–1876, already at the site of the future Seifert block. The south half of the Patterson block was destroyed by fire on 3 December 1982. The central fire wall of brick showed its value in preserving the north half.

Fig. 5. Seifert block, built in Iowa City in 1900. The facade has been altered in recent years. (author)

the large and bulky parts and the Victorian polychromy. Rather, the whole enclosed block is smoothed out. Linear elements define the shapes precisely. There are only remnants of rich Queen Anne decoration in the pediment and the central arch. The light and skillful ornamentation, the taste and respect for proportions, and the correctness of the Ionic capital suggest that the Seifert block was designed by an architect who controlled the tinsmith's modeling of pilasters and entablatures. This expression of Neo-Renaissance style is intermediate between the architectural statements made by Schaeffer Hall and those made by the Patterson block. Moreover, the variations appear to be part of a local dialogue concerning aesthetics. Lemuel Patterson, who commissioned the Patterson block, had his law offices on the second floor of the Seifert block, and it was his daughter who had this new front applied. It appears, then, that the Seifert block was her criticism of her father's building.

Among the several other examples of Iowa City's Neo-Renaissance style is the George Gay block (Fig. 6). Gay arrived in Iowa City in 1902 and two years later constructed the corner section. At intervals of two years, he added two more sections. He employed a basic Neo-Renaissance formula: a brick and tin front with little more than garlanded friezes and modillioned cornices to evoke the style of the Columbian Exposition. That the design was not by an architect is made clear by the placement of the circular windows between the rectangular ones. They destroy the sense of continuous support that should rise from the ground through the cast-iron columns and upward through brick walls to the cornice. For several years, the building was considered an eyesore, and it was enthu-

Fig. 6. George Gay block, built in Iowa City in 1904. The building has been demolished. (author)

siastically demolished for urban renewal. Nevertheless, the builder and the patron had clear notions of the beauty they sought. Not a little was owed to the brickmason. Machine-pressed bricks laid in thin mortar beds made a smooth, almost textureless surface against which the garlanded friezes were set like jewels. This basic Neo-Renaissance style reappeared in several other blocks in the city.

An English friend once remarked that while passing a group of houses almost completed, he saw a carpenter nailing planks over the face of one. When questioned about their purpose, the workman replied, "Them's Chudor." Similarly, these commercial buildings of turn-of-the-century Iowa City are Renaissance, shopkeeper's Palladian. If Tudor can be expressed by a few planks and stucco, then Renaissance can appear as sheet-metal friezes against a brick wall. It is a diluted Renaissance, but to the builder, merchant, and citizen it was an interpretation of the Renaissance as ordered beauty. In the slower pace of the day, these austere beauties were savored by pedestrians who appreciated the patron's effort to keep Iowa City up-to-date by participating in the nationwide post-Columbian Neo-Renaissance and the City Beautiful Movement. At the same time, the front of the commercial block was like a great signboard from which the hieroglyphs of style proclaimed the modernism of the block and presumably of the goods to be had inside.

In espousing the new style, these merchants fell into a pattern known in other times and places. A paramount example is the mercantile patronage of early Renaissance art and architecture in the city of Florence during the fifteenth century. This practice continued in nineteenth-century American cities. In early Baltimore, for example, the prominent editor Hezekiah Niles often noted the construction of new buildings as ornaments to the city. Baltimore had to achieve a reputation as safe and up-to-date in order to maintain the commerce that was the basis of its existence. Buildings in a modern style contributed to this desirable image.[6] Clearly, the needs that operated on their predecessors also induced the merchants of Iowa City to adopt the latest style in architecture.

Perhaps it is easier to define the interaction between high art and popular art in a small city, where the buildings stand face-to-face and side-by-side. Any definition of architecture must recognize emotional, symbolic, and economic needs as shaping forces not only in high art but in the vernacular as well. The progress of the Neo-Renaissance style in Iowa City is an instructive example. The board of regents took the first step with the design of Schaeffer Hall at the University of Iowa. Widespread rejection of the plan gave way very quickly to the merchants' acceptance of the Neo-Renaissance style. Gradually, and with variations, the crisp lines of this historical style and its attendant associations with modernity and orderly urban spaces became part of the popular architectural vocabulary. Once its statements were understood, elements of the style were abbreviated, rendered in malleable sheet metal, and applied to architectural surfaces. The shopkeeper's Renaissance was ensconced.

6. Among the many references to new buildings, see especially the discussions in Niles's *Weekly Register*, 19 September 1812, pp. 45–48, and 19 November 1825, p. 177.

The author owes thanks for continued support from the administrative officials of the University of Iowa. Nancy Brcak, Jean Sizemore, and Judy Van Wagner have contributed valuable service as research assistants.

Abstracts: Vernacular Architecture Forum Conferences, 1982–1984

1982: North Carolina

1. W. Frank Ainsley. Which Side of the Tracks?: Social Geography and Vernacular Architecture in Three North Carolina Railroad Towns

2. LeAnne Baird. Evolution of Landscape in Northeast Cherokee County, Texas, 1830–1930

3. David R. Black. Rehabilitation of the Boyette Slave House and Its Stick Chimney

4. Frances Downing. Shape-Grammar: The Other-Than-Arbitrary Method for Defining Built Artifacts

5. Leonard T. Garfield. A Century of Criticism: Architectural Historians and Vernacular Commercial Architecture, 1876–1976

6. Douglass C. Reed. The Log Frame as Conceptual Technology

7. Rudolf L. Schreiber. Highlandtown: Culturally Significant Architectural Alterations in a Baltimore Neighborhood

8. Barbara Collins Turner. Afro-American Settlements in the Tidewater Region: Highland Beach

9. Michael Ann Williams. House Plans and Folk Patterns of Spatial Use in the Upland South

1983: Wisconsin

10. Arnold R. Alanen. Corporate Vernacular: Communities and Housing in Michigan's Copper Country

11. Thomas Carter. North European Log Construction in the Mormon West

12. David Denman. Ste. Genevieve and the Issue of Town Planning in the Mississippi River Valley, 1700–1815

13. Kathryn B. Eckert. The Vernacular Tradition in the Sandstone Architecture of the Lake Superior Region

14. Darrell D. Henning. The Norwegian Two- and Three-Room Traditional House Type in America

15. Stephen E. Ludwig and Michael Koop. German-Russian Folk Architecture in Southeastern South Dakota

16. William T. Morgan. Vernacular Architecture of Central Minnesota

17. David Murphy. Bohemian-American Log Technology in Northeastern Nebraska

18. Gerald L. Pocius. Mass Housing and Its Impact on Traditional Forms in a Newfoundland Community

19. Labelle Prussin. Gender-Related Vernacular Expression in the Built Environment

20. John Michael Vlach. The Brazilian House in Nigeria

21. Ellen Weiss. Methodist Camp Meeting Grounds: Regional Modes

22. Christopher L. Yip. The Vernacular Architecture of Chinese-American Agricultural Settlements in California

1984: Delaware

23. Simon J. Bronner. The House on Penn Street: Conflict and Creativity in the Back-to-the-City Movement

24. Patricia Irvin Cooper. Toward a Revised Understanding of American Log Building

25. Jonathan Fricker. The Origins of the Creole Raised Plantation House

26. Kingston Heath. John Dewey Revisited: Teaching Vernacular Architecture by Doing

27. Jan Leo Lewandoski. The Plank Framed House in Northeastern Vermont

28. Julie Riesenweber. Domestic Spatial Order: Salem County, New Jersey, 1700–1774

29. Myron O. Stachiw. Impermanent Architecture in the City: Examples from Nineteenth-Century New England

30. Dell Upton. Black and White Landscapes in Eighteenth-Century Virginia

1. W. Frank Ainsley

Which Side of the Tracks?: Social Geography and Vernacular Architecture in Three North Carolina Railroad Towns

Vernacular architectural form and structure are important subjects of study, but of equal significance is the way ordinary buildings are sited and distributed. The counting and mapping of buildings can provide the foundation for a greater understanding of the social and economic forces that shaped a community. This study of three railroad towns in North Carolina represents an enlightening case study.

In the middle of the nineteenth century, the towns of Warsaw, Faison, and Clarkton, North Carolina, evolved as agricultural collection stations on the Wilmington and Weldon and the Carolina Central rail lines. Comprehensive architectural inventories of these towns and their immediate vicinities revealed some clear patterns in the arrangements of buildings. The commercial-warehousing-industrial districts of each town were situated around the railroad tracks—the avenues of transport to which they were economically tied. In most cases, these business zones also buffered the residential areas from the tracks.

Within the residential districts, a mapping of various dwelling types revealed subtle geographic distinctions. More desirable—and therefore more costly—building sites were usually located upwind of the the railroad, but still in close proximity to the station. There thus exists physical evidence of the more ephemeral perception in each town that there is a "right" and a "wrong" side of the tracks.

As always, careful analysis of the evidence reveals, however, that there exists no simple cause-and-effect relationship. Spatial patterns in each of these three railroad communities were created by several factors: the preexisting agrarian divisions of land, the location and orientation of the railroad itself, the occupations, incomes, and social positions of original and subsequent owners.

2. LeAnne Baird

Evolution of Landscape in Northeast Cherokee County, Texas, 1830–1930

In 1980 and 1981, Exxon Coal U.S.A. funded a cultural resource survey of a 35,500-acre potential lignite mine site in Cherokee, Rusk, and Smith counties, Texas. Two hundred forty-eight archaeological and architectural resources were identified during the field investigation. This work, conducted by Environment Consultants of Dallas, provided the basis for this study of a historic landscape as it evolved between 1830 and 1930.

The study area in northeast Cherokee County encompasses approximately forty-five square miles. Within this rural district, the boundaries of neighborhoods were identified through the use of local oral traditions. Then all the buildings in the area were examined so that remnant architectural features could be interpreted within the context of changing rural communities.

The history of northeast Cherokee County can be divided into six settlement and development phases. From 1820 to 1850, initial settlers entered the region and began to engage in traditional small-scale corn and cotton cultivation. Between 1850 and 1870, the population of the area continued to increase, and a few churches and schools were established. Beyond the borders of the study area, a number of urban centers began to develop. In the last quarter of the century, seven distinct rural communities emerged in northeast Cherokee County. In 1872, the construction of a railroad several miles north of the project area provided residents with limited—but improved—access to urban markets. Throughout the nineteenth century, the agricultural economy remained similar to that of the Deep South. Nevertheless, in northeast Cherokee County, little class distinction existed among landlords, tenants, and yeoman farmers.

Between 1900 and 1925, agriculture became more diversified, although cotton continued to be the primary cash crop. Rural neighborhoods came to be identified less as groupings of households and more as geographic places distinguished by the presence of stores, sawmills, cotton gins, and churches of various denominations. After 1925, cotton production was replaced first by truck farming and subsequently by cattle production. As a result, farm tenancy declined and more young people sought work in nearby cities. Because of this decrease in population, the rural neighborhoods of northeast Cherokee County lost their cohesiveness and, eventually, their distinct identities.

Of all building types, houses are the most reflective of broad cultural change. They are also the feature of the built landscape most likely to be left standing. Sixty-seven old houses in the survey area were documented and sorted into three groups according to materials and building technology. Seven folk houses survive from the years before 1880. Of the forty-six houses dating from 1880 to 1920, eighteen are of folk plan, eighteen are of unstandardized vernacular design, and ten have a popular-culture origin. For the period dating from 1920 to 1940, there are five folk houses, five vernacular houses, and four dwellings of popular-culture design. Folk houses are more or less evenly distributed throughout the most habitable portions of the study area. Popular-culture houses, on the other hand, are clearly contained within neighborhood boundaries. Vernacular houses cluster along major roads, or on the outskirts of established neighborhoods. After 1925, almost no new house construction occurred within neighborhood boundaries, reflecting the breakdown of traditional rural community identities.

3. David R. Black

Rehabilitation of the Boyette Slave House and Its Stick Chimney

Early in 1981, a rehabilitation of the antebellum Boyette slave house in Johnston County, North Carolina, was carried out under the supervision of the Restoration Branch of the North Carolina Division of Archives and History. Because of its construction, condition, and original association with the domestic life of a neglected socioeconomic group, this dwelling is an especially interesting subject for preservation.

The Boyette slave house is of saw-cut plank construction with saw-cut full dovetail joints (Fig. 1). Its chimney is unique among surviving North Carolina buildings in that it is composed entirely of pine splints. The chimney structure is tied to the building at the base of the shoulder by a through-wall tenon and peg. While the two doors centered on opposite sides of the building are original features that reflect standard con-

struction for nineteenth-century slave houses and kitchens, the window in the gable end and the roof overhang that shelters the chimney appear to date from the early twentieth century, when the building was used as a school.

Rot and termites destroyed most of the squared-log foundation and several of the lower planks. As a result, the structure was wracked considerably out of plumb, compressing the existing joints and endangering the stick chimney. Initial stabilization work consisted of carefully jacking the building to a level and nearly plumb position. Severely deteriorated planks and all of the foundation logs were replaced with new wood.

Because wracking had so widened the surviving dovetail joints that they could no longer support the building, some method of unobtrusively pinning the corners together had to be found. On the end of the building where the least damage had occurred, the corners were stabilized with sixteen-penny hot-dipped galvanized cut nails driven into small holes drilled diagonally from one dovetail down into its contiguous member in the perpendicular wall. On the chimney wall, where the damage was worst, reinforced structural epoxy adhesives were used in a similar fashion. Half-inch holes were drilled, and

Fig. 1. Boyette slave house in Johnston County, North Carolina, before rehabilitation. (author, courtesy of North Carolina Division of Archives and History)

threaded galvanized steel rods were inserted. Around these rods was poured structural epoxy adhesive. When the epoxy had cured, the holes were covered with a colored sealant.

The stick chimney was relaid from the shoulder down, using splints cut from planks that had been removed from the walls of the structure. A very soft mortar mix of sand, clay, lime, and white Portland cement approximating the original clay pargeting was used to reface the chimney.

4. Frances Downing

Shape Grammar: The Other-Than-Arbitrary Method for Defining Built Artifacts

The full text of this paper appears in Frances Downing and Ulric Flemming, "The Bungalows of Buffalo," *Environment and Planning B* 8 (1981):269–93.

Parametric shape grammar is a technique that defines and generates shapes, shape relationships, and their potential transformations, making it possible to form an appropriate building typology. This method of analysis utilizes a strict rule system to identify all possible shapes for spaces within a particular typology and to enumerate their potential combinations. These same rules exclude all spaces and relationships that do not fit the typology, thus establishing a firm physical definition of a specific building type. To develop a parametric shape grammar, the researcher must identify a set of conventions that govern the arrangement, types, shapes, and juxtaposition of spaces.

This essay applies the principles of shape grammar to the American bungalow, a complicated and widespread house form. While the bungalow can be understood through social or stylistic analysis, the construction of a parametric shape grammar allows for pattern and rule recognition not possible with traditional methods. Spatial organizations of bungalow plans follow a rather well defined set of conventions that reflect three broad classes of requirements. They are functional, contextual, and formal.

The first stage of analysis usually involves a geometric pattern that determines certain universal characteristics, both formal and contextual. A second stage develops a graphic diagram following rules of application for primary spaces by identifying their functions and describing their conventional juxtapositions. A third stage identifies vertical and horizontal

systems of circulation. Succeeding stages deal with the functional areas of the plans in greater detail. The result is an enumeration of bungalow plans that includes all possible combinations of elements and rules for assemblage (Fig. 1).

The parametric shape grammar can be beneficial to researchers by helping to establish a definitive typology for a group of like artifacts. Besides enumerating the variations of the theme that exist in typologies, the grammar can identify missing types in a sample and even generate new plans that fit the typology.

Fig. 1. An enumeration of classes of bungalow plans, based on the principles of parametric shape grammar. (author, courtesy of *Environment and Planning B*)

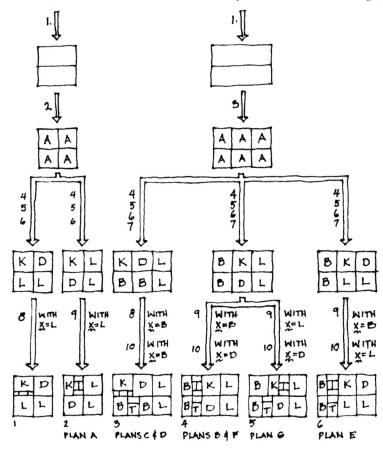

5. Leonard T. Garfield

A Century of Criticism: Architectural Historians and Vernacular Commercial Architecture, 1876–1976

This essay is part of a larger unpublished study of vernacular commercial architecture in the United States. Research was funded in part by a Rackham Predoctoral Fellowship awarded at the University of Michigan in 1980.

The vernacular commercial architecture of America's late nineteenth-century cities has long had its critics—less frequently, its champions. This paper considers both, reviewing a body of scholarly and popular analysis that ranges from disparaging statements in the architectural journals of the late nineteenth century to mid-twentieth-century attempts to understand vernacular commercial buildings in a historical context.

In the last quarter of the nineteenth century, vernacular commercial architecture provided both a new shape for the American urban landscape and a new subject for architectural critics who deplored the "tumultuous incoherence" of the ubiquitous commercial buildings.[1] Aesthetic values, it was feared, had been doomed by pecuniary concerns.

Architectural historians sustained this critique well into the new century, deriding the economic expediency of commercial vernacular buildings as well as their stylistic inadequacies. At the same time, an emerging group of writers and painters, including Sinclair Lewis and Edward Hopper, perceived vernacular commercial design as a powerful metaphor for America's spiritual malaise. Indeed, the literature that

1. *American Architect and Building News,* 1 January 1876, p. 3.

presented the first "realistic" portraits of modern America created a lingering image of an architectural wasteland in the country's commercial centers.

While early twentieth-century scholars largely agreed with one critic's assertion that America's "vigorous industrial expansion completed the architectural collapse" of good design,[2] a later school of architectural historians, inspired by the achievements of the Chicago School, initiated a reappraisal. Searching for antecedents for the modern skyscraper, historians in the mid-twentieth century found significance in the technical achievements and economic emphases of nineteenth-century vernacular commercial buildings. Sigfried Giedion, Carl Condit, John Kouwenhoven, and others celebrated "the transmutation of vernacular building . . . into a genuine architectural style."[3] In so doing, critics simultaneously imparted a new importance to commercial vernacular design and identified a historical context for modernism.

In the 1960s and 1970s, interpretations of vernacular commercial buildings sustained a kind of democratization, as scholars identified the tradition as an architecture for the masses that embodied both the virtues and the faults common to all the popular arts. Other critics replaced evaluations of style with the theories of an-

2. Ralph Gabriel, "Introduction," in Talbot Hamlin, *The American Spirit in Architecture* (New Haven: Yale University Press, 1926), p. 6.

3. Carl Condit, *The Chicago School of Architecture* (Chicago: University of Chicago Press, 1964), p. 9. See also Sigfried Giedion, *Space, Time, and Architecture: Growth of a New Tradition* (Cambridge: Harvard University Press, 1941), and John Kouwenhoven, *Made in America: The Arts in Modern Civilization* (Garden City: Doubleday and Company, 1948).

thropology, social history, and cultural geography, thereby relating vernacular commercial buildings to the larger context of American urban development. The task of this essay is to put a century of architectural criticism into historical perspective. By charting and explaining changing responses to a common building type, it attempts to shed new light on evolving attitudes toward America's architectural heritage.

6. Douglass C. Reed

The Log Frame as Conceptual Technology

It is a commonly held notion that log housing was both temporary and crude when built by people settling along a frontier. Careful fieldwork is beginning to indicate, however, that many of these initial settlement houses were well planned and built for permanence. Contrary to popular notions, these houses, though small, were often quite refined, nicely finished, and planned to allow for future expansion.

This essay summarizes the most recent physical and documentary evidence concerning the intentions of frontier log house builders and dwellers. The discussion focuses not on floor plans or ethnic influences except where they are relevant to an understanding of log building as a conceptual technology. Rather, several houses are examined to establish their initial construction, original appearance, and sequence of growth.

Architectural historians have carefully examined diffusion, ethnography, floor plans, and styles of embellishment, yet they have rarely considered the planning of a site or the treatment of the structure itself. Many houses were carefully situated on ground that

was artificially changed to suit the needs of the owner. Houses may have started out small, but they were often enlarged along the lines initially planned by the original builder/owner.

Other elements of log technology have been similarly overlooked or misunderstood. Many architectural historians believe that whitewash on log walls indicates that this was the original—and intended final—finish for the building. In actuality, the treatment was meant to be a temporary solution until the green logs used to construct the shell of the building had dried out sufficiently to accept plaster and siding.

Even a cursory examination of the literature of material culture reveals that log buildings have received frequent and intensive investigation. Yet recent study in the field and among documentary sources indicates that the buildings and the technology that produced them still have much information to yield.

7. Rudolf L. Schreiber

Highlandtown: Culturally Significant Architectural Alterations in a Baltimore Neighborhood

Highlandtown, a neighborhood in east Baltimore, was laid out and filled with two-story brick row houses at the beginning of this century. With few exceptions, the houses originally had little exterior ornamentation other than white marble steps and stained-glass transoms above the doorways. As the neighborhood grew older and larger, these houses came to be occupied serially by German, Irish, Polish, and Italian immigrants. These newcomers, like many other immigrants who came to America between 1900 and 1950, did not have the opportunity to build their own houses. Any architectural manifestations of their previous cultural experience had to be added onto the existing plain housing stock they occupied.[1]

The building techniques employed by immigrants in the construction of rural buildings have been a major concern among students of material culture, but the architectural contributions of the larger population of urban immigrants who bought or rented extant houses have hardly been examined. This paper attempts to recognize some of those contributions by identifying the kinds of changes that urban immigrants made or intended to make to their new homes. In this process, it is important to distinguish between changes motivated by cultural or ethnic traditions and those made for practical reasons. One informant, for example, felt that his house was incomplete because it had no cellar space in which he could prepare and store salt pork and sauerkraut, as his Polish father had taught him. Normally, the addition of a basement would not seem culturally motivated, but, in this context, it clearly was.

Some architectural alterations can be found simply by examining pictorial resources, but, in order to determine the motivation behind changes, this study also incorporates oral histories of Highland-town residents that were collected by the Baltimore Neighborhood Heritage Project. These oral histories represent a valuable group of potential informants who can fill in the details concerning how and why changes were made to Highlandtown houses and sites.

The ultimate objective of this study is to determine what role ethnicity played in the modification of these Baltimore row houses, but other questions are

1. See Read's essay elsewhere in this volume.

equally significant. How important is architecture in immigrants' perceptions of their domestic environment? Does one individual make changes in response to those made by neighbors? Do the changes represent an intention to assimilate, to maintain cultural identity, or to create a "hybrid" of images that incorporate both Old and New World traditions?

8. Barbara Collins Turner

Afro-American Settlements in the Tidewater Region: Highland Beach

In the summer of 1892, Maj. Charles R. Douglass, son of abolitionist Frederick Douglass, attempted to visit a restaurant in the Maryland resort community of Bay Ridge. He and his wife were refused service because they were black. Angered by the incident, Douglass walked along the beach, where he met by chance a family who owned and farmed land in the area. He discovered that they were interested in selling some of their property, and he began to purchase land from them with the intention of establishing a resort community for blacks.

The following year, Douglass had his tract of land laid out in a grid of individual lots, each averaging about an acre in size. In 1894, Douglass himself built the first house in the community, which he named "Highland Beach." Thirteen cottages were erected at the resort within the next decade. By 1930, some thirty residences had been built at Highland Beach by prominent Afro-Americans.

Despite their origins from all parts of the Mid-Atlantic Region, many of these individuals had known one another before they built houses at Highland Beach. These ties developed as an indi-

rect result of the racist and segregationist practices that prevailed at the time. Even famous blacks were generally barred from public accommodations in the South and also in exclusionary communities of the North. Segregated facilities for blacks were frequently inferior and unappealing. In response, many blacks made a practice of opening their homes to traveling associates, who used letters of introduction from mutual friends to smooth the process. In this way, a tradition of empathy and hospitality developed. Highland Beach was a setting in which members of this close-knit black society could create a recreational atmosphere together.

Highland Beach cottages are situated formally along a rectilinear plan, with the facades oriented toward shared corridors. In most cases, however, the decorative emphasis of each dwelling is on the side that faces Chesapeake Bay, rather than on the front. Typically, the one-and-a-half-story beach cottages are set on masonry piers, constructed of wood frame, and clad with weatherboards or shingles. Although architectural style is less important than form and siting, modest Victorian and Colonial Revival trim is common, and many of the houses have elements associated with the bungalow house type.

What is the importance of Highland Beach? This late nineteenth-century resort community makes a contribution toward reversing the notion that Afro-Americans have not participated actively in their own culture. Most American blacks are the descendants of unwilling immigrants whose bondage, it has been assumed, prevented them from expressing their native cultural identities. Once freed, their long-acculturated descendants set up positions near the margins of the dominant and discriminating Anglo-American social order, where they presumably went about producing correspondingly marginal versions of Anglo-American culture. It has never adequately been established that the strong African heritage of black Americans, coupled with their unique oppressed position in American social, economic, and political structures, has produced a distinct sense of community, identity, and aesthetics. Highland Beach is an integral part of that story.

9. Michael Ann Williams

House Plans and Folk Patterns of Spatial Use in the Upland South

For a more complete development of these ideas, see the author's dissertation, "Homeplace: The Social Use and Meaning of the Folk Dwelling in Southwestern North Carolina," University of Pennsylvania, 1985.

The study of past and present domestic spatial patterns through the methods of oral history and ethnography provides insights into both the nature of cultural change and the relationship of house form and room use. This type of investigation is especially rewarding in the rural Upland South, where the construction of traditional dwellings often persisted into living memory. Using data collected from fieldwork in northeastern Mississippi and southwestern North Carolina, this essay explores the nature of domestic architectural and spatial change.

During the early twentieth century, profound changes occurred in the spatial use of folk houses in the Tennessee hills of northeastern Mississippi. The majority of folk houses at the turn of the century were variants of the double-pen plan with a rear ell or shed kitchen. The use of this plan was generally traditional in nature, except for the increasing impulse to isolate cooking and eating in the rear kitchen. The two main rooms of the double-pen house were the "sitting room," the informal domestic center of the household, and the "parlor," which was reserved primarily for formal interaction. The lack of designated bedrooms in this spatial arrangement and the presence of beds in every room except the kitchen suggest a pattern of generalized room use. However, oral history reveals that the spatial system was actually complex and layered. While giving primacy to distinctions between formal and informal living space, the system actually maximized privacy within the small house by allowing beds in the rooms without acknowledging their function.

A few decades later, the system of spatial use changed, as construction of traditional folk houses declined. Even those families that continued to live in older dwellings altered their spatial arrangements. The traditional sitting room and parlor of the double-pen house became living room and bedroom. While giving new priority to the recognition of a private bedroom, the new system eliminated the arena for formal interaction without actually creating more privacy. Significantly, this change was usually accomplished without physical alteration to the structure, indicating an independence of house plans from systems of room use.

Somewhat earlier, similar changes in spatial use occurred in mountainous western North Carolina. In this region, however, the central-passage house was more common during the early twentieth century than it was in northeastern Mississippi. A typical physical alteration to these North Carolina dwellings involved the abolition of the central hallway. While the removal of the hallway appears to be a result of changing spatial patterns, evidence suggests that there was a historically rooted ambivalence to the central passage resulting from a conflict between house form and spatial use. Rather than acting as a formal circulation space, the central passage was frequently used as an informal living space, despite the awkwardness of its size and shape and the absence of a direct source of heat. People eventually removed the passage altogether, creating a two-room plan that was more compatible to local systems of spatial use.

Oral history suggests that the relationship between house form and spatial use is more malleable and subtle than inferences from form alone suggest. Systems of spatial use can change without physical alteration to the dwelling, and, under certain circumstances, people may choose house types that are incompatible with their preferred system of spatial use. Rather than leaving an understanding of past spatial use to hypotheses based on house form, vernacular architecture scholars need to make a study of spatial use within specific cultural contexts and to let their findings through oral history and ethnography inform interpretations of the more distant past.

10. Arnold R. Alanen

Corporate Vernacular: Communities and Housing in Michigan's Copper Country

The company town is an important element in the history of American architecture and planning. Although the traditional company town is no longer as commonplace as it once was, it is important to note that the United States has hosted the development of more versions of the corporate-sponsored community than any other nation in the world. Nevertheless, the company town—especially its physical characteristics—has been for the most part ignored by scholars and investigators.

While surveys of company towns do exist,[1] one region of the United States that has been completely overlooked is the Lake Superior region of northern Michigan, Wisconsin, and Minnesota, which encompasses one copper- and six iron-ore ranges. The process of extracting these metals generated the construction of hundreds of mining towns between the 1840s and the 1920s. Not all these communities were totally company-sponsored, but they all were subject to the vagaries of a single industry and a single employer.

This essay considers the general characteristics of company towns in one area of the region, Michigan's Copper Country.[2] Company towns in this area may be classified as *locations*, mostly residential

assemblages situated around a mining operation, or as *townsites*, more autonomous communities usually established by speculators and laid out in grid patterns. Within the framework provided by this typology, other matters concerning layout, plantings, house forms, construction materials, degrees of permanence, and concern for appearance are treated.

From these descriptions, it becomes clear that the central issue of company-town formation was *control*. Employers might build more commodious workers' dwellings or encourage the planting of gardens, but the motive for such improvements was an understanding that such accommodations made the miners more contented or reliable. Indeed, the entire social and economic hierarchy of the community was expressed and reinforced in the plan and architecture of the company town. Rows of identical "well-regulated" miners' houses were generally devoid of any ornamental detailing. For those better placed along the scale of employment—from shift bosses, mechanics, and carpenters to agents and mining captains—available houses were progressively more spacious, better sited, and more finely detailed.

While general statements concerning the place of company towns in the history of America—or even the history of Michigan's Copper Country—must await consideration of their social and economic contexts, it is undeniable that these forms of corporate vernacular design and planning have lessons to teach. At odds with the uncritical view of the American past as unfailingly based on democratic principles are these commu-

nities, where most of the population lived and worked according to the restrictions of "the managers of the mining company [who] control everything, and allow no business that is not conducted by themselves."[3]

11. Thomas Carter

North European Log Construction in the Mormon West

An expanded version of this paper was published as "North European Horizontal Log Construction in the Sanpete-Sevier Valleys," *Utah Historical Quarterly* 52 (1984):50–71.

In the second half of the nineteenth century, intense missionary activity in the Scandinavian countries by the Church of Jesus Christ of Latter-day Saints resulted in the arrival of nearly thirty thousand immigrant converts to the Mormon Zion in Utah. Previous historical studies of this immigration have stressed the rapid assimilation of the Scandinavians into what has been considered a rigidly authoritarian and homogeneous Mormon society. Old World folkways, including the techniques of log construction, are thought to have been discarded quickly as Swedes, Norwegians, and Danes adopted the language and customs of the dominant Anglo-American Mormon culture.

Failure to recognize survivals of immigrant folk culture is due partly to faulty survey methodologies, but it also reflects a deeper assumption that Mormonism, as a quintessentially American religion, actively and successfully stifles all forms of ethnic expression. Recent studies in history, anthropology, and folklife have begun to

1. See especially John W. Reps, *The Making of Urban America: A History of City Planning in the United States* (Princeton: Princeton University Press, 1965), pp. 414–38; and Reps, *Cities of the American West: A History of Frontier Urban Planning* (Princeton: Princeton University Press, 1979), pp. 194–237, 456–522.

2. Other studies by the author have focused on the entire Lake Superior mining region or have been oriented toward communities on Minnesota's iron ore range. See Arnold R. Alanen, "The Planning of Company Communities in the Lake Superior Mining Region," *Journal of the American Planning Association* 45 (July 1979):256–78; Alanen, "Documenting the Physical and Social Characteristics of Mining and Resource Based Settlements," *Association for Preservation Technology Bulletin* 11 (1979):49–68; and Alanen, "The 'Locations': Company

Communities on Minnesota's Iron Ranges," *Minnesota History* 48 (Fall 1982):94–109.

3. William E. Curtis, "Calumet, A Unique Municipality," *Chautauquan* 29 (April 1899):34.

chip away at the monolithic interpretation of nineteenth-century Mormon society. A descriptive study of north European horizontal log architecture in Utah can make a useful contribution to the ongoing reappraisal of immigrant life in the early settlements of the Mormon West.

This study grew out of a larger survey of nineteenth-century Mormon vernacular architecture and deals specifically with several representative homesteads in the heavily Scandinavian settlements of the Sanpete and Sevier valleys in central Utah. Attention is given to particular house plans, timber-fitting techniques, and corner-timbering methods. Norwegian and Swedish antecedents for these practices are identified and discussed within the context of Scandinavian immigration to Utah in the period between 1850 and 1890. While the study is outwardly directed toward the origins and diffusion of elements of North European material folk culture, a more general concern involves rethinking traditional historical interpretations of nineteenth-century life in Mormon Utah.

12. David Denman

Ste. Genevieve and the Issue of Town Planning in the Mississippi River Valley, 1700–1815

French explorers first entered the Mississippi River Valley late in the seventeenth century. In the opening years of the eighteenth century, French settlers established permanent communities in the region. They built houses, cultivated fields, traded with the Indians, hunted, and trapped for furs. Over the next sixty years, five principal villages were founded: Cahokia, Kaskaskia, St. Louis, and the old and new sites of Ste. Genevieve.

This paper examines the way French colonial authorities and *habitants* visualized and created their settlement landscapes. Because of an especially large quantity of documentary material, the focus of this study is on Ste. Genevieve. Through analysis of written sources, it has been possible to re-create maps of Ste. Genevieve at several stages of growth: in 1785, 1792, and 1815.

The Renaissance version of the ancient Roman rectilinear town plan was firmly fixed in the minds of seventeenth-century French colonial officials. Obviously, the French colonies in America represented an opportunity to impose rational, grid-like town plans onto an untouched terrain. Montreal, New Orleans, and St. Louis—as well as other French-American communities—exhibit evidence of original grid plans. As time passed, however, villages and parishes developed distinct identities that were the result, in part, of modifications of the original Renaissance models. What factors effected these changes?

In Ste. Genevieve, the Mississippi River forced major adaptations that included, in 1785, the removal of the entire village site from the riverside alluvial plain to the surrounding low hills. At the new site, evidence clearly indicates some impulse to reestablish an orderly plan of square blocks, each with about three hundred eighty feet to a side. Topography, however, mitigated attempts to regularize streets and lots. Between the forks of the Gaboury Creek, where the center of the new village was located, flood plains and terraces challenged the guiding rectilinear ideal.

More important still is clear evidence of a settlement bias with social and economic class origins. Both the reconstructed town plans and the surviving buildings indicate a systematic differentiation of

residential patterns in the community. *Habitants* of higher social and economic position appear to have concentrated their residential holdings in the area between the forks of the creek. The religious and administrative focus of Ste. Genevieve was also located within this central community segment. In outlying areas of the village, on lots with boundaries that consistently follow geographic convenience, documentary sources and standing structures suggest that early *habitants* were of a lower economic and social class than were those who lived near the center of town.

What is to be made of all this? It seems clear that an influential or organizing element of the Ste. Genevieve community was committed to the Renaissance idea of town planning. The planners were challenged, however, not only by the terrain and the waterways but also, more significantly, by competing social and economic interests in the community. In short, the ideal of rational, rectilinear town plans was absorbed by one class and not another. Both the documentary evidence and the architectural evidence point to such a class division.

13. Kathryn B. Eckert

The Vernacular Tradition in the Sandstone Architecture of the Lake Superior Region

Red sandstone architecture gives the rugged landscape around Lake Superior a distinct identity. From 1870 to 1910 the prosperity of the region's mining, lumbering, and shipping industries created a need for all kinds of buildings. For a sturdy, permanent building material, architects, builders, and clients preferred the sedimentary rock found in the Jacobsville geological formation and the Bayfield group of formations that lie in a four-hundred-mile-long belt from Sault Sainte Marie, Michigan, to Duluth, Minnesota. People chose sandstone for construction rather than brick or wood for practical as well as romantic reasons. It was easily extracted in large blocks, cheaply shipped by water, carvable, and durable. Moreover, during the late nineteenth century it was aggressively promoted. Finally, and perhaps most importantly, it symbolized solidity, security, permanence, and success.

Field inspections and searches of geological and mineral records have identified nearly fifty quarry sites clustered at Marquette and Portage Entry, Michigan, at Bayfield, Wisconsin, and scattered along the shore of Lake Superior (Fig. 1). These were developed and operated by some seventy companies based in large midwestern cities and in small cities in the lake region. Surveys of extant buildings and historic photographs have verified the existence of hundreds of buildings constructed wholly or largely of stone in more than a dozen towns located within the boundaries of the Jacobsville and Bayfield geological formations.

This essay relates the location of the quarries in the geological formations to the settlements in which the stone was used. It discusses the role of local investors in promoting the use of sandstone. It also analyzes the vernacular sandstone structures of builders and stonemasons, contrasting them with the cultivated designs of trained architects. Emphasis is on the environmental, social, and economic forces that interacted to produce this distinctive regional architecture.

Red sandstone lost favor with changes in architectural fashion and building technology. Popularization of steel frame construction increased the demand for lighter-weight building materials that could serve as sheathing for the metal skeletons. In 1893, the Chicago World's Columbian Exposition generated a renewed interest in the forms and motifs of classical design, which required white, smooth-cut stone and cleanly molded clay products. Nevertheless, this distinctive regional red sandstone architecture not only represents an important aspect of the character of the last quarter of the nineteenth century, it also illustrates the persistence of the vernacular tradition.

14. Darrell D. Henning

The Norwegian Two- and Three-Room Traditional House Type in America

Norwegian immigrants arrived in the New World with the usual load of cultural baggage. As with other rural European peoples, their heritage included a long tradition in building forms and construction techniques. One of the several house types brought to America by Norwegian newcomers was a two- and three-room structure (Fig. 1). Its many variations were retained in this country for at least two generations. This essay is drawn from ongoing research on Norwegian-American material culture—a culture in transition.

The two- and three-room house apparently had its beginnings in Norway during the Middle Ages. A one-room, one-story, open-hearth house with a door in the gable end protected by an extended roof was the forerunner of the house type (Fig. 2A). The next step in its development involved enclosure of the entrance, resulting in a two-room house (Fig. 2B). Moving the entrance from the gable-end wall allowed the new room to be further divided, completing the basic development of the type (Figs. 2C and 2D).

Although the form appears to be evolutionary, each stage of the development has its own subsequent history. Even after the introduction of partitioned versions, the single-room type continued to be constructed, but usually its function was changed from dwelling to storehouse or granary. Structures of this sort are found in Norway, as well as among farm building inventories of first- and second-generation Norwegian-American farmsteads.

The first step beyond the one-

Fig. 1. Photo, taken about 1891, of quarrying conducted by the Portage Entry Redstone Company in Jacobsville, Michigan. The finished blocks of stone typically measured eight by four by two feet and were sold to builders by the cubic foot. (Michigan Technological University Archives and Copper Country Historical Collections)

Fig. 1. Norwegian-American two- or three-room house in Worth County, Iowa. Photo taken around 1910. (courtesy of Vesterheim)

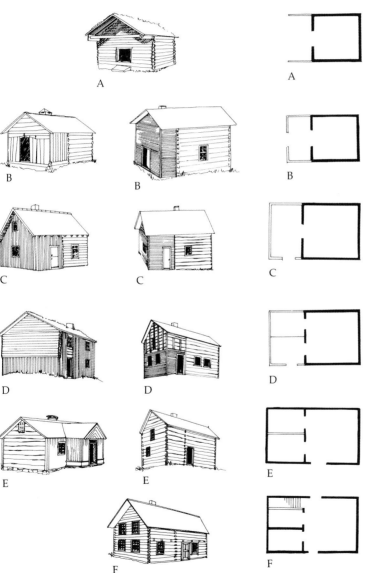

Fig. 2. Variations of a form: the two- and three-room house in Norway and America. (Dana Jackson)

room type, the two-room form with a gable-end entrance, was used for dwelling construction well into the nineteenth century. In Norway, it often was used as the summer dwelling on the upper pasture of a seasonally split farm. The house form reached America completely intact, and, since the split-farm system apparently was never practiced, it was employed as a year-round dwelling. Not only the form but also the basic construction method persisted in the New World. The main room, or *stue*, was usually constructed of hewn logs. The smaller room might also be built of logs, or it might be constructed of wood framing that was attached to the main log structure, or of wood framing set beneath a timber extension of the *stue*. When not built entirely of logs, the two parts of the house normally had common sills and plates, or these members were connected with dovetail or lap joints.

When the entrance was shifted from the gable-end to the long wall, a number of variations were possible. If the door was located in such a way as to give access to the smaller room, an asymmetrical facade was the result. If this space was subdivided, the front room, or *forestue*, served only as an entryway to the *stue* and to the loft, if there was a second floor (Fig. 2D). The rear half of the new, partitioned space became either a bedroom or an annex to the kitchen. If the door was placed to provide direct entry to the *stue*

(Fig. 2E), the smaller rooms were most often used as a pantry and a bedroom. Second-floor space was accessible by way of a stair located in the pantry. A late variation of this house type included a tripartite division of the smaller end of the house formed simply by enclosing the stair (Fig. 2F).

As with other variations of the form, these developments were found both in the Old World and in America. A functional change peculiar to American examples often involved placing the kitchen in one of the smaller rooms, rather than incorporating it into the *stue*, as had been the custom in Norway. Many American examples of the form also sustained the addition of a second exterior door to the *stue*, usually opposite the traditional one (Fig. 2F).

Most differences between the Old World and the New World construction follow expected patterns. Casement windows were supplanted by readily available double-hung sash windows. Steeply pitched roofs clad with wooden shingles replaced low sod roofs, and cast-iron stoves were installed in place of stone fireplaces. Some details of construction do not follow Old World practices and are difficult to explain. Log construction techniques have a long tradition in Norway and exhibit numerous regional differences. The use of *langdraget*, a long grooved cut along the length of the logs designed to create tight-fitting joints, was standard in Norway but is found rarely in America. The common Norwegian-American practice was to use a full dovetail corner joint with spaces left between the logs. These spaces were filled with chinking material such as mud, clay, or plaster. Unlike other European settlers, the Norwegian immigrants employed wooden spacers—either pegs or butterfly wedges set into slots—to keep logs in place around doors and windows and to stabilize the gaps between the logs. In Norway, this technique was usually associated with the construction of barns, rather than dwellings.

The two- and three-room rural house type—as well as log construction—is associated in America with Norwegian immigrants and their descendants, but the building forms and construction techniques are not limited to Norwegian or even to Scandinavian builders. It is necessary, then, to consider that there was more than one European source for these traditions. Nevertheless, between 1825 and 1900, over a half-million Norwegian immigrants arrived in America. Many of these people settled in rural areas of the Midwest, and their contribution to vernacular architectural traditions must not be overlooked.

15. Stephen E. Ludwig and Michael Koop

German-Russian Folk Architecture in Southeastern South Dakota

The results of this study were published as Michael Koop and Stephen E. Ludwig, *German-Russian Folk Architecture in Southeastern South Dakota* (Vermillion: State Historical Preservation Center, 1984). Copies are available for $5.00 from the center at P.O. Box 417, Vermillion, SD 57069.

This essay summarizes the results of an architectural survey conducted in 1982 under the direction of the State Historic Preservation Center of South Dakota. In the course of the study, twenty German-Russian farmsteads were recorded, and some twenty other sites associated with the same ethnic group were identified in the southeastern part of the state.

The term *German-Russian* refers to a group of people who migrated in the eighteenth and nineteenth centuries from German-speaking regions of central Europe to the unsettled steppe country of Russia. Under the reigns of Catherine the Great and Alexander I, the settlers enjoyed toleration and economic incentives to establish communities that reinforced their cultural cohesion. In 1871, the Russian government abrogated the privileges of the German-speaking colonists and began to suppress their distinct ways of life. As a result, they emigrated once more.

Between 1873 and 1918, thousands of German-Russians settled on the plains of South Dakota. They brought with them not only their accustomed ways of living and farming but also distinct architectural traditions. Examination of standing structures indicated that German-Russian folk building practices had been transplanted directly to the region in the 1870s and had survived there for about forty years.

The characteristic German-Russian house type is a one-story, gable-roofed, rectangular dwelling of varying dimensions but with consistent proportions. Typically, a house is one and a half to two times longer than wide. Although the structure is low-roofed, it always contains a loft. Other characteristic features include a central chimney, symmetrically placed fenestration on at least one long wall, a central doorway, and two windows on each gable end. Interior space is divided into two or three bays that are one or two rooms in depth. Commonly, a small gable- or shed-roofed extension shelters the main entrance, and a rectangular barn is connected to one gable end of the house. The combined building is sited in a north-south direction to provide protection from winter winds. Other notable features of the house type include a combined furnace and bake oven known as a "Russian oven," and whitewashed or painted surfaces.

Among the German-Russian houses built before 1890, seven traditional masonry construction materials were identified. Six of these employ puddled clay as material for load-bearing walls, sun-dried brick, or mortar. Around 1880, there occurred a shift from the preference for thick-walled earth or masonry construction toward the use of commercially dressed balloon frame construction. Nevertheless, the most significant elements of the German-Russian house type endured until the time of the First World War.

16. William T. Morgan

Vernacular Architecture of Central Minnesota

This paper was extracted from a book written by the author with Marilyn S. Brinkman entitled *Light from the Hearth: Central Minnesota Pioneers and Early Architecture* (St. Cloud, Minn.: North Star Press, 1982).

This essay presents the results of several years of architectural fieldwork carried out in a seven-county area of central Minnesota. The goal was to identify and record structures that represent the vanishing social and architectural heritage of that region. The buildings studied were constructed between 1860 and 1900. They included houses, churches, schoolhouses, barns, granaries, smokehouses, corncribs, small-animal shelters, and other miscellaneous outbuildings. Over two hundred structures were photographed, and the best examples of each building type were measured. Where buildings were

abandoned, written sources were sought for background information. In other cases, interviews provided an invaluable record of building history, family history, and rural life-styles.

Central Minnesota was settled largely by people from several European nations who arrived directly from their homelands, rather than from the eastern United States. The region, therefore, is invaluable for the study of European-transplanted building techniques and forms that were not initially influenced by Anglo-American adaptations. Out of this stream of late nineteenth-century immigration, there emerged four major building traditions that are of special importance to the field of vernacular studies.

After a brief period during which temporary structures were used, immigrants turned to the abundant wood supplies found in the region. Central Minnesota still contains hundreds of hewn-log houses, barns, and outbuildings. Erected by Slovenian and German immigrants who began arriving in the 1850s, these structures more strongly resemble the European medieval building traditions than do those structures erected by westward-moving American pioneers. Slovenian settlements in Brockway and Krain townships, for example, host a number of log buildings fashioned in the style of medieval rural Yugoslavia.

While the predominant form of log construction was horizontal, vertical log houses also can be found in central Minnesota. Although this type of structure is usually associated with French post-in-sill construction, the Minnesota houses were apparently built by Scandinavian and Slovenian craftsmen. It is not known whether these builders were acquainted with the similar French traditions. The few surviving ex-

amples of upright hewn-log houses show a refined level of craftsmanship: hand-hewn mortise-and-tenon joints, smoothly adzed surfaces, and skilled methods of wall construction.

A highly developed tradition of stone construction is the third important architectural characteristic in central Minnesota. While stone piers and foundations abound, the best and most significant masonry is found in wall construction. German farmers made fairly wide use of this material, and their smokehouses have survived with particular tenacity.

Since immigrants to central Minnesota arrived rather late in American frontier history, they had advanced technology at their disposal. In the latter decades of the nineteenth century, frame construction, commercially finished board sheathing, and brick flues for store-bought stoves became commonplace. Though traditional house forms remained popular, there began to appear L- and T-plan houses with classical or Gothic decorative trim. These structures indicate the growing influence of Anglo-American building traditions.

These observations, drawn from the first study of central Minnesota's vernacular architecture and ethnic heritage, indicate how much remains to be done. Future studies should strive to integrate social and architectural histories of other ethnic traditions, historical periods, and regions of Minnesota.

17. David Murphy

Bohemian-American Log Technology in Northeastern Nebraska

Students of vernacular architecture have long been interested in log architecture, particularly in the antecedents and development of the distinctly American log construction that played such an important role in the westward settlement of this country. The long-standing debate on antecedents has alternately attributed primary importance to the Swedes of the Delaware Valley or to the Germans of southeastern Pennsylvania. While no one would argue that a study of American log technology in Nebraska can inform the argument over antecedents, other historical circumstances—principally the transplantation of large numbers of European immigrants directly to the Plains region—do provide interesting comparative material. Indeed, it is this direct migration, innocent of the acculturating forces of the previous hundred and fifty years in the eastern United States, that makes research into the early log architecture of the Great Plains both difficult and rewarding.

A superior log technology was introduced into northeastern Nebraska by settlers from central Bohemia in the last half of the nineteenth century. Three major diagnostic features of eighteen extant log buildings provide strong circumstantial evidence in support of an east-central European source for American log technology: the universal existence of chinks between the logs, the use of hewn logs on houses and some barns while other barns and outbuildings are constructed of unhewn logs, and the prevalence of full dovetail notching on houses and some barns while V, saddle, and square notches occur occasionally on barns and other outbuildings. Additional features enhance the diversity and sophistication of the Bohemian-American technology. These include the use of the vertical double notch on the chinked hewn logs of one house and the cantilevered plate log of another, the presence of vertical mortised posts for door and window jambs

in some houses, the practice of dovetailing interior log partition walls to exterior walls, and the occasional appearance of beamed ceilings in place of joists.

The challenge is to continue research and fieldwork relative to the antecedent question, both in the United States and in Europe. Future studies need to be both spatial and temporal, and they must account adequately for ethnicity, particularly in environments where more than one ethnic tradition has currency or where survival rates are greatly reduced. Additionally, it is important to distinguish between major and minor buildings, permanent and temporary ones, first-generation and later constructions. A clearer understanding of how log technologies were selected, modified, and diffused in the eastern United States will contribute to better appreciation of the American character, both as it developed in the forested East and as it confronted unfamiliar conditions on the treeless midcontinental plains.

18. Gerald L. Pocius

Mass Housing and Its Impact on Traditional Forms in a Newfoundland Community

An expanded version of this paper will appear in the author's forthcoming book entitled *Living Spaces: Landscape Structures in a Newfoundland Community*.

Standard works dealing with vernacular architecture often take a negative stance toward recent mass-housing forms. Some writers directly make this assertion, while others imply as much by neglecting to investigate any architectural forms that were built after a certain date or that have clear popular-culture origins. Moreover,

the research that is conducted on modern housing tends to emphasize the form and original design of the house rather than its spaces and their uses. Does modern mass housing indeed represent a break with vernacular building traditions? This essay proposes an answer to that question.

For this study, all of the structures in Calvert, Newfoundland, were recorded—regardless of their date of construction. Floor plans and the number and types of rooms were the focus of attention. Spatial distinctions and similarities among buildings of different periods were documented, and patterns of domestic organization were examined. The resulting information was grouped around several questions. How were spaces in old houses used in the past, and how are those same rooms used today? How do these patterns compare with the utilization of rooms in new examples of mass design? How do residents adapt to new spaces, such as dining rooms and recreational rooms? A related matter is the relationship of mass-housing designs to constructed versions. Since even modern houses are still owner-built in Calvert, it is possible for individuals to alter mass-produced plans to meet local needs.

Out of myriad mass-housing types available to builders, one standard plan is now the most common in Calvert. Not surprisingly, it is a plan that maintains the scale and major spatial units common to earlier traditional forms. Since room functions in the community still emphasize many long-standing practices like visiting and Christmas mummering, the kitchen remains a community room—the setting for most social activity. The living room is often used on formal occasions, such as wakes and visits by clergymen. Play for children takes place outside the home, rather than in the basement recreational room. Indeed, the basements of modern houses often assume functions—such as boat building—that were previously relegated to outbuildings.

It is clear that a kind of spatial homeostasis has caused new structures to be altered quickly to conform to traditional patterns of use. The mass housing of today, then, does not mark a clear break with the building of the past. In spatial terms, new houses are similar to earlier forms. Furthermore, this spatial continuity of room uses calls into question the notion that external architectural forms constrain values and behaviors. At least in Calvert, people find ways to get around these introduced forms, continuing to live some aspects of their daily lives much as they have in the past.

19. Labelle Prussin

Gender-Related Vernacular Expression in the Built Environment

A revised version of this paper will appear in the proceedings of the Conference on People and Physical Environment Research that was held in Melbourne, Australia, in June 1985.

Architectural values constitute a part of every cultural system. Furthermore, although every cultural system constitutes a unique whole, it also includes within its parameters a number of subsets or subcultures. Assuming that men and women constitute distinct subcultures, it follows that the architectural values inherent in any culture reflect gender-related differences. Indeed, studies show that men and women do relate differently to space: they use it, look at it, design it, and conceive of it in different ways. Even more spe-

cifically, women speak about their domiciles in distinctly different ways than men do. They value the objects in and around their habitats quite differently, and they invest the artifacts of their residential environments with different meanings.

In nomadic cultures, it is traditionally the women who have carried responsibility for creating, erecting, maintaining, and striking the domestic habitat. The whole of a woman's personality is involved in the creation of her dwelling. Thus, the study of nomadic architecture can provide a particularly fruitful field of research into the nature of gender-related questions of cognition, perception, and meaning in the built environment. Nomadic architectures can thus function as expressive indicators of the social, emotional, and aesthetic components of gender-related subsets in any culture.

Even a cursory survey of nomadic cultures reveals a cluster of elements that suggests the intimate relationship between the world of women and the domestic habitat. The languages of the Tuareg of north and west Africa and the Fulbe of west Africa provide striking examples. The Tuareg word *ehen*, meaning "tent," is used simultaneously to refer to the marriage ceremony, as well as to an entire lineage group. The Fulbe term *kakool* has equivalent uses. Thus, physical reality is linked to an entire set of moral and social values.

What is there in the nomadic environment that accounts for these unique gender-related meanings and that distinguishes them from vernacular architecture in general? This essay suggests some answers. First of all, maintenance and renewal, as a way of personalizing and symbolizing space, is reinforced in the nomadic building technology by the recur-

rent mounting and striking of the domestic envelope. In addition, the fabrication of materials essential to the creation of the habitat occurs within the dwelling itself—the spatial setting is integral to the process of producing and reproducing the architecture. Furthermore, small-scale changes are easier to manipulate in a tent and require less investment of materials and labor. Personal identity is also reinforced by the fact that clothing and housing materials are both the result of the same production technology. As a consequence, associative iconographies are woven into the spatial metaphor that surrounds both the body and the residence. Finally, the materials of dwelling construction are also evocative of early tactile experiences associated with childhood well-being and thereby provide for sensory and psychological continuity in the built environment.

In examining the concept that men and women constitute discrete subcultures, it is important to acknowledge biological differences but more important still to stress behavioral and symbolic differences. Attention to these distinctions as they are manifested in the built environment of nomadic cultures can contribute much to an understanding of the creative process, as well as to its expression within the larger cultural context.

20. John Michael Vlach

The Brazilian House in Nigeria

A revised version of this essay appears in "The Brazilian House in Nigeria: The Emergence of a 20th-Century Vernacular House Type," *Journal of American Folklore* 97 (1984):3–23.

Most historical studies concerning the diffusion of house types trace building forms from the Old World to the New. This paper reverses the usual approach, demonstrating that the genesis of one African building pattern can be found in South America. Today, approximately two-thirds of all houses built in southwest Nigeria are versions of what is locally termed the "Brazilian house." Such structures are typically two rooms wide, three rooms deep, and either one or two stories high. They are so common that they have come to be associated with the Yoruba people, the most numerous ethnic group in the region.

Brazilian house types, the *sobrado* and the *térreo,* were introduced to Nigeria in the middle of the nineteenth century through the coastal city of Lagos by repatriated ex-slaves from Brazil. Eventually, these immigrants—most of whom had Yoruba roots—constituted 10 percent of the population of Lagos and were especially dominant in building trades. The houses they built were based on their Brazilian experiences and became prototypes for many of the dwellings built in Lagos and in other coastal settlements.

Inland diffusion of the Brazilian house form was initiated during the 1920s and 1930s, when indigenous Nigerians began to consider it an appropriate way to display their wealth and status. The dwelling type enjoyed a second wave of popularity during the 1960s, when Nigeria gained political independence from Britain. At that time, simpler variants of the Brazilian house were constructed by rural farmers and other members of the working class. In these cases, the houses follow the forms of traditional domestic structures, incorporating only the passageway from the imported Brazilian type.

There were other models of new house construction that Nigerians might have used. Most prominent among these are the building of colonial European residents, or the dwellings of repatriated slaves from Sierra Leone. The Yoruba preference for a Latin American house type suggests that they wanted a building form that had been contributed to their landscape by descendants of long-lost cousins, rather than one associated with white oppressors or their agents.

21. Ellen Weiss

Methodist Camp Meeting Grounds: Regional Modes

This summary was drawn from material in the author's forthcoming book on Wesleyan Grove Campground, to be published by Oxford University Press in 1986.

The full history of that peculiar American invention, the Methodist camp meeting, has yet to be written. Because such meetings were never an official part of the denomination, their identification, analysis, and preservation are best achieved locally. Yet, there are many characteristics and issues common to all of these important nineteenth-century sites.

The buildings and site plans of campgrounds differed North from South as early as 1830, fourteen years before the Methodist Church split over the issue of abolition. In the first half of the century, northern campgrounds kept to "primitive" forms: cloth tents ringing a tree-shaded audience area with a preacher's stand and a straw-filled pen that served as the "altar" at one end. Wooden cabins were derided as giving a "low and ludicrous" shantytown appearance.

Southern campgrounds were characterized by a range of wooden structures—also called "tents"—that were arranged in various ways. There were concentric squares of party-wall tents, separate cabins connected by continuous front porches, and party-wall dog-trot versions. Southern campgrounds were also distinguished by "tabernacles," great gable- or hip-roofed wooden structures with open sides that sheltered the preacher and his entire audience (Fig. 1).

While southern campgrounds show a remarkable continuity from antebellum times to the present, northern meeting grounds were radically changed after the Civil War. A unique two-story cottage with decorative trim was first built at Wesleyan Grove on Martha's Vineyard, and it quickly became popular at other campgrounds. At about the same time,

Fig. 1. Little Texas tabernacle in Macon County, Alabama. The structure dates from about 1850. (author)

a complex new site plan was developed: a wheel-like form with preaching space in the center and tents or cottages ranging along the "spokes." This new plan became popular among four northern states over the next two decades. Also during the latter half of the nineteenth century, northern campgrounds were built near rail lines and next to bodies of water. These locations tended to make the meeting facilities larger and more recreational.

Despite a growing resort-like atmosphere, the function of campgrounds remained quite serious. The literature of nineteenth-century forest revivals suggests social and religious aims similar to those of more overtly Utopian communities. Perfectionist goals were intertwined with a collective spirit and with dreams of a better society. Camp-meeting theorists wove these notions into metaphors taken from Exodus, comparing revivalists to Hebrews fleeing for the safety of the wilderness. They cited ancient Jewish festivals, particularly *Sukkoth*, as precedents: the convictions of a dispersed and persecuted people could be strengthened through group bonding in tribal love. Even with the numerical triumph of Methodism at mid-century, revivals were considered beneficial, for they rescued individuals from isolation in a greedy and competitive world and returned them to a wilderness community of belief and human warmth.

For these reasons, the natural qualities of the campground settings were integral to their architectural character. Nineteenth-century accounts make it clear that intimacy with nature—the mossy loam underneath and the rustling leaves overhead—was necessary to create a sense of distance from everyday affairs, a psychic release that made the evangelical experience possible.

Camp meetings existed throughout the nation in the last century. For generations of Americans, they represented significant religious, social, and personal experiences. Thus, recording and analyzing Methodist campgrounds is one important step toward understanding nineteenth-century American culture.

22. Christopher L. Yip

The Vernacular Architecture of Chinese-American Agricultural Settlements in California

An expanded version of this paper will appear in Michael Fazio, ed., *Proceedings of the Fourth Annual Chautauqua in Mississippi* (Oxford: University Press of Mississippi, forthcoming).

Chinese-Americans formed an important part of the California labor force during the late nineteenth and early twentieth centuries. With the completion of the transcontinental railroad in 1869, many Chinese shifted their energies from railroad construction to land reclamation and agricultural labor in the Sacramento-San Joaquin Delta of northern California. The farms of the delta were usually large, and many tracts were owned by investment companies that fostered a system of tenant farming.

In this region, the houses of the Caucasian farmers and landowners tended to line the embankments and man-made levees of the delta islands, while the Chinese and other tenants were relegated to the back swamps in the centers of the islands, where an unpleasant peat dust prevailed. Among these rural delta holdings were scattered river towns with ethnic sections, or Chinatowns, that accommodated the commercial and social needs of the Chinese laborers and served as winter quarters for unemployed seasonal farmworkers.

These delta Chinatowns were not composed of the tile-roofed structures common to Guandong Province from which most of the Chinese had emigrated. Rather, they were modest adaptations of the wood-framed American buildings of the delta. The Chinatown buildings reflected the needs of the predominantly male farm-laboring population. These included residential hotels, shops, restaurants, gambling houses, and brothels. Farmworkers came to the Chinatowns to collect mail, send letters and money back to their home villages in China, make purchases, and escape from the labor of the fields.

Chinatowns in the delta were characterized by tightly packed lots along narrow streets. The closely placed buildings were simple, efficient, and inexpensive. Because they were legally barred from owning land, the Chinese had no incentive to build expensive or elaborate structures. Two-story buildings were numerous, for they provided more square footage on a cramped lot, and the upper story could be used as a refuge in case of flood. A typical two-story building was about twenty-four feet wide and sixty feet long, oriented toward the levee and the main street. The usual metal-covered gable roof was partly concealed at the street end by a parapet wall.

Multiple and changing functions were housed within these structures. Spaces facing a street were good for shops, restaurants, dance halls, and other commercial purposes. Rooms toward the middle of a building could be used as storage or as boarding space for farmworkers during the idle season. The back room could serve as a kitchen, fitted with a traditional Chinese brick oven that was open in the front for firewood and at the top for a wok.

When the delta Chinatowns were constructed, there were no detached single-family dwellings, for there were few families among the immigrant Chinese population. This began to change at the end of the nineteenth century, when the Exclusion Acts and the mechanization of agriculture effected a decrease in the total Chinese rural population, while simultaneously increasing the proportion of the rural population that was organized into family groups. The Chinatowns were accordingly modified to accommodate more complex domestic arrangements, and spaces at the edges of the communities were turned into vegetable gardens.

Throughout the twentieth century, the Chinese-American population of the delta has continued to decline. The centralization of canneries near urban centers and the social disruptions caused by World War II accelerated the migration of younger Chinese-Americans toward the educational and employment opportunities of the cities. As a result, the vitality of these important delta Chinatowns has been all but extinguished.

23. Simon J. Bronner

The House on Penn Street: Conflict and Creativity in the Back-to-the-City Movement

This essay will appear in expanded form in the author's *Grasping Things* (Lexington: University Press of Kentucky, 1986).

There is a cultural question raised by the back-to-the-city movement of the late 1970s and early 1980s. Members of the upper middle class move into urban working-class neighborhoods, renovating rowhouses to suit their

own tastes. These tastes tend toward plain surfaces, clean lines, and sparse trim. By contrast, working-class homeowners typically rely on "bricolage," a layering of varied colors and textures, to create a design and to maintain a structure.[1] What is emerging here is a conflict of class-specific aesthetics and implicit criticisms of alternate ways of life worked out in architectural form and decoration.

Cal Yoder, who lives on Penn Street in Harrisburg, Pennsylvania, provides an illustration. His house is layered with contrasting colors of paint, shapes, and coverings, all in keeping with the decorative system favored by his working-class neighbors, but more richly applied (Fig. 1). Young urban professionals living nearby find Yoder's house garish. As he perceives more of a threat from the newcomers, who use his lack of formal education to back up an image of general working-class ignorance and shiftlessness, Yoder has added still more embellishments. The designs he uses have

1. See Read's essay elsewhere in this volume.

Fig. 1. Facade of Cal Yoder's house on Penn Street in Harrisburg, Pennsylvania. Photo taken in June 1984. (author)

become symbolic gestures of defiance in the face of professional-class criticism, and affirmations of the local, informal social networks established by Yoder and his blue-collar neighbors.

Architecture plays such an important symbolic role because it is so visible. To cultural critic Lewis Mumford, architecture's symbolism takes on importance, too, because it reflects a wide variety of social facts and "the empirical tradition and experimental knowledge that go into their application, the processes of social organization and association, and the beliefs and world outlooks of a whole society."[2] The appearance of Yoder's house, for example, proclaims his informal learning, communal bonding, and ambivalence toward middle-class notions of professionalism and work.

Using "decoration" to describe what Yoder does implies that it is

2. Lewis Mumford, *The Culture of Cities* (New York: Harcourt, Brace, and World, 1938), p. 403.

secondary and frivolous. In reality, decoration has become central to the control of space and connections with community, since the structure of houses is predefined, and selection—especially for the lower classes—is limited. Decoration becomes socially important because it is used by the dominant classes to identify the occupant's propriety, rationality, and level of social organization. It provides a visible index of conformity. Indeed, the indecorous resident appears to lack self-control.

In the "embourgeoisement" of the city, decoration becomes part of the agent-client market system and the culture of consumption. "Bricolage," the alternative aesthetic system of lower-class homes, is based on creative processes involving inventive recycling, face-to-face exchange of information, and communal interaction. The result is the dramatic emergence of "housing classes" defined by "taste cultures" that are anchored in occupation, income, social organization, and race. In other words, status is assigned not just by how much money is made but also according to the type of work done, the way the community is defined, and how goods and services are consumed.

All art and creativity require collective action and systematic thinking. When art is invoked, and when it is sliced apart, power and ethical relations are involved. Why? The ability to make and alter things has the potential of influencing others. It identifies the individual's role in, and relationship to, a larger system. The power to shape and control objects is also the power to reshape self and community. Architecture, because it is so public, is the "essential commanding art."[3]

3. Ibid.

24. Patricia Irvin Cooper

Toward a Revised Understanding of American Log Building

The upland log house, with its hewn logs, half-dovetail or V notching, one-and-a-half-story form, rafter roof, studded and weatherboarded gables, brick or stone chimney, and one- or two-room plan, has been often photographed and studied. But it has not been correctly understood. This essay considers accepted notions concerning the origin, diffusion, and typing of log architecture, challenging these statements on the basis of field and documentary evidence. Recent work confirms that the upland log house was not the only American log dwelling type. It was one of three types of log dwellings built in the colonial era and through much of the nineteenth century. There were, in addition, the woodland or frontier cabin and the lowland log house (Fig. 1).

The woodland cabin, the first shelter on newly settled lands, was built of round logs, the ends often left protruding raggedly beyond saddle notches. It was raised to only one story; gable ends of short logs were laid up to the roof ridge, and pole purlins or "ribs" were laid lengthwise across the cabin to support the roof covering of riven boards. The floor was of dirt or puncheons. There was, at most, one window, and the chimney was composed of sticks and clay.

The lowland log house is characterized by a one-story form, frequently built with a one-room or a dogtrot plan. Logs are hewn with half-dovetail or square notches, or they are left round with saddle or—rarely—diamond notches. The hewn log with V notching is not found. The houses have weatherboarded gables and rafter

Fig. 1. A lowland log house in Tattnall County, Georgia, about 1922. Extended plates carry the roof to the outer plane of the stick-and-clay chimney. There was usually no access to the attic. The detached kitchen is located to the right. (courtesy of Georgia Department of Archives and History)

roofs. Extended plates carry the roof past one gable end of the house so that it shelters the chimney. The chimney itself is built of sticks and clay. Among later examples, shaped stones or bricks are more common materials.

In the field of vernacular architectural studies, the most commonly accepted theory for the origin of American log construction is Fred Kniffen and Henry Glassie's attribution to the Schwenkfelders and Moravians who originally settled in Pennsylvania in the 1730s.[1] Careful examination of the evidence, however, reveals that log construction existed both before the arrival of these groups and well beyond the stream of settlement from southeast Pennsylvania to the west and southwest.

The earliest log house now surviving in Georgia, for example, is a dogtrot dwelling erected on the inner coastal plain about 1785 by a settler from southeastern Virginia. Although few log structures survive in the coastal regions of the Carolinas, there are nonetheless eighteenth- and even seventeenth-century references to log construction in those areas. Among these is William Byrd's 1728 description of dwellings that were, beyond a doubt, built of horizontally laid and corner-notched logs.[2]

Not only did log construction appear too early, it also occurred too generally to be assigned completely to the Pennsylvania cultural hearth. The woodland cabin was found in new settlements everywhere. The upland log house became the common log structure not only of the upland South but also of the eastern mountains, the bluegrass region, the old Northwest, and lands beyond the Mississippi River. The lowland log dwelling, of more restricted distribution, is found in the coastal regions of the Carolinas, Georgia, Alabama, and westward into the fall lines, as well as in parts of upland Georgia and Tennessee. All these regions are well beyond the boundaries of direct settlement from the supposed Pennsylvania system of migration.

It is therefore necessary to conclude that American log construction was based on Swedish-Finnish models built along the Delaware River and carried southward by migration and perhaps also by trade in the naval stores. Dismissal of the Swedes and Finns on the Delaware River as a source of log building resulted from a misreading of both Swedish and German settlement history. While German immigrants were numerous, many of them were originally city dwellers who knew nothing of log construction. The majority of later German immigrants came from regions with strong traditions in half-timbered construction; like the English, Welsh, and Scotch-Irish, they had to learn the technique of log building.

The Swedish colony was comparatively small, but initial settlement was augmented by continued immigration and by traditionally large families that retained some of their Old World practices. In the middle of the eighteenth century, the Swedes still spoke and held church services in their native language. They remained a rural people, building and inhabiting log houses and barns. Seventeenth- and eighteenth-century descriptions make it plain that these log houses were usually one story in height, built of hewn or round logs, and heated by corner fireplaces set into stick-and-clay chimneys. While most of these buildings were single-pen structures, at least one dogtrot house, or "paired cottage," survives.[3]

This essay argues that the woodland log house type and the lowland log house form were both of Swedish-Finnish origin. Only the upland log house has structural and formal features that make its Pennsylvania-German origins clear. There thus are two hearths of American log construction: the Pennsylvania-German tradition recognized by Kniffen and Glassie and the Swedish-Finnish tradition of the Delaware Valley.[4]

25. Jonathan Fricker

The Origins of the Creole Raised Plantation House

The full text of this paper was published in *Louisiana History* 25 (1984):137–53.

The Creole raised plantation house is among the best known symbols of Louisiana's cultural

1. Fred Kniffen and Henry Glassie, "Building in Wood in the Eastern United States: A Time-Place Perspective," *Geographical Review* 56 (1966):59.

2. Louis B. Wright, ed., *The Prose Works of William Byrd II of Westover: Narratives of a Colonial Virginian* (Cambridge: Belknap Press of Harvard University Press, 1966), pp. 174, 206.

3. Bartlett Burleigh James and J. Franklin James, eds., *Journal of Jasper Danckaerts 1679–1680* (New York: Scribner's, 1913), p. 98; Adolph B. Benson, ed., *Peter Kalm's Travels in North America*, 2 vols. (New York: Wilson-Erickson, 1937), 1:82; 2:726–28; Israel Acrelius, *A History of New Sweden*, trans. William M. Reynolds (Ann Arbor: University of Michigan Microfilms, 1966), p. 310.

4. Terry Jordan also makes this attribution for the woodland cabin. See Jordan, "A Reappraisal of Fenno-Scandian Antecedents for Midland American Log Construction," *Geographical Review* 73 (1983):93–94.

heritage. Yet its origins are widely misinterpreted. This is partly because the Creole house type has received little serious study over the years. As a result, there has been no scholarly voice to contradict the mythmakers. This essay attempts to document the popular myths and to examine the true origins of Creole architecture.

The Creole raised house is a regionally distinctive form of architecture that persisted in southern Louisiana for almost two centuries. It appeared early in the colonial period, and vestiges of the type were built as late as 1880. Creole plantation houses are characterized by one main story that is raised on brick piers well above ground level. Rooms open through sets of French doors onto broad porches or galleries. There are no interior halls; all circulation takes place by way of the galleries. Most Creole houses exhibit frame construction filled in with brick nogging or with a mixture of mud and Spanish moss known as *bousillage*. Many examples feature *cabinets*, or small rooms set at each end of the gallery. The form is also distinguished by a broad overhanging roof that appears to shelter the house like an umbrella.

Because of its design, the Creole house copes well with Louisiana's hot, wet, flood-prone climate. This has given rise to the popular notion that the house type originated in the Gulf Coast–West Indies area as a direct response to the local tropical conditions. The view has a somewhat patriotic appeal. Here, after all, is a colonial house type that actually originated on this side of the Atlantic.

In considering the supposed New World origins of the Creole plantation house, however, several points must be emphasized. First, pioneer societies seldom produce innovative architecture.

Furthermore, Creole-type houses appeared in many parts of New France, not just in the hot, wet places that are thought to have generated them. More important still are nineteenth- and early twentieth-century photographs of late medieval French farmhouses that clearly show architectural features normally associated with Creole plantation houses, including elevated main stories, galleries, *cabinets*, and broad overhanging roofs. These photographs indicate that the Creole raised plantation house has direct French ancestry. It evolved and changed somewhat in Louisiana, but this was the further development of an existing tradition—not the birth of a new architectural form or style.

Creole architecture, then, like other American colonial forms, sprang from European traditions. Unlike most of the others, however, the Creole type remained true to its folk roots. English and Spanish colonial architecture eventually came under the influence of classical Renaissance ideals, but French colonial architecture remained essentially medieval. For that reason, the Louisiana Creole house occupies a very special place in America's colonial legacy.

26. Kingston Heath

John Dewey Revisited: Teaching Vernacular Architecture by Doing

The full text of this paper was published as "Architectural Education and Change: John Dewey Revisited or Taking the Classroom to the Mountains: The Field School on Early American Building," *Montana Educational Review*, Spring 1984, pp. 10–13.

The challenge facing colleges in preparing students for this era of great change involves not so much selection of subject matter as teaching students *how* to learn. Modern society, with its computers, calculators, and microwave ovens, too often stresses immediate end product over an understanding of *process*. This is especially true when large university classes mandate "objective" exams that stress the short-range goal of memorization. Such educational experiences provide nothing more than veneers of understanding. Educators have then failed to prepare students to respond to concepts, apply principles, develop ideas. In a changing society with fluctuating vocations and fields of study, it is not enough to prepare students for passive test-taking in subjects that fit the requirements of current job-market trends. They must be taught to think and apply their ideas in a resourceful manner so that they will be flexible enough to adapt to changing circumstances.

Each summer for four weeks, students of the Montana State University School of Architecture receive firsthand experience with various building techniques, such as post-and-beam construction, scribe log construction, Hudson Bay log construction, balloon framing, and geodesic dome construction. The work is done on an eleven-acre mountain site just outside Bozeman, Montana. The purpose of this Field School on Early American Building and Crafts is to provide working models of John Dewey's "learning by doing" principle.[1] The program stresses *process* in the educational system. Traditional crafts and restoration skills are taught, appreciation of the skills and techniques of the an-

1. John Dewey, *The School and Society* (Chicago: University of Chicago Press, 1900), pp. 1–28.

cient housewright is achieved, alternative energy sources are explored, and the proper use and care of tools is stressed. More important than these matters, however, is the hands-on method of instruction that preserves the cognitive process of past builders by employing the same tools and methods. It is the emphasis on internalizing knowledge that distinguishes this program.

At the field school, students attempt to become aware of subtle changes in historical and technological developments through immersion in simulated history. Students are encouraged to see architecture through the eyes and minds of the past. By reexperiencing the methods of past builders in similar contexts, it is often possible to judge the shortcomings and accomplishments of historical developments in ways not possible through a simple reliance on written sources. For example, was the balloon frame really an 1832 invention, or did it actually evolve from post-and-beam construction?[2] When such questions are tested in the field rather than merely examined through slides, diagrams, and matboard models, the answers gain more credibility.

If, however, sitting passively in the classroom does not result in Dewey's desired internalization of knowledge, neither does the performance of a job guarantee insight and understanding. At the field school, projects do not operate in a historical vacuum. Each of the field exercises is buttressed by weekly two-hour slide lectures that identify tools, explain framing members, and establish historical perspectives and philosophical bases for the projects. The goal is

to create an ongoing field laboratory for the study of building history.

What is a newly built Rhode Island stone-ender doing in Montana?[3] More to the point, how is squaring a timber preparing students for the challenges of a modern society? The activity itself may prove irrelevant in terms of direct academic transfer, but the learning process is of the greatest importance. Students who study different building principles and practices by testing them in the field are really learning in a long-lasting manner about scholarly investigation, concept development, problem solving, and critical analysis— all tools of learning necessary to meet modern challenges.

27. Jan Leo Lewandoski

The Plank Framed House in Northeastern Vermont

The full text of this paper was published in *Vermont History* 53 (1985):104–21. Reprints are also available from the author at RD 1, Greensboro Bend, VT 05842.

Northeastern Vermont was first settled in the post-Revolutionary period, and the early buildings of the region reflect the stylistic and technological conventions of the day. From 1780 to 1830, at least one-third of the dwellings constructed in northeastern Vermont were plank framed. It is these structures that are the focus of this essay.

Plank framing is a method of construction involving pieces of timber usually of substantial width (from nine to twenty-eight inches) and sawn to a uniform thickness (from one-and-a-half to four inches) that are placed vertically between sills and plates to form the walls of a building. Set edge to edge, these planks take the place of some or all of the vertical load-bearing members of the frame, and often of the diagonal bracing as well. The planks also serve as exterior sheathing, as an interior base for lath or paneling, as framing for doors and windows, and, perhaps unintentionally, as a kind of insulation. In the fully developed form common in parts of northern New England, all posts, studs, and braces are replaced by planks. The majority of plank-framed dwellings are one or one and a half stories with square or rectangular plans. A number of full two-story plank-framed buildings have also been identified.

Little is known of this substantial framing tradition because it is usually concealed within the walls of a structure. For this study, three approaches were used. A survey of all old structures within a sample district was conducted to establish the frequency with which the construction form appears. Interviews were conducted with twenty-seven Vermont tradespeople, all of whom have a working knowledge of plank frames. Finally, thirty-eight plank-

2. Paul E. Sprague, "The Origin of Balloon Framing," *Journal of the Society of Architectural Historians* 40 (1981):311–19.

3. The major ongoing project of the Field School on Early American Building is a reconstruction of an eighteenth-century Rhode Island stone-ender. Stone-enders were transplanted from Wales to New World locations in northern Rhode Island and northeastern Connecticut, where they were well suited because of the availability of lime and gneiss stone. Built predominantly during the late seventeenth century, stone-enders utilized an entire gable-end wall of stone or brick to provide for as many as three fireplaces in the hall, the chamber above, and the kitchen outshot. Entrance was through a door at the center of the house, and structural additions were made to the side opposite the stone end.

frame buildings were intensively examined.

Three distinct types of plank framing were identified in northeastern Vermont. The earliest type of plank construction involves the use of corner and intermediate posts to stiffen the frame between sill and plates. The second and most widespread type of plank construction is composed of planks without posts. In this form, the planks are set into rabbets or mortises in the sills and plates (Fig. 1). Less frequent in appearance is a plank-without-post construction in which the planks are simply attached to the exterior surface of the sills and plates (Fig. 2). A wide variety of techniques for affixing planks, carrying joists, and bracing the frame is used.

It is clear from this study that plank framing did not represent a primitive or isolated folk practice, but rather a widely used alternative to timber framing. Several factors may account for its popularity in northeastern Vermont at the turn of the nineteenth century. In a newly and rapidly settled area, a shortage of skilled labor and an extraordinary demand for new construction made the simplified joinery of plank framing popular. Since a relatively few planks can take the place of all posts, studs, braces, and sheathing, production time and costs were greatly reduced. Moreover, large-dimension timber, essential for both the stability and speed of plank construction, was readily available on freshly cleared land. Finally, the exposing of a building frame was no longer popular in New England by the time of the Revolution, and planking created a uniform wall surface, making possible a more finished interior appearance. This advantage may account for the special popularity of the construction technique during the Federal period.

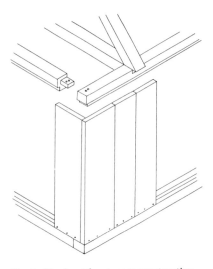

Fig. 1. Plank-without-post construction at the Weed-Reynolds house, built about 1820 in Stannard, Vermont. The planks are spiked to rabbets in the sills and plates. (author, courtesy of *Vermont History*)

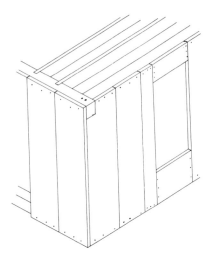

Fig. 2. Plank-without-post construction at the Parker house, built about 1850 in East St. Johnsbury, Vermont. The planks are spiked to the outside faces of the sills and plates, except at each upper corner, where a length of plate intersects and bears upon the plank. (author, courtesy of *Vermont History*)

28. Julie Riesenweber

Domestic Spatial Order: Salem County, New Jersey, 1700–1774

Material for this essay appears in the author's thesis, "Order in Domestic Space: House Plans and Room Use in the Vernacular Dwellings of Salem County, New Jersey, 1700–1774," University of Delaware, 1984.

Domestic spatial order operates on two architectural levels: those of form and use. The residents of eighteenth-century Salem County, New Jersey, planned and used the rooms of their dwellings in ways that were both comfortable and meaningful to them. Social conventions regarding domestic life determined the nature of this comfort and meaning. Domestic spatial order was, then, the physical expression of values, attitudes, and ideas.

The use of rooms in the eighteenth-century domestic vernacular architecture of Salem County demonstrates that members of this community were concerned with the explicit spatial categorization of objects and activities that had seemed inappropriately combined in one-room dwellings. Most of the county's residents built houses with two or more rooms, where they distinguished between the public and private domains of their lives. They combined formal and public activities such as dining and sitting in one room, while isolating private activities such as sleeping at the other end of the house or on the second floor.

Also classed as private were those objects, activities, and individuals, such as servants and slaves, that were stigmatized by their associations with work and dirtiness. Work-oriented rooms were thus also separated from the clean and refined spaces that contained formal, public objects and activities. Separate kitchens and outbuildings facilitated this segregation, indicating that eighteenth-century Salem County residents considered work even more private than sleeping.

Most of the community's members felt that two- and three-room dwellings based on the familiar Anglo-American hall-parlor plan sufficiently met their needs. A dwelling with two or three rooms on the lower floor contained enough distinct spaces to allow the occupants explicit differentiation between those activities that, in their minds, belonged apart. This was particularly true when there were a few outbuildings, including one with facilities for cooking.

The eighteenth-century inhabitants of Salem County valued tradition over innovation with respect to house form and use. The architecture was based on principles of accretion rather than on any progressive vision, and additions were made in ways that did not compromise the traditional appearance of the dwellings. Extensive rebuilding was not a phenomenon in colonial Salem County. Economic well-being allowed individuals to make additions to their dwellings or to erect more outbuildings, but it did not contribute to any new perception of what constituted a home. Even the wealthiest of the county's inhabitants continued to build and inhabit houses in traditional ways.

29. Myron O. Stachiw

Impermanent Architecture in the City: Examples from Nineteenth-Century New England

The study of impermanent architecture has focused largely on the Chesapeake region, where this form of building was a viable choice for many sectors of society during the seventeenth century. Surviving archaeological and architectural evidence suggests that impermanent Chesapeake architecture was replaced by more permanent building types in the early eighteenth century.[1] In many contexts, however, impermanent building remained a common practice for over two hundred years—particularly in urban areas, where socially and economically marginal groups were segregated into ghetto-like neighborhoods.

Archaeological investigations during 1982 in Providence, Rhode Island, revealed surprisingly intact evidence of such dwellings and outbuildings.[2] Two occupations separated by three feet of clean sand fill were uncovered. The earliest stratum represented Snowtown, a late eighteenth- and early nineteenth-century settlement of free blacks and poor Anglo-Americans situated on the marshy north shore of a tidal cove. The buildings were located only several hundred yards from rows of substantial dwellings, warehouses, and wharves owned by merchants and craftsmen.

There was archaeological evidence of a number of structures, including the remains of one dwelling's flooring, room partitions, and hearth. Also discovered were postmolds for two hole-set structures of undetermined function, a wood-lined well, and several wood-lined pits. In contemporary documents, Snowtown was generally described as a community of ill repute occupied by a promiscuous and transient population. During race riots in 1832, a white crowd tore down a number of buildings in the community. This action may have prompted the subsequent covering of the area with sand from a nearby hill.

The second layer of occupation was situated on and into the fill level. It was established predominantly by Irish immigrants, although some of the earlier population remained. Archaeological evidence of building includes remains of a small center-chimney house with no foundations, two outbuildings with wood-lined cellars, a stone-lined well, and a small outbuilding foundation. Like the community it replaced, this neighborhood remained on the urban fringe, cut off from the more substantial commercial and residential districts of the city by rail yards and slaughterhouses. Nineteenth-century descriptions of similar settlements of the poor and newly immigrated in other New England cities make it clear that this community was not unusual. Impermanent building was a practice common to the lower social classes throughout the nineteenth century and into the twentieth.

1. Cary Carson et al., "Impermanent Architecture in the Southern American Colonies," *Winterthur Portfolio* 16 (1981):135–97. For samples of impermanent architecture in colonial New England, see James Deetz, "Plymouth Colony Architecture: Evidence from the Seventeenth Century," in *Architecture in Colonial Massachusetts*, ed. Abbott Lowell Cummings (Boston: Colonial Society of Massachusetts, 1979), pp. 43–59.
2. Janice Artemel et al., *Providence Cove Lands Phase III Report* (Washington, D.C: Federal Railroad Administration, 1984).

30. Dell Upton

White and Black Landscapes in Eighteenth-Century Virginia

The full text of this essay was published in *Places: A Quarterly Journal of Environmental Design* 2 (1985):59–72.

This study of colonial Virginia argues that a historic landscape must be interpreted as the complex creation of many groups with varied and sometimes conflicting social roles, rather than as a unified reflection of the values of a dominant group. Although the landscape of eighteenth-century Virginia is often treated as such a unified artifact, it incorporates the ideals and perceptions of poor whites and of blacks as well as those of the planter elite. The domestic complexes of the gentry, the subjects of standard architectural histories, drew on academic design sources but adapted them to accommodate the requirements of the Chesapeake slave society. In contrast to the planter's house were the nearby dwellings of the slaves—typically poorly built, tiny log structures shared by several people and surrounded by gardens and public areas that were an essential part of the slave's space.

Contemporary evidence confirms that most poor whites lived in similar rude circumstances, suggesting that, in some respects, the slaves' houses merely reflected their status as poor people in Virginia.

The quarter and the planter's house were part of a shared landscape that carried different meanings for each group. The planter constructed his dwelling at the center of a complex of domestic and farm buildings that outsiders commonly compared to villages. In fact, the plantation complexes had many of the same civil, economic, and social functions as villages, except that, on the plantation, all of these elements served the interests of one individual— the planter himself.

At home, as well as at church and court, where the gentry were also prominent figures, the landscape was arranged to emphasize the central, dominant position of the planter. In all these environments, this point was partially made through the use of physical barriers such as terraces, gates, steps, and entry passages.

Slaves, on the other hand, had a different perception of the plantation terrain. They created and inhabited an alternate landscape located in the uncontrolled spaces about the planter's domain. Back stairs, work buildings, quarters, outlying subsidiary farms, and corresponding zones on neighboring plantations were all knitted together by woodland paths, fields, and waterways. In this manner, black and white, elite and common landscapes were viable and contrasting perspectives on the same geography.

Notes on the Contributors

W. FRANK AINSLEY holds a Ph.D. in geography from the University of North Carolina at Chapel Hill. He currently teaches at the University of North Carolina at Wilmington, where he specializes in cultural, historical, and urban geography. He has participated in various studies of vernacular architecture in North Carolina, many of which were conducted in cooperation with the North Carolina Division of Archives and History. His publications include "Folk Architecture in Early Twentieth Century Ethnic Agricultural Colonies," in *SEASA 83: Design, Pattern, Style; Clarkton and Its Historic Resources*; and *The Historic Architecture of Warsaw, North Carolina*.

ARNOLD R. ALANEN is chairman of the Department of Landscape Architecture at the University of Wisconsin at Madison. He holds a B.A. in architecture and M.A. and Ph.D. degrees in geography from the University of Minnesota. He also has been a Fulbright graduate fellow and a visiting research professor at the University of Helsinki. In 1983, he received an award of merit from the American Society of Landscape Architects for his role in developing and editing *Landscape Journal*, published by the University of Wisconsin Press. His primary research and teaching interests are in the areas of landscape and town planning history, with special emphasis on immigrant groups, vernacular architecture, and ordinary landscapes of the Lake Superior region.

ROBERT L. ALEXANDER earned his Ph.D. at the Institute of Fine Arts of New York University. He is author of *The Architecture of Maximilian Godefroy* and of numerous articles on nineteenth-century art and architecture. He has also written about the art of the ancient Near East. Since 1961, he has taught art history at the University of Iowa.

LEANNE BAIRD received her B.A. in folklore from the University of Nebraska at Lincoln, where she also completed graduate coursework in historical geography and architectural history. From 1980 to 1983, she served as head of the architecture and history division of Environment Consultants, Inc. She is joint author of a number of cultural resources technical reports, has prepared nominations for the National Register of Historic Places, and has written the texts of several Texas state historical markers. She is currently an independent historic preservation consultant.

DAVID R. BLACK received an M.S. in historic preservation from the Columbia University School of Architecture and Planning in 1976. Since 1977, he has worked as a preservation and restoration specialist for the North Carolina Division of Archives and History. He has also served as a consulting architectural conservator on projects throughout the southeast. Among his publications are *Maintaining and Renewing Your Old House*, a buildings restoration manual prepared for Racine, Wisconsin, and *Historical Architectural Resources of Downtown Asheville, North Carolina*. Currently he is architectural conservator and partner in the firm of Black and Black Preservation Consultants.

KENNETH A. BREISCH has a Ph.D. in art history from the University of Michigan. Since 1981, he has administered the Survey and Planning Program for the Texas Historical Commission. Over the years, he has lectured and written on the subject of architectural books and treatises and on architectural photography in the nineteenth century. He is currently pursuing research interests in ethnic architecture and Norwegian immigration in Texas, in addition to writing a book on the architecture of American public libraries.

SIMON J. BRONNER is assistant professor of folklore and American studies at the Pennsylvania State University at Middletown. He is author of *Chain Carvers: Old Men Crafting Meaning* and editor of *American Material Culture and Folklife* and *American Folk Art: A Guide to Sources*. He has also recently served as editor of the journal *Material Culture* and as president of the Pennsylvania Folklore Society.

THOMAS CARTER has a Ph.D. in folklore from Indiana University. He is currently an architectural historian with the Utah Division of State History and an adjunct assistant professor at the University of Utah School of Architecture. He has published several articles on the vernacular buildings of the Mormon West and is in the process of revising his dissertation, "Building Zion: Folk Architecture in the Mormon Settlements of Utah's Sanpete Valley," for publication. Carter has served as a member of the board of directors of the Vernacular Architecture Forum.

EDWARD A. CHAPPELL is director of architectural research at Colonial Williamsburg Foundation, where he is responsible for interpretation and conservation of historic buildings. Previously, he carried out rural and urban surveys as an archaeologist for the Virginia Historic Landmarks Commission and as an architectural historian for the Kentucky Heritage Commission. He has also taught architectural history at the College of William and Mary . His essay "Acculturation in the Shenandoah Valley: Rhenish Houses of the Massanutten Settlement" was recently republished in *Common Places: Readings in American Vernacular Architecture*. Chappell is a founder of the Chesapeake Farm Buildings Survey and a current member of the Vernacular Architecture Forum board of directors.

PATRICIA IRVIN COOPER attended Oberlin College and received a masters degree in foreign studies at the University of Maryland. Early in her career, she was a French teacher. For seven years, she worked for the Historic Preservation Section of the Georgia Department of Natural Resources doing architectural surveys and National Register nominations. She has also served as Rambles Chairman for the Georgia Trust for Historic Preservation. Her essay "A Quaker-Plan House in Georgia" was published in 1978 in *Pioneer America*.

DAVID DENMAN received an M.A. in history from the University of Missouri at Columbia in 1980. He has initiated and helped complete a study of the late eighteenth- and early nineteenth-century architecture of the community of Ste. Genevieve, a project that was funded by the National Endowment for the Humanities. Denman is currently on the staff of the Missouri Heritage Trust, where he has begun to study

and develop a preservation plan for Hermann, an early German community in Missouri.

FRANCES DOWNING has received degrees in architecture from the University of Oregon at Eugene, and she is now working on her Ph.D. in architecture at the University of Wisconsin at Milwaukee. She has taught architecture at the State University of New York at Buffalo, the University of Wisconsin, and Arizona State University at Tempe. Downing's interests include the influences of vernacular tradition on architectural design and the role of imagery in the design process. She has published in *Environment and Planning B* and the *Western New York Society of Architectural Historians Journal*. She is also a member of the board of directors of the Vernacular Architecture Forum.

KATHRYN B. ECKERT received an M.A. in art history and a Ph.D. in American studies from Michigan State University. She has been awarded a grant from the Eastern National Parks and Monuments to prepare a publication on the sandstone quarries of the Apostle Islands. In 1984, she planned and conducted an architectural tour through northern Michigan for the Society of Architectural Historians. Eckert is the Deputy State Historic Preservation Officer for the Michigan History Division and a former member of the Vernacular Architecture Forum board of directors.

JONATHAN FRICKER graduated from Cornell University in 1975 with a B.A. in architectural history. From 1975 to 1977, he worked for the New Jersey State Historic Preservation Office as director of the National Register program for the southern counties of the state. Since 1977, he has worked with the survey and National Register programs of the

Louisiana State Historic Preservation Office. He is currently senior architectural historian for the Louisiana state office.

LEONARD T. GARFIELD received a B.A. in history from Wooster College and an M.A. in American studies from the University of Michigan, where he is also a doctoral candidate. His dissertation research has focused on the relationship between urban morphology and commercial architecture with particular emphasis on the development of American vernacular commercial forms. He has served as a historian with the historic preservation division of the State Historical Society of Wisconsin and is now working as an architectural historian for the State of Washington Office of Archaeology and Historic Preservation.

PAUL GROTH holds a degree in architecture from North Dakota State University and a Ph.D. in geography from the University of California at Berkeley. He has taught in North Dakota and at the New Jersey School of Architecture. He has also carried out architectural surveys for the State Historical Society of Wisconsin. He is now assistant professor in the departments of Architecture and Landscape Architecture at Berkeley. He has published articles on street grids, screened porches, and environmental education. Currently, he is working on a book about the history of permanent residence in urban American hotels. Groth is a member of the board of directors of the Vernacular Architecture Forum.

KINGSTON HEATH received an M.A. from the University of Chicago and a Ph.D. in American studies from Brown University. He has worked on restoration and interpretation projects at Plimouth Plantation and Mystic Seaport. More recently, he has served as a preservation consultant and architectural historian for the state of Montana. He is currently associate professor of architectural history and preservation at the Montana State University School of Architecture.

DARRELL D. HENNING holds a B.A. in anthropology from the University of Missouri and an M.A. in history museum training from Cooperstown. He studied historic farm buildings and farm plans for the Nassau County Historical Museum in New York, and he was the recipient of a New York State Arts Council grant to study rural architecture on Long Island. Since 1970, Henning has been curator of the industrial and open-air sections of the Norwegian-American Museum in Decorah, Iowa. In 1973, he received a grant to study nineteenth-century rural architecture in Norway, and the results of that study now inform his consideration of Norwegian-American architectural traditions.

ARLENE HORVATH holds a B.A. in English from Pennsylvania State University and an M.A. in American civilization from the University of Pennsylvania, where she is also now a doctoral candidate. Her dissertation research concerns nineteenth-century table furnishings and foodways in Chester County, Pennsylvania. Horvath has worked as registrar and assistant curator of the Chester County Historical Society. In 1979, she won the Thomas U. Walter Award for the best architectural paper presented before the Philadelphia Chapter of the Society of Architectural Historians.

THOMAS C. HUBKA holds architecture degrees from Carnegie-Mellon University and the University of Oregon. He has taught courses in design, nineteenth-century architectural theory, and vernacular architecture at the University of Oregon, the University of Wisconsin, and, most recently, at the Massachusetts Institute of Technology. He also practices architecture in Maine, where years of fieldwork resulted in his recent book *Big House, Little House, Back House, Barn: The Connected Farm Buildings of New England*. Hubka is a recipient of the Abbott Lowell Cummings Award for vernacular architecture studies and a current member of the board of directors of the Vernacular Architecture Forum.

JANET HUTCHISON was educated at Duke University and the University of Pennsylvania. From 1980 to 1982, she worked as an archaeologist and preservation specialist for the North Carolina Division of Archives and History. She is currently a doctoral candidate in American studies at the University of Delaware.

MICHAEL KOOP has been involved in studies of vernacular and ethnic architectural traditions in Wisconsin, Montana, and South Dakota. He is now working on his M.A. degree at the University of Wisconsin.

JAN LEO LEWANDOSKI has studied politics at Syracuse, Northwestern, and McGill universities and has taught history and politics at the college level in Vermont and Quebec. More recently, he has established a business in restoring, repairing, moving, and reproducing old buildings in New England and New York. His publications include "Early Lithic Sites: A Note from Thoreau's Journal," in *Bulletin of the Early Sites Research Society*, and "A Factor in the Collapse of Old Barns in Vermont," in *Vermont History*.

RICHARD LONGSTRETH holds a Ph.D. in architectural history from the University of California at Berke-ley. He is currently associate professor of architectural history and director of the graduate program in historic preservation at George Washington University. He chairs the preservation committee of the Society of Architectural Historians and serves on the editorial board of the *Journal of Architectural and Planning Research*. Additionally, Longstreth is a member of the board of directors of the Vernacular Architecture Forum. He is coauthor of *Architecture in Philadelphia* and author of *On the Edge of the World: Four Architects in San Francisco at the Turn of the Century*.

STEPHEN E. LUDWIG holds an M.A. in literature from Syracuse University and is completing a thesis in historic preservation at the University of Wisconsin at Madison.

HOWARD WIGHT MARSHALL took M.A. and Ph.D. degrees in folklore from Indiana University. He has worked at the Smithsonian Institution and the Library of Congress American Folklife Center. He has also taught at Earlham College, George Washington University, and Kansas State University. Currently, Marshall is director of the Missouri Cultural Heritage Center and associate professor of art history and geography at the University of Missouri at Columbia. He has written *Folk Architecture in Little Dixie: A Regional Culture in Missouri* and, with Richard E. Ahlborn, *Buckaroos in Paradise: Cowboy Life in Northern Nevada*. He is a former member of the Vernacular Architecture Forum board of directors.

CHRISTOPHER MARTIN holds an M.A. in American studies and folklife from George Washington University. He has served as folklife consultant for the city of Alexandria, where he worked primarily with archaeological and architectural features in the community's historic black neighborhoods. He has also been a researcher at the Library of Congress Archive of Folk Culture and an architectural surveyor for the North Carolina Division of Archives and History. He is currently folklorist for the North Dakota Council on the Arts.

DAVID MOORE received a B.A. in history from the University of Texas. From 1977 to 1980, he was employed as a historian with the National Register program of the Texas Historical Commission. Since 1980, he has worked as a preservation consultant—most recently as a principal in the firm of Hardy, Heck, and Moore. He has written a number of studies of Texas architecture and is now researching the subject of Norwegian immigration into Texas.

WILLARD B. MOORE received a Ph.D. in folklore from Indiana University. His publications on material culture include "An Indiana Subsistence Craftsman," in *Material Culture Studies in America,* and "Metaphor and Changing Reality," in *The Ethnic and Regional Foodways of the United States.* He has also completed a chapter for a Minnesota Historical Society book on the foodways of the Southeast Asian Hmong people who have settled in St. Paul. Currently, Moore is conducting a survey of Minnesota's folk art under the terms of a National Endowment for the Arts grant to the University of Minnesota Art Museum.

WILLIAM T. MORGAN is associate professor of American studies at St. Cloud State University in Minnesota. In 1978, he worked as senior architectural historian for a Historic American Buildings Survey of Missouri's Little Dixie. He has also been coordinator of a summer course in the techniques of log construction taught in northern Minnesota. Morgan is author of "Strongboxes on Main Street: Prairie Style Banks," published in the journal *Landscape,* and "Sauk Centre as Artifact: The Architecture, Painting, and Literature of Sinclair Lewis' Home Town," in *Sinclair Lewis at a Hundred.*

DAVID MURPHY received a degree in architecture from the University of Nebraska, where he has also done graduate work in the study of vernacular buildings. He joined the staff of the Nebraska State Historical Society and initiated the Nebraska Historic Buildings Survey in 1974. Murphy has recently been appointed acting Deputy State Historic Preservation Officer in Nebraska, and he is a member of the Vernacular Architecture Forum board of directors.

GERALD L. POCIUS received a Ph.D. in folklore and folklife from the University of Pennsylvania. He is now assistant professor of folklore and a member of the archaeology unit at Memorial University in Newfoundland. He has served on the editorial board of the *Material History Bulletin* and on the executive committees of the Folklore Studies Association of Canada and the Society for the Study of Architecture in Canada. He is also a member of the Vernacular Architecture Forum board of directors. Pocius has written *Textile Traditions of Eastern Newfoundland* and numerous essays on various aspects of material culture.

LABELLE PRUSSIN was educated in architecture, anthropology, and art history at the University of California at Berkeley and Los Angeles and at Yale University. She earned her Ph.D. in 1973. She has served as architect and planner for the government of Ghana and has taught at Ghana's University of Science and Technology in Kumasi. She has also taught at the University of Texas, the University of Michigan, and the University of Washington, where she is currently professor of architecture. Prussin has published extensively on the subjects of African and Islamic architecture. Her most recent work is *Hatumere: Islamic Design in West Africa.*

ALICE GRAY READ holds a masters degree in architecture from the University of Pennsylvania. In 1983, she edited *Via 6: Architecture and Visual Perception.* She is currently a practicing architect in Boston, where she studies vernacular architecture as a resource for design.

DOUGLASS C. REED studied early American cultural arts and historic preservation at Antioch College and George Washington University. He has worked extensively with the rehabilitation and renovation of old buildings and is now president of Preservation Associates, Inc., of Hagerstown, Maryland. Reed is an area representative to the Maryland Historical Trust Board of Trustees, and he has served as chairman of the planning commission of Sharpsburg, Maryland.

JULIE RIESENWEBER studied anthropology and worked as a historical archaeologist at the University of Kentucky. In 1984, she received an M.A. in early American culture from Winterthur Museum. She has worked at the Kentucky Museum at Western Kentucky University and is currently a historian on the staff of the Kentucky Heritage Council.

RUDOLF L. SCHREIBER received a B.A. in American studies from Case Western Reserve University and an M.A. in American studies from the University of Maryland. In 1982 and 1983, he taught at the University of Mainz in West Germany as part of a cultural exchange program. He is currently working as a researcher for a law firm in Washington, D.C.

MYRON O. STACHIW holds a B.A. in anthropology and an M.A. in American studies from Boston University. He was in charge of industrial history for a Massachusetts Historical Commission cultural resources survey of Worcester County and has worked extensively as a historical archaeologist throughout New England. Stachiw is currently a research historian at Old Sturbridge Village.

WILLIAM TISHLER graduated from Harvard University. He is now professor of landscape architecture at the University of Wisconsin at Madison. A past president of the Vernacular Architecture Forum, Tishler has written extensively on landscape architecture and historic preservation. His professional work includes preparation of the master plan for Old World Wisconsin. Currently, he is conducting the research and fieldwork for a book on the rural architecture of Wisconsin's many ethnic groups.

PAUL B. TOUART received a B.A. in art history from the University of Delaware. Since 1977, he has worked as an architectural surveyor for the Maryland Historical Trust and the North Carolina Division of Archives and History. With survey catalogs of Cecil County, Maryland, and Davidson County, North Carolina, in press, Touart is now studying the buildings of the lower Eastern Shore of Maryland. He is also a participant in the Chesapeake Farm Buildings Survey.

BARBARA COLLINS TURNER has studied architecture, urban design, and city planning at Syracuse University, the State University of New York at Buffalo, and the University of Pennsylvania, where she is now a doctoral candidate. She has been an assistant professor at Morgan State University and a consultant with the Development Planning Research Group in Baltimore. She currently works as a planner in the Philadelphia mayor's office.

DELL UPTON holds a Ph.D. in American civilization from Brown University. He has worked as an architectural historian at the Virginia Historic Landmarks Commission and has taught architectural history at the University of Virginia, George Washington University, and Case Western Reserve University. He now teaches in the department of architecture at the University of California at Berkeley. He is the editor of the *Vernacular Architecture Newsletter* and, with John Michael Vlach, of *Common Places: Readings in American Vernacular Architecture*. Upton is author of numerous studies of vernacular architecture, the most recent of which is *Holy Things and Profane: Anglican Parish Churches in Colonial Virginia*.

JOHN MICHAEL VLACH earned a Ph.D. in folklore from Indiana University. He has taught folklore at the University of Maryland, the University of Texas, and Boston University. Currently, he is director of the folklife program and associate professor of American studies and anthropology at George Washington University. Vlach is author of *The Afro-American Tradition in the Decorative Arts* and *Charleston Blacksmith*. He is also editor, with Dell Upton, of *Common Places: Readings in American Vernacular Architecture*.

ELLEN WEISS received a Ph.D. from the University of Illinois at Urbana-Champaign. She has worked at the Rhode Island Historical Preservation Commission and has taught architectural history at the University of California at Berkeley, the University of Illinois, Dartmouth, the Rhode Island School of Design, the Boston Architecture Center, and the University of Manitoba. In addition to several essays of criticism of contemporary architecture, Weiss has written studies of various nineteenth-century architectural topics that have appeared in *Architecture Plus*, *Nineteenth Century*, and the *Journal of the Society of Architectural Historians*.

CAMILLE WELLS studied history and architecture at Wake Forest University and the University of Virginia. She is a doctoral candidate in history at the College of William and Mary, where she also teaches. She has worked as an excavator for the Virginia Research Center for Archaeology, an architectural surveyor for the state historic preservation offices in Kentucky, North Carolina, and Maryland, and a research fellow at the Colonial Williamsburg Foundation. Wells is editor of the first *Perspectives in Vernacular Architecture* and a member of the board of directors of the Vernacular Architecture Forum. She is also a participant in the Chesapeake Farm Buildings Survey.

MARK R. WENGER was educated in architecture and environmental design at North Carolina State University and the University of North Carolina at Charlotte. He has also earned a masters degree in architectural history from the University of Virginia. Currently with the Department of Architectural Research at Colonial Williamsburg Foundation, Wenger has also taught at the College of William and Mary. In 1984, he received a Mellon grant to edit for publication the newly discovered eighteenth-century travel journal of Sir John Perceval.

MICHAEL ANN WILLIAMS holds a Ph.D. from the University of Pennsylvania Department of Folklore and Folklife. She has worked as an assistant historian for the Historic American Buildings Survey and as an architectural surveyor for the North Carolina Division of Archives and History. She is author of *Marble and Log*, an architectural catalog based on her work in Cherokee County, North Carolina, as well as several essays on vernacular architecture traditions in western North Carolina. Currently, she is professor of folklore at Western Kentucky University and a member of the board of directors of the Vernacular Architecture Forum.

CHRISTOPHER S. WITMER received a B.A. in American studies from Pennsylvania State University and a masters degree in landscape architecture from the University of Wisconsin at Madison. In 1979, he received a fellowship to study at Historic Deerfield in Massachusetts, and he has worked for the Historic Buildings Survey on a project in El Paso, Texas. Witmer now manages the Main Street Project for Williamsport, Pennsylvania.

JOSEPH S. WOOD holds degrees in geography from Middlebury College, the University of Vermont, and Pennsylvania State University. Since 1977, he has taught cultural geography at the University of Nebraska at Omaha, where he is now associate professor. In 1984 and 1985, he was visiting professor of geography at South China Normal University in Guangzhou. Wood is also the author of several articles on the New England village. He is currently pursuing research interests in the American urban landscape and material life in China.

BARBARA WYATT was educated in history at Hartwick College and in regional planning at Utah State University. She has conducted historic buildings surveys for the Texas Historical Commission, the Utah Historical Society, and the Rocky Mountain Regional Office of the National Park Service. For the past five years, she has served as chief of the survey and planning section of the Wisconsin State Historical Society. Her most recent role is as head of the computerization subcommittee of the National Conference of State Historic Preservation Officers. Wyatt is also a member of the Vernacular Architecture Forum's board of directors.

CHRISTOPHER L. YIP holds degrees in environmental design, architecture, and architectural history from the University of California at Berkeley. He has participated in historic resources surveys of the Berkeley campus and of San Francisco's Chinatown. As a research fellow at the University of Hong Kong, he studied colonial building on the South China coast. Yip teaches in the College of Design and Planning at the University of Colorado at Boulder.

Index